PLATFORM WORK IN EUROPE

PLATFORM WORK IN EUROPE

Towards Harmonisation?

Edited by
Maria Teresa CARINCI
Filip DORSSEMONT

INTERSENTIA
Cambridge – Antwerp – Chicago

Intersentia Ltd
8 Wellington Mews
Wellington Street | Cambridge
CB1 1HW | United Kingdom
Tel: +44 1223 736 170
Email: mail@intersentia.co.uk
www.intersentia.com | www.intersentia.co.uk

Distribution for the UK and
Rest of the World (incl. Eastern Europe)
NBN International
1 Deltic Avenue, Rooksley
Milton Keynes MK13 8LD
United Kingdom
Tel: +44 1752 202 301 | Fax: +44 1752 202 331
Email: orders@nbninternational.com

Distribution for Europe
Lefebvre Sarrut Belgium NV
Hoogstraat 139/6
1000 Brussels
Belgium
Tel: +32 (0)800 39 067
Email: mail@intersentia.be

Distribution for the USA and Canada
Independent Publishers Group
Order Department
814 North Franklin Street
Chicago, IL 60610
USA
Tel: +1 800 888 4741 (toll free) | Fax: +1 312 337 5985
Email: orders@ipgbook.com

Platform Work in Europe. Towards Harmonisation?

ISBN 978-1-83970-164-1
D/2021/7849/111
NUR 823

British Library Cataloguing in Publication Data. A catalogue record for this book is available from the British Library.

The Authors would like to thank Giulia Cassano, Silvia Magagnoli and Tommaso Maserati for the collaboration in editing the book.

CONTENTS

LIST OF CASES

SUPRANATIONAL

COURT OF JUSTICE OF THE EUROPEAN UNION

EUROPEAN COURT ON HUMAN RIGHTS

NATIONAL

BELGIUM

FRANCE

GERMANY

ITALY

NETHERLANDS

SPAIN

UNITED KINGDOM

LIST OF AUTHORS

Maria Teresa Carinci
Full Professor, University of Milan, Italy

Nicola Countouris
Director of the Research Department at the European Trade Union Institute (ETUI), Belgium; Professor of Labour Law and European Law, University College London (UCL), United Kingdom

Filip Dorssemont
Full Professor, Catholic University of Louvain (UCLouvain), and Visiting Professor, Free University of Brussels (VUB), Belgium

Fernando Fita Ortega
Associate Professor of Labour and Social Security Law, University of Valencia, Spain

Barbara Gomes
Assistant Professor in Labour Law, Polytechnic University of Hauts-de-France, France

Antoine Jacobs
Emeritus Professor of Labour Law, Social Security Law and Social Policy, Tilburg University, the Netherlands

Fabienne Kéfer
Full Professor of Labour Law, University of Liège, Belgium

Rüdiger Krause
Full Professor of Civil Law and Labour Law, University of Göttingen, Germany

Luca Ratti
Associate Professor of European and Comparative Labour Law, University of Luxembourg, Luxembourg

Tatiana Sachs
Assistant Professor in Labour Law, Paris Nanterre University, France

INTRODUCTION

Maria Teresa CARINCI and Filip DORSSEMONT*

The idea for this book came about when we met in Milan in 2018 and, over a Milanese Veal Cutlet and a glass of red wine, we were discussing the phenomenon of platform work – then in its infancy, but which would soon explode throughout Europe – and the legal status and protections platform workers[1] should be granted. At the time, it seemed that platform work was confined to marginal sectors of the labour market (the riders in the food delivery sector and the drivers of taxi-hailing services) and involved a small portion of the national labour markets. However, it quickly spread to many other forms of work (from baby-sitting and dog-sitting to doing small household chores, to cleaning services, shopping services and grocery delivery, to name just a few), gradually involving – partially due to the pandemic – an increasing number of workers.

After that first conversation, a seminar was held in Milan in October 2019 that was attended by the authors of the contributions collected in this book. That exchange of opinions, which highlighted many similarities between European legal systems, gave rise to the idea for this volume, which – thanks to the time that has passed – is much richer in content than the reports originally presented at the Milan seminar. Judges have intervened in all (or almost all) the legal systems in recent years, and in some legal systems even the legislators have intervened, to classify and, to some extent, protect platform workers, which will be clear from reading the national reports.

This book contains a number of national reports (Belgium, France, Germany, the Netherlands, Italy, Spain and the United Kingdom), other more transversal reports dealing with the issue of fundamental (collective)

---

* Full Professor at University of Milan and Full Professor at Catholic University of Louvain (UCLouvain), Visiting Professor at Free University Brussels (VUB).

1 The term is used with a wide meaning here. For a more accurate distinction, see M.T. CARINCI and F. DORSSEMONT, 'Platform Work in Europe: A Comparative Analysis' *in this volume*, infra, section 1.

workers' rights, as well as the applicable European legal framework. The conclusions focus on a comparison of the legal systems analysed in the national reports.

However, an analysis of 'work via platform' inevitably requires jurists to go further, to ask themselves a crucial question: is the notion of subordinate work, as it emerged and was consolidated during the 20th century, still able to encompass and provide workers in this new millennium with suitable protection?

Indeed, one cannot hide the fact that 'work via platform' is the epiphenomenon, the tip of the iceberg, of an epochal transformation of work. Thanks to new technologies, it is now possible to find and engage workers only for the time strictly necessary to perform the service and then constantly change the organisation of work by providing the worker with automated and impersonal instructions. This occurs by way of constantly reprocessing, using algorithms, the data collected in real time by the tools provided to the worker, such as the data collected by the geolocation system incorporated in the app placed on riders' smartphones, the exoskeleton worn by a worker in the warehouse of a distribution company or the detection of Internet connections located on the employee's computer. In short, new technologies now make it possible to create a man-machine integrated circuit – which operates using algorithms that constantly reprocess the data – in which the worker risks decisive insecurity and exasperating exploitation.

With reference to the workers used by the platforms, not only does case law in many countries still operate under the assumption that the classic notion of subordination should be used (as emerges from the national reports reported in this volume), but collective bargaining also now seems to be moving in the same direction. For instance, on 29 March 2021, Just Eat, on the one side, and the major Italian trade unions, on the other (CGIL, CISL and UIL), signed the first company collective employment agreement governing the employment relationship of riders as subordinate workers. The autonomous union of riders ('RidersXiDiritti': 'Riders for Rights'), which took an active role in the negotiations, also signed up to this contract by way of a separate protocol.

The Just Eat collective agreement therefore clearly demonstrates that the legal framework of subordinate work – which the system imposes on the worker whenever the platform exercises, also by way of the algorithm, the typical powers of the employer (directive, disciplinary and control power) – is not in itself incompatible with the organisational model chosen by the platforms. The platforms can, therefore, continue to profitably develop their business and, at the same time, give the workers the protections that the law provides for when the employment relationship is of a subordinate nature. On the contrary, as shown by the collapse of its share price on 30 March 2021, for Deliveroo – which, unlike Just Eat, is firm in rejecting the claims of the riders – compliance with the labour law rules and accrediting the platform as an entity that is attentive to social sustainability can contribute to creating added value and to gaining new market shares.

The collective agreement stipulated by Just Eat grants riders, in particular, application of the protection, in terms of workplace health and safety, provided for by subordinate work contracts. In addition to the coverage guaranteed by insurance and social security bodies, it provides for, *inter alia*: private life insurance; civil liability insurance covering damage to third parties; work breaks, holidays, leave and weekly rest; a precise definition of working hours (which includes the time in which the worker is waiting for orders at the designated hub); the guarantee that each work shift will last at least 2 hours; remuneration calculated on the basis of working time – which is higher in the case of night work, additional work and overtime; severance pay; and reimbursement of expenses per kilometre.

The progress made by this contract is undeniable if one compares the situation to that of platform workers who are considered 'pure' autonomous or 'coordinated and continuous' workers.[2] At the same time, however, a careful analysis of the Just Eat contract highlights how the platforms – even within the new legal framework of subordination – have worked to obtain the greatest possible flexibility of the rules governing the subordinate employment relationship. The collective employment contract in question,[3] in fact, contains a series of provisions aimed specifically at guaranteeing the company maximum flexibility in the employment relationship: the possibility to use, for a certain period of time (9 months) and without any quantitative limitation, staff leasing contracts and fixed-term employment contracts; the possibility to use the intermittent on-call employment contract; and the overwhelming possibility to hire riders on a vertical and horizontal part-time employment contract (which is, in fact, classified as

2 See M.T. Carinci, 'Platform Work: Case Law Approaches And Regulatory Choices. The Italian Case' *in this volume*.

3 Which, as a company collective agreement, is authorised to derogate from the national collective agreement for the category (in the specific case the national collective agreement for the logistics, transport, goods and delivery sector).

'the common form of work in the company') on the basis of three working-hour categories (10, 20 or 30 hours) which will then be spread over the course of the week according to a schedule agreed by the worker and the company on a weekly basis, but which will be subject to variations – in terms of timing, without additional charges, and with minimum notice of 2 days – at the platform's unilateral decision. It is also envisaged that the company can offer employees so-called 'open shifts', namely open time slots when the worker is free (at least this is the provision on paper) to accept or not.

The contract does not, however, specify whether or how the platform will continue to monitor the performance of the worker moment by moment (e.g. the route taken, the time taken, etc.) or to draw up worker rankings. In this regard, the collective agreement contractual clause provides, on the one hand, that the app installed on the worker's phone have a geolocation system, which is defined as a 'work tool essential to carry out the assignment', and, on the other hand, it specifies that the data collected, apart from having to be treated in accordance with the provisions of the EU's General Data Protection Regulation (GDPR), will not be used for disciplinary purposes. This, as is clear, does not rule out the fact that the data can be collected and processed for other purposes, such as to measure the productivity of the workers, to extend their working hours and even to favour them in the allocation of overtime, among other issues.

The crucial issue, however, remains – that is, the need to make transparent the data collection and processing by the algorithm used to manage employment relationships. It would be desirable for the legislator to intervene at this fundamental moment in time – perhaps along the lines of the regulations on workplace health and safety – and to require the platforms (and any other employer) to 'disclose' the algorithm to a specific trade union representative (an *ad hoc* union representative elected by the workers and appointed to monitor the algorithms' functioning and their impact on employment relationships).

PART I

NATIONAL PERSPECTIVES

PLATFORM WORK

The Belgian Case

Fabienne KÉFER*

1. INTRODUCTION

The classification of the relationship between platforms and app-based workers is not governed by any Belgian-specific regulation. Ordinary law

* Full Professor of Labour Law at the University of Liège, fkefer@uliege.be.

rules are therefore the only ones that qualify this relationship. A specific piece of legislation concerned almost exclusively the taxation of the income made through platforms and the social charges. It did not regulate the relationship between workers and the platform. This legislation will be presented in brief.

This chapter starts by discussing the importance of the phenomenon of platform workers in Belgium (section 1) before turning to the classification of the work relationship by case law (section 2) and by statutory law (section 3) and addressing legislative projects (section 4). Before concluding, a short section presents, in a few words, the organisation of the defence of platform workers' interests (section 5).

However, before going further, a brief observation is needed. Belgium is a federal state. Consequently, the competence regarding the regulation of online platforms is shared between the federal and federate levels of power. Regulations of cab companies, for example, fall within federate jurisdiction. As far as social law is concerned, the competences remain predominantly federal, which is why focus will be put on this level of power.

2. IMPORTANCE OF THE PHENOMENON OF PLATFORM WORKERS IN BELGIUM

There is no official statistical data with regard to the number of workers involved in the platform economy. There is unofficial and incomplete data, which dates back to 2019: for a population of just over 11 million inhabitants, the number of Uber drivers was estimated to be between 500 and 2000 and the number of Deliveroo riders was estimated to be around 2,600. These are mere approximations. In the meantime, bicycle delivery companies have multiplied and developed their activity in more and more cities, so that the actual figures are in fact different.

The sectors of activities are very varied if one looks at the platforms' websites (gardening, dog-sitting, shopping, baby-sitting, cleaning, language teaching, etc.).[1]

1 List of online platforms available at https://economie.fgov.be/fr/themes/entreprises/economie-durable/economie-collaborative/les-plateformes-actives-en.

3. CLASSIFICATION OF THE RELATIONSHIP BY CASE LAW

In Belgium, a court has not yet ruled on the legal classification of the relationship between platforms and platform workers. There are, however, things happening which relate to platform work.

Firstly, the Labour Prosecutor's Office opened a criminal investigation in October 2017. The Labour Prosecutor's Office leads the Labour Inspectorate's investigation concerning the nature of the working relationship between the Deliveroo platform and the Deliveroo riders. The investigation has lasted more than two years and has now reached a new stage. One of the difficulties encountered in the pursuit of this investigation is the refusal of the riders to testify. They fear that the authorities may suspect them for tax fraud on the grounds that they had not reported the revenues made through their work on any platform.

The investigation is now closed. The Labour Prosecutor's Office had several options: not to prosecute because it considers that there is no offence; refer the matter to the criminal court; or refer the matter to the Labour Court.[2] The office chose the third option in December 2019. The case will therefore be settled by the Brussels Labour Court by applying the rules related to the nature of the working relationship which will be discussed below. The outcome of the trial is not expected for several months.

It has to be noted that only a few workers decided to participate in the suit. One might have expected that all the riders heard during the judicial investigation would have joined the proceedings. This is indicative of the fact that a significant number or riders, for various reasons, prefer not to have employee status.

Secondly, two Deliveroo riders brought claims before the *Commission administrative de règlement de la relation de travail* (Social Ruling Commission).[3] The Commission is empowered to make assessments of the nature of working relationships. It is composed of civil servants working in social security entities and is chaired by a judge. The procedure followed by this Commission is administrative and may result in an opinion on the legal status of a working relationship. The rulings of the Commission

---

[2] Art. 138*bis*, para. 2, du Code judiciaire.

[3] Art. 329 de la loi du 27 décembre 2006 relative à la nature de la relation de travail.

are not binding on labour courts, who retain the power to make the final decision.

In both cases brought before the Commission, it was concluded that the riders were Deliveroo employees.[4] It should be stressed that given their administrative nature, said proceedings are not contradictory. Deliveroo was not a party to the proceedings and was, consequently, unable to argue that the Deliveroo riders are self-employed. Naturally, Deliveroo lodged an appeal before the Labour Court. These two decisions were overturned for procedural reasons. The Court found that the Social Ruling Commission could not issue an opinion as long as the criminal investigation of the Labour Prosecutor's Office was on-going.[5]

A similar administrative decision was taken in October 2020 concerning an Uber driver.[6]

As for the other platforms, there are, to my knowledge, no on-going disputes over the legal status of the working relationship between them and the platform workers.

4. CLASSIFICATION OF THE RELATIONSHIP BY STATUTORY LAW 'À DROIT CONSTANT'

Belgian social law is designed according to a binary system, which means that it is based on the binary divide between employees and self-employed individuals. There is no third status (unlike Italy or Spain, for example). This dichotomy, which dates back to the Fordist period, is regularly criticised in connection with the evolution of the world of work and working patterns. However, there are many voices against the creation of a third status.[7] Thus far, there is no political will to move away from the binary system.

Some platforms like Takeaway.com make use of temporary workers. However, in most cases, the contracts of riders and drivers exclude subordination. This does not mean that parties do not have an employment contract. The first section examines if the legal provisions allow the judge

---

4 Commission administrative de règlement de la relation de travail, 23 February 2018, *J.L.M.B.*, 2018, p. 863, et note Q. Cordier.

5 Tribunal du travail francophone de Brussels, 7è chambre, 3 July 2019, R.G. 18/2076/A, unpublished.

6 Commission administrative de règlement de la relation de travail, 26 October 2020.

7 See F. Kéfer, Q. Cordier and A. Farcy, 'Quel statut juridique pour les travailleurs des plateformes numériques?' [2019] 31 *Revue de Droit Social/Tijdschrift voor sociaal recht* 47–48, and references.

to classify the relationship between an app-based worker and a platform as an employment relationship (section 3.1). The second section considers the effects of reclassification as an employment contract (section 3.2). The third section discusses the minimum protection rules for platform workers if they have self-employed status (section 3.3). Lastly, the fourth section presents the specific provisions already mentioned in the introduction to this chapter (section 3.4).

4.1. PROVISIONS RELATED TO THE CLASSIFICATION OF THE WORKING RELATIONSHIP

4.1.1. The Nature of the Working Relationship Act of 27 December 2006

Most of the platforms' terms and conditions exclude the classification of the working relationship as an employment contract: workers who agreed on the terms and conditions – and they cannot work if they do not – are therefore seen as independent contractors.

In some cases, this classification corresponds to reality. Indeed, there are many platforms whose role is limited to matching requesters with service providers. These platforms do not exercise authority over the service provider and do not intend to do so. This is the case of Listminut.[8] This platform works as intermediary for the fulfilment of tasks like handiwork, gardening, cleaning, baby-sitting and so on. It plays no role other than that of an intermediary (except to collect the payment). It does not exercise the authority that characterises the employment contract.[9]

The classification of the relationship as self-employed is more questionable for delivery or transport platforms. The employment contract could be imposed because these platforms do not limit themselves to playing the role of intermediary; their role is more extensive. These platforms more or less structure the organisation of the activity. It is their algorithm that designates the service provider and manages the evaluations. The platform is able to exercise closer control over the service provider. This is the reason why the question of the existence or absence of a legal subordination link arises and deserves to be addressed in terms of the provisions of the Nature of the Working Relationship Act of 27 December 2006.

---

8 https://listminut.be/fr/howitworks.

9 This is in consideration of this fact that the law proposals referred to below (section 4) outline some rules of protection for platform workers, based on a self-employed status.

In order to put an end to a degree of legal uncertainty while seeking to combat some forms of social fraud, a programme act of 27 December 2006 was adopted. Title XIII (art. 328 et seq.) of this act constitutes the so-called Nature of the Working Relationship Act. It sets out the principles in this area. Simply put, parties will freely choose the nature of their working relationship as far as they do not contravene the law of public order, public morals and mandatory laws (art. 331). The legislator does not give preference to one or the other form of collaboration; the choice of self-employment is just as legitimate as that of salaried employment.

The judge must give precedence to the classification provided by the parties to the contract. He will disregard it only if the effective performance of the contract proves incompatible with the conventional classification and will reclassify the convention and apply the relevant social security scheme (art. 331–332). Therefore, the judge cannot limit himself to finding that the legal classification that the plaintiff wishes to see applied is plausible. The court will still have to find that the conventional classification is incompatible with the performance of the contract.

In its assessment, the court will take into account 'general criteria' laid down by the legislator (art. 333) and 'specific criteria' to be determined by the king. However, the sovereign power of the court to assess the nature of a particular working relationship is preserved (art. 339). The general criteria adopted are intended to establish legal and not economic dependence:

a) The will of the parties expressed in the contract
b) Freedom to determine working time (schedules, holidays, justification of absences, etc.). According to the parliamentary papers of the Act, the obligation to work certain hours due to commercial or organisational constraints is not in itself an indication of subordination.[10] For the *Cour de cassation* (judicial Supreme Court), the 'freedom to determine working time' criteria relates to 'whether or not independence with regard to use of time during the working period in which the work is to be carried out or the person carrying out the work is to be available according to the agreement between the parties'.[11] In the

10 *Doc. parl.*, Chambre, 2006–2007, n° 51-2773/1, p. 216.

11 Cass., 18 October 2010, *Pasicrisie*, 2010, p. 2662, n° 610: 'l'indépendance ou non en matière d'emploi du temps au cours de la plage de travail pendant laquelle le travail doit être effectué ou l'exécutant du travail doit être disponible selon l'accord conclu entre les parties'.

same decision, the court provides an interesting clarification for work performed through platforms:

> The fact that the person carrying out the work is free to decide whether or not to accept an offer of work from his employer and, where appropriate, to refuse it, does not therefore prevent the employer, once he has accepted the work, from disposing of the labour and assigning it in accordance with the provisions of the contract. The mere fact that [the worker] has full freedom to take up the offer of work or not does not imply that the person performing the work is also free in the determination of working time once the assignment has been accepted.[12]

Essentially, the brevity or irregularity of performance and the worker's freedom to refuse the proposed task or assignment do not preclude the formation of a contract of employment.

c) Freedom to determine work organisation (definition of tasks, modalities of execution, ability to subcontract, etc.).

d) The possibility of exercising hierarchical control. Hierarchical control does not correspond to the qualitative control of services, which is present in many commercial agreements. It is the control of an employee that can lead to internal sanctions.[13] It supposes the insertion in the structure of a department or company.[14] Uber drivers or Deliveroo riders are truly integrated in a service organised by the platform. The platform exercises a certain form of direct control over them, notably by sanctioning them if they do not accept enough tasks when they are connected to the app or if they choose to cancel tasks,[15] which has strong affinities with hierarchical control.

---

12 'La circonstance que celui qui exécute le travail dispose de la liberté de donner suite ou non à une offre de travail de son employeur et qu'il peut, le cas échéant, la refuser n'empêche donc pas que, dès qu'il a accepté le travail, l'employeur dispose de la main d'œuvre et affecte celle-ci selon les dispositions du contrat. Le simple fait que (le travailleur) ait toute liberté de donner suite ou non à l'offre de travail n'implique pas que celui qui exécute le travail soit également libre dans l'organisation du temps de travail une fois la mission acceptée'.

13 *Doc. parl.*, Chambre, 2006–2007, n° 51-2773/1, pp. 217–18.

14 J. Clesse, 'La qualification juridique de la relation de travail' in J. Clesse and F. Kéfer, *Questions de Droit Social*, vol. 94, No. 21., CUP, Anthemis, Louvain-la-Neuve 2007, p. 242.

15 See, among others, V. De Stefano, 'The rise of the "just-in-time workforce": on-demand work, crowd work and labour protection in the "gig-economy"' [2016] 37 *Comparative Labor Law & Policy Journal* 471, 491–92.

If one of these criteria is met (just one is sufficient), the judge may reclassify the working relationship.[16] It is therefore not excluded, in light of these elements, that the judges called upon to examine the classification of the relationship uniting the platform and the platform workers may consider that the classification chosen by the parties does not correspond to the performance that they give of their agreement and reclassify it as an employment contract. This is compounded by the fact that Belgian judges are attentive to what is decided abroad; and yet, more and more foreign decisions are reclassifying the working relationship of workers via app as an employment contract.

4.1.2. *The Presumption of Employment Contract in the Transportation Sector*

Provisions 337/1 and 337/2 of the same Act establish a presumption regarding the nature of the working relationship for workers active in certain sectors including the transport of goods and/or persons on behalf of third parties.[17] The implementation of this presumption is linked to a list of criteria set out in a Royal Decree of 29 October 2013.[18] If more than half of the criteria are met, the working relationship is presumed to be salaried. If less than half of the criteria are met, the working relationship is presumed to be on a self-employed basis. These criteria do not relate to the exercise of authority, but to economic dependency.

Five of these criteria are related to the level of involvement of the service provider in the financial risk: (a) the management of the undertaking; (b) the purchasing policy; (c) the price determination; and (d) whether the provider's remuneration is flat-rate and is not linked to the result or the volume of services provided (f). The other criteria are the existence or

16 Cass., 6 December 2010, *Pasicrisie*, 2010, p. 3097; Cass., 26 March 2013, *Pasicrisie*, 2013, p. 793; Cass., 10 October 2016, *Pasicrisie*, 2016, p. 1932; W. Van Eeckhoutte, *Handboek Belgisch Arbeidsrecht*, No. 426, Wolters Kluwer, Mechlin 2014, p. 241; J. Clesse, Q. Cordier and F. Kéfer, 'Le statut social des travailleurs de plateforme' in J. Clesse and F. Kéfer, *Enjeux et défis juridiques de l'économie de plateforme*, vol. 187, CUP, Anthemis, Limal 2019, pp. 160–62.

17 Art. 337/1, para. 1er, 3°, de la loi-programme du 27 décembre 2006.

18 Arrêté royal du 29 octobre 2013 pris en exécution de l'article 337/2, para. 3, de la loi-programme (I) du 27 décembre 2006 en ce qui concerne la nature des relations de travail qui se situent dans le cadre de l'exécution des activités qui ressortent du champ d'application de la sous-commission paritaire pour les taxis et de la commission paritaire du transport et de la logistique, uniquement pour les activités de location de voitures avec chauffeur et de taxis collectifs.

absence of an obligation of result (e); the obligation to perform the work personally (g); the fact of working for a single principal or, on the contrary, of appearing as a company in the eyes of third parties or clients (h); and, finally, the involvement of the principal in the leasing or provision of the vehicle (i).

Because of the significant lack of clarity with which the text of the Royal Decree was written, the interpretation of these criteria is very controversial. The courts have not yet ruled on their application to workers via app. In the literature, it can be observed that their application to platforms such as Uber or Deliveroo leads, according to one interpretation, to retaining the presumption in the head of the platform and to rejecting the presumption in the other interpretation.[19]

If the presumption of employment contract is upheld by the judge, it is a simple presumption, which the platform could overturn by establishing that the worker is not subordinate. In order to do so, the platform must rely on the four general criteria set out in the Act of 27 December 2006. This is not an easy task, but it is not impossible either.[20]

4.1.3. The Presumption of Employment Contract for Students

Article 121 of the Employment Contract Act of 3 July 1978 contains a presumption of salaried status for students. A significant number of Deliveroo riders are students and could invoke this presumption.[21] It is a simple presumption which the platform could overturn by establishing that the student is not a subordinate. To do so, the platform should rely on the four general criteria set out in the Act of 27 December 2006, which would be far from simple.

4.1.4. Extension of Social Security Law to Some 'Employed-Like Persons'

The employee versus Self-Employed dichotomy affects the social security system. Belgian law has created several social security schemes. There

---

19 See F. Kéfer and Q. Cordier, 'Le travailleur 2.0. Contribution à l'étude de la dépendance dans l'environnement numérique' in L. Dear and E. Plasschaert, *Le contrat de travail revisité à la lumière du XXIè siècle*, Larcier, Brussels 2018, pp. 69–72 and 77 and references.

20 W. van Eeckhoutte, 'Les frères Jacques c. Délubéro' in V. d'Huart and F. Kéfer, *Casus de Droit Social*, vol. 191, CUP, Anthemis, Limal 2019, pp. 97–101.

21 See W. van Eeckhoutte, 'Les frères Jacques c. Délubéro', above n. 20, pp. 93–95.

are three main schemes: employees, self-employed individuals and civil servants. The classification of the working relationship is therefore of crucial importance for the determination of the scheme: the scheme for employees – described by the Social Security for Employees Act of 27 June 1969 – is much more favourable than that for self-employed persons.

However, exceptionally, an independent contractor can benefit from the social security scheme for employees. Indeed, the king may extend the scope of application of the Social Security for Employees Act of 27 June 1969 to workers who perform work in a manner similar to that of a contract of employment.[22] The aim of this formula is to reach workers who are in a situation of economic dependence comparable to that of an employee, even though they are not in a state of legal subordination, or cannot prove it.[23] According to the Court of Cassation,

> Persons who perform work on terms similar to those of a contract of employment are not those who, whether or not under a contract of employment, work under the authority or in a relationship of subordination; (…) these provisions apply only to persons who work in circumstances similar to those in which work is performed in a relationship of subordination.[24]

Therefore, these individuals are in a hybrid situation.

Such an extension was made under certain conditions in favour of carriers of goods, carriers of persons and cab drivers by Article 3 of the Royal Decree of 28 November 1969.[25]

Do platform workers benefit from such an extension? Regarding bike deliveries, Article 3, 5° of the Royal Decree of 28 November 1969

---

22 Art. 2, para. 1er, 1°, de la loi du 27 juin 1969 révisant l'arrêté-loi du 28 décembre 1944 concernant la sécurité sociale des travailleurs.

23 J. Clesse, P. Delooz, R. Manette and V. Neuprez, 'L'assujettissement à la sécurité sociale des travailleurs salariés. Règles générales et questions particulières' [1993] *Actualités du Droit* 1156; W. van Eeckhoutte, *Handboek Belgisch Socialezekerheidsrecht*, No. 155, Wolters Kluwer, Mechlin 2017, p. 89.

24 Cass., 9 April 1979, *Pasicrisie*, 1979, p. 945: 'Les personnes qui exécutent un travail selon des modalités similaires à celles d'un contrat de travail ne sont pas celles qui, en vertu ou non d'un contrat de travail, travaillent sous l'autorité ou dans un lien de subordination; (…) ces dispositions ne visent que des personnes qui travaillent dans des circonstances ressemblant à celles où le travail est effectué dans un lien de subordination'.

25 Art. 3, 5° à 5°*ter*, de l'arrêté royal du 28 novembre 1969 pris en exécution de la loi du 27 juin 1969 révisant l'arrêté-loi du 28 décembre 1944 concernant la sécurité sociale des travailleurs.

extends the scope of application of the 1969 Act to persons who transport goods ordered by an undertaking by means of vehicles which they do not own or whose purchase is financed, or whose financing is guaranteed, by the operator of that undertaking and to that operator. Couriers use their own bicycles or scooters, so the conditions for extension are not met.

Regarding car drivers, the situation is more complex. Some drivers could benefit from the extension of the scope of application of the 1969 Act. The technical conditions are too complex to be detailed here.[26] It is sufficient to bear in mind that in certain cases, Uber drivers can benefit from the social security of employees even if they are considered as independent contractors.

It would not be prohibitively difficult to extend this advantage to all workers via app. The king could complete Article 3 of the Royal Decree of 28 November 1969 in order to extend the scope of the application of 1969 Act to platforms workers. In this scenario, the legal person paying the workers' benefits would be assimilated to the employer for the purpose of the Act.

4.2. THE EFFECTS OF A RECLASSIFICATION OF THE WORKING RELATIONSHIP

The classification operation may lead to a reclassification, that is, the finding that the working relationship is a contract of employment. This case raises many legal questions.

The reclassification of the working relationship as an employment contract would ensure that the employer complies with rules on minimum wages, working time, holidays, dismissal, well-being at work, maternity protection and so on. It would lead to the recognition of an employee status under social security law and particularly to legal protection against workplace accidents.

The conclusion that the worker is an employee as a result of a judicial reclassification of the working relationship would nevertheless raise a series of questions that are complex, to say the least.

These questions arise from the fact that Belgian employment law does not contain any legal framework for occasional work, except the

---

26 For more detail, see F. Kéfer and Q. Cordier, above n. 19, pp. 72–74.

regulation of temporary employment[27] and so-called flexi-jobs,[28] which are not applicable in this case. The zero-hours contract is not recognised in Belgian Law. In the absence of specific rules, it is therefore necessary to apply the ordinary law of the employment contract.

The first question concerns the delimitation of the working time, that is, the time during which the worker is at the disposal of the employer, at the mercy of an unforeseen call (art. 19, pt. 2, of the Labour Act of 16 March 1971). What is the status of the waiting time between two runs for a Deliveroo rider? Is this included in the working hours, or is it not included in the working hours?

Upstream of this first difficulty, the question of the time limits of the employment contract inevitably arises. Should one consider that the service provider is employed from the moment he registers on the platform until the deactivation of the account by the platform or its deletion by the worker? This interpretation is implausible. Does the contract rather begin at the moment of connection, which constitutes a declaration of availability, or does it begin at the moment the provider accepts a task, so that it only covers the actual time of performance? Do the connection periods constitute sequences of execution of a single contract, or is a new micro-contract concluded for each new connection? One may consider linking the services to each other and consider that they constitute the discontinuous execution of the same employment contract. But one may also consider seeing a separate employment contract in each connection period so that the disconnection coincides with the end of the employment contract. These are some of the questions that one might ask and to which the answer is not self-evident.

4.3. MINIMUM PROTECTION FOR SELF-EMPLOYED INDIVIDUALS

If the court does not invalidate the classification chosen by the parties, the platform worker is lawfully occupied under a self-employed status. As such, he enjoys less protection than an employee.

---

27 Art. 7 et s. de la loi du 24 juillet 1987 sur le travail temporaire, le travail intérimaire et la mise de travailleurs à la disposition d'utilisateurs.

28 A so-called flexi-job contract of employment can be concluded between an employer and an employee already employed for at least 4/5th time with another employer or several other employers during a reference period or a pensioner. In practice, the parties must conclude a framework contract, in writing, which contains at least the

The self-employed status is not homogenous, particularly because of the diversity of the types of contracts concluded (mandate, partnership, agency, management, brokerage, provision of service, etc.) and because the rules on access to the profession or the deontology may be specific to certain professions.

There is, however, a kind of common self-employed status that is socially protected. Firstly, certain standards benefit both employees and the self-employed. Thus, the personal scope of application of the Freedom of Association Act of 24 May 1921 and Anti-Discrimination Act of 10 May 2007 is not limited to employees, but also extends to the self-employed.[29] Similarly, health insurance and family allowances are available to both employees and self-employed persons.[30] The self-employed also have insurance compensation in the event of incapacity for work and maternity;[31] a so-called bridging right in the event of bankruptcy (in particular, consisting of the granting of a financial benefit for 12 months and maintenance for four quarters of rights in terms of health insurance and compensation);[32] a family assistant's allowance granted for a maximum of 12 months in the event of serious illness or palliative care for a relative, or care for a disabled child;[33] and a retirement and survivor's pension.[34] Mention may also be made of the provisions relating to compulsory closing hours and weekly rest periods contained in the Opening Hours in Trade,

---

identity of the parties, the terms and conditions for proposing a flexi-job employment contract, the job description, the salary and the reproduction of an excerpt from the Act. They conclude a flexi-job employment contract for each occupation. It is necessarily a fixed-term contract, which may be written or verbal (Social Matters Act of 16.11.20015).

29 Art. 4, 1°, et art. 5, para. 2, de la loi du 10 mai 2007 tendant à lutter contre certaines formes de discrimination; art. 5, 1°, et art. 6, para. 2, de la loi du 10 mai 2007 tendant à lutter contre la discrimination entre les femmes et les hommes; art. 4, 1°, et art. 5, para. 2, de la loi du 30 juillet 1981 tendant à réprimer certains actes inspirés par le racisme et la xénophobie.

30 Art. 32, 1°*bis*, et 2°, de la loi relative à l'assurance obligatoire soins de santé et indemnités, coordonnée le 14 juillet 1994, et art. 1/1 de la loi générale du 19 décembre 1939 relative aux allocations familiales.

31 Arrêté royal du 20 juillet 1971 instituant une assurance indemnités et une assurance maternité en faveur des travailleurs indépendants et des conjoints aidants.

32 Loi du 22 décembre 2016 instaurant un 'droit passerelle' en faveur des travailleurs indépendants.

33 Arrêté royal du 22 septembre 2015 accordant une allocation en faveur du travailleur indépendant qui interrompt temporairement son activité professionnelle pour donner des soins à une personne.

34 Arrêté royal n° 72 du 10 novembre 1967 relatif à la pension de retraite et de survie des travailleurs indépendants.

Crafts and Services Act of 10 November 2006, provisions which aim to maintain a balance between the private life of self-employed traders and the interests of consumers.[35] Finally, the self-employed worker can protect his main residence against foreclosure by making a statement before a notary.[36]

This common legal status could be further developed. Considering that in the next few years, pluriactivity will be a reality for many workers and that everyone will be obliged to manage his or her employment portfolio, W. van Eeckhoutte proposed a common core of rules for the termination of a working relationship, whether salaried or self-employed: observance of a reasonable notice period; motivation for unilateral dismissal; and equal treatment with regard to social security law.[37]

4.4. PLATFORM WORKERS' SPECIFIC REGULATION

As mentioned above, the imposition of the income made through approved platforms is governed by a specific regulation.

What is this specific legislation? The regulation is a quite technical, and this chapter will attempt to simplify so as to be as clear as possible. Simply put, labour courts remain free to consider the employment relationship between the platform and the service provider as a contract of employment. It is therefore theoretically possible for labour law to apply to the relationship between the platform and the platform worker. If a judge qualifies a relationship as a contract of employment, this would simultaneously entail, on the one hand, the application of standard provisions of labour law, employee social security, health and safety provisions and so on, and, on the other hand, taxation of the revenue made and the payment of employee social security contributions.

---

35 Projet de loi relatif aux heures d'ouverture dans le commerce, l'artisanat et les services, Exposé des motifs, *Doc.*, Chambre, 2005–2006, n° 2486/1, p. 4. See, in particular, on this issue, J. Clesse, 'À propos du travail indépendant …' in M. Westrade and S. Gilson, *Le statut social des travailleurs indépendants*, Perspectives de droit social, Anthemis, Limal 2013, p. 15; W. van Eeckhoutte, 'Vers une harmonisation du droit du travail pour les travailleurs indépendants ?' in S. Gilson and P. Vanhaverbeke, *La rupture du contrat de travail : entre harmonisation et discrimination*, Jeune barreau de Mons, Anthemis, Limal 2015, p. 607.

36 Art. 72 et s. de la loi du 25 avril 2007 portant des dispositions diverses (IV).

37 W. van Eeckhoutte, above n. 35, p. 618.

However, when the employment relationship is classified as independent – either because the status is not contested in court or because the judge finds that the relationship does not involve any subordination – a specific tax regulation provides for a very advantageous tax regime (a contribution equivalent to 10 per cent of income) for the revenues received by a self-employed worker through the digital economy. Platform workers who benefit from the advantageous tax regime are also exempted from the social charges for which self-employed workers are responsible. In other words, one faces with an activity as a self-employed person generating an income as a self-employed person. This activity is not considered as an economic activity and is not taken into account either to participate in the financing of social security or to constitute a career giving entitlement to social security benefits.

Activities pursued by platform workers are therefore not considered as 'economic activities' by the Belgian legislature. This is surprising, because the legislature declared that its intention was also to fight tax fraud; however, the system it sets out resembles legalised money laundering.

The benefit from this tax and social charges exemption is possible only if some conditions are met, especially if the income does not exceed 6,390€ per year (2021 amount) as far as the services were provided via approved platforms and if the beneficiaries were private individuals (P2P).[38]

Between 2018 and 2020, the legislature had gone one step further. Not only had it abolished the 10% tax contribution, but in addition and above all it had – supposedly for reasons of legal certainty – excluded platform workers from the scope of application of a large part of the laws that make up labour law (Employment Contracts Act; Act on the Protection of Remuneration; Act on Collective Labour Agreements; Act on Working Hours; Act on Health and Safety at Work, etc.) and of all social security law, both that concerning employees and that concerning the self-employed. In other words, even if a judge came to the conclusion that the platform provider was an employee, labour law and social security law for employees could not be applied. The Act establishing this regime was annulled by the Constitutional Court.[39]

---

38 Article 37*bis* du Code des impôts sur les revenus (CIR92); article 5*ter* de l'arrêté royal n° 38 du 27 juillet 1967 organisant le statut social des travailleurs indépendants.

39 C.C., 23 April 2020, n° 53/2020, available at https://www.const-court.be/public/f/2020/2020-053f.pdf.

5. LEGISLATIVE PROPOSALS

Two legislative proposals had been introduced by the opposition in 2018. They included provisions on the establishment of a minimum level of protection for self-employed workers who perform platform work.[40] In view of their content, these proposals bear similarities with provisions inserted in France in the Labour Code. One sets the minimum gross hourly wage for service providers (14.00€), but refers to the king the difficult task of delimiting the working hours of service providers.[41] The other provides for relative immunity from civil liability for service providers in the platform economy, modelled on that enjoyed by employees,[42] accompanied by civil liability of the platform for damage caused to third parties by service providers; the text does not, however, specify what is meant by 'third parties'. It also provides for the obligation to take out insurance covering at least extra-contractual liability, as well as insurance covering 'bodily injury and incapacity for work caused to workers on the occasion of or as a result of the performance of activities on the platform or on the way to and from such activities and for illness contracted as a result of the benefits'.[43] Finally, it is stated that platforms that provide their services to a number of service providers determined by the King must be approved. The right to disconnect from the app was not included.

The two proposals were ultimately not passed in Parliament. It is as yet too early to tell if these proposals will be brought before Parliament again.

6. THE ORGANISATION OF THE DEFENCE OF PLATFORM WORKERS' INTERESTS

The organisation of the defence of platform workers' interests should be examined in several stages.

Prior to October 2017, meal deliveries by bike riders were mainly done through the Take Eat Easy platform and then through the Deliveroo platform, after Take Eat Easy had gone bankrupt.

---

40 Proposition de loi visant à encadrer et garantir protection et rémunération aux travailleurs de l'économie de plates-formes, *Doc.*, Chambre, 2017–2018, n° 2912/1 and Proposition de loi visant à garantir une rémunération minimale aux travailleurs de l'économie de plates-formes agréées, *Doc.*, Chambre, 2017–2018, n° 3116/1.

41 Art. 2 de la proposition de loi n° 3116/1.

42 See art. 18 de la loi du 3 juillet 1978 relative aux contrats de travail.

43 Art. 3, para. 2, de la proposition de loi n° 2912/1.

The originality of the concept of this collaboration lay in the fact that the riders were employees of another platform, SMart. SMart is, above all, a platform for artists (*Société mutuelle pour artistes*). This undertaking, whose activities have diversified over the years, aims to enable legally independent workers to perform an activity while benefiting from the social security of employees within the framework of a so-called employee-entrepreneur status.[44]

In practical terms, the riders were hired by SMart under successive fixed-term employment contracts concluded for very short periods. SMart made its riders available to Take Eat Easy and then Deliveroo. SMart collected the total amount of the riders' fees. SMart then converted these amounts into wages and applied social security contributions and tax deductions. SMart then paid the net amount to the workers, to which it still applied a 6.5 per cent deduction for 'operating expenses'. SMart had obtained from the platform a minimum daily working time, a minimum wage, a partial reimbursement of the costs of the smartphone subscription and bicycle maintenance. This arrangement concerned the Take Eat Easy and Deliveroo riders only, but not the workers on other platforms. It seems that the traditional trade unions did not have much influence during this period, since the role of trade unions was played by SMart to some extent. This was not necessarily well received by the unions.

SMart's creativity flourished through a transgression of Belgian legal frameworks, which are too narrow for the social innovations it promotes.[45] Indeed, its scheme raises several legal questions. The justification for the succession of fixed-term contracts seems doubtful in light of Article 10 of the Employment Contract Act of 3 July 1978. In addition, there are questions about the way in which, in practice, provisions concerning the working hours of part-time workers were respected. Finally, a series of questions arises from the fact that SMart did not exercise any of the prerogatives associated with an employer. SMart did not exert authority as the employer. The arrangements made with food delivery platforms were entirely illegal from the point of view of labour law and social security law. On the one hand, the Temporary Work, Temporary Employment and the Provision of Workers Act of 24 July 1987 subjects the provision of

---

44 S. Graceffa, *Refaire le monde … du travail: une alternative à l'ubérisation de l'économie*, Les Éditions Repas, Valence 2016; see also V. Xhauflair, B. Huybrechts and F. Pichault, 'How Can New Players Establish Themselves in Highly Institutionalized Labour Markets? A Belgian Case Study in the Area of Project-Based Work' [2018] 56(2) *British Journal of Industrial Relations* 370.

45 S. Graceffa, above n. 44, p. 47.

personnel to a strict framework. On the other hand, under Belgian law, a worker cannot choose his social security scheme; it is imposed by public policy regulations. A worker who is not subordinate cannot be subject to the scheme for employees, unless the law or the king has extended to him the scope of application of the 1969 Act. The social Criminal Code penalises fraudulent subjection to social security of employees (art. 221).[46]

In October 2017, Deliveroo put an end to the collaboration with SMart. This was due to Deliveroo's desire to standardise the status of riders in Europe. In addition, the platform had legitimate concerns that the collaboration arrangement with SMart would be illegal: there was a risk that it could be considered as being bound to its riders by employment contracts on the basis of Article 31, para. 3, of the Act of 24 July 1987.[47] Since the end of this collaboration, *Deliveroo* has been contracting directly with riders.

The traditional unions have attempted to regain control. It is with the support of the Christian Trade Union that the two aforementioned cases were brought before the Ruling Commission. In September 2019, the Christian Trade Union launched the 'United Freelancers' initiative (trade unionism of self-employed workers; self-employed without staff or collaborative/associative economy). Its objective is to 'move the lines' in the Belgian social context. The intention is to defend all workers in the grey zone in the same way as the union defends employees.[48] There is also a collective of couriers, which is more of a forum (based on Facebook) than a real union defending workers' interests. At present, platform workers have gained the sympathy of traditional trade unions (the Socialist Trade Union has also undertaken to support them). The collective of couriers does not replace traditional unions, which are much more powerful, and more professional in defending the interests of working people.

With regard to the legal obstacles to such an organisation like the one launched by the Christian Trade Union, two points are to be highlighted. Firstly, there is no provision in Belgian law which prohibits 'mixed' trade unionism or even a freelancers' association. Secondly, the Christian Trade

46 See also C. Van Olmen and K. Devloo, 'De "Uberisatie" van het Belgisch arbeidsrecht' in *L'économie du futur. Le futur de l'économie*, Le droit des affaires en évolution, Bruylant, Brussels 2016, p. 147.

47 Article 31(1) prohibits the provision of personnel. Article 31(3) proclaims that, in the event of violation of this prohibition, the user (*Deliveroo*) and the worker are bound by an employment contract concluded for an indefinite period.

48 https://www.unitedfreelancers.be/home-fr.

Union is considering concluding collective agreements for the benefit of freelancers.

The legal nature of this type of agreement raises difficulties. There is, in fact, no mechanism for receiving such an agreement in the state legal order, given the current state of law. Such agreements are not prohibited, but they have no normativity. In such circumstances, how could the judge, in the event of a conflict, consider such an agreement? Similarly, their position in the hierarchy of norms is not settled. The absence of a legal status comparable to that of a collective labour agreement gives rise to a second difficulty: the agreement can only have effect between the signatory parties and is not binding on platform workers. In order for them to be able to claim to be the holders of rights drawn from this type of agreement, a detour through another legal mechanism would have to be made. This detour is, in any case, quite perilous.

Moreover, given the European Court of Justice's (ECJ) *FNV Kunsten* judgment, one cannot yet say what the future holds for this type of association.[49] There is a serious risk that any agreements concluded by organisations representing platform workers to ensure a minimum income will come up against Article 101 of the Treaty on the Function of the European Union (TFEU), unless the service providers are deemed to be falsely self-employed within the meaning of the ECJ.[50]

---

49 Case C-413/13, *FNV Kunsten Informatie en Media c. Staat der Nederlanden*, ECLI:EU:C:2014:2411. See P. Pecinovsky, 'Het recht op collectief onderhandelen voor economisch afhankelijke zelfstandigen' [2019] *Revue de Droit Social/ Tijdschrift voor sociaal recht* 542–44; A. Lamine and F. Dorssemont, 'Quels droits collectifs pour le travailleur de plateformes?' in A. Lamine et C. Wattecamps, *Quel Droit Social pour les travailleurs de plateformes*, Anthemis, Limal 2020, pp. 321–30.

50 On the meaning the Court give to the concept of 'false self-employed' see para. 33 and seq. The court juxtaposes elements that relate to economic dependence with a conventional definition of the concept of employed person that takes account of legal subordination alone. Is it to be inferred from this that European competition law does not regulate collective agreements concluded on behalf of economically dependent providers; or must it be established that these providers are in fact (legally) subordinate workers? The question remains unresolved. See, e.g. V. De Stefano, 'Non-Standard Workers and Freedom of Association: A Critical Analysis of Restrictions to Collective Rights from a Human Rights Perspective' [2015] 123 *Working Papers del Centro Studi Diritto del Lavoro Europeo Massimo D'Antona* 1, 22–23, available at http://csdle.lex.unict.it/docs/workingpapers/Non-Standard-Workers-and-Freedom-Of-Association-a-Critical-Analysis-af-Restrictions-to-Collective-Ri/5448.aspx; comp. S. Hennion, 'Les limites d'application du droit de la concurrence aux conventions collectives conclues au profit de la protection sociale de travailleurs indépendants' [2015] 12 *La semaine juridique – Édition générale (JCP G)* 341; C. Robin, 'La notion d'entreprise, le droit de la concurrence et la convention collective de travail' [2015] 43 *Revue Lamy de la concurrence* 15–16.

7. CONCLUSION

Labour law was built on the model of the Fordist enterprise, that is, the factory with mass production, which is characterised by a unity of place and working time, a strong verticality in interpersonal relations and a collective organisation of workers employed in the same factory, among other factors. Social security law was also modelled in reference to the full-time factory worker. It is from this period that the employed/self-employed dichotomy dates.

This model no longer corresponds to today's worker, who enjoys greater autonomy in the design and the execution of his work. This autonomy, which both threatens and protects the worker, appears to be a central element in the reflection on the future of work itself, as carried out by Belgian and international scholars.[51] The changes in the organisation of work brought about by Uberisation are likely to give a new impetus to reflection on the *raison d'être*, function and consistency of the legal and social protection of the worker in the 21st century. The essential elements characterising the employment contract are being called into question. It is above all subordination that is affected. What is the status of platform workers? Are they employees or self-employed individuals? The destabilising effects of this model on labour relations are certainly significant. If one adopt a diachronic perspective, the upheavals brought about by the phenomenon of Uberisation (i.e. outsourcing, triangulation of labour relations, increased flexibility making it possible to offer companies a 'just-in-time workforce'[52] by eliminating the cost of unproductive time, and so on) perhaps appear less as a mutation than as an exacerbation, favoured by digital technology, of a trend observed for several decades. That trend is the casualisation of work, on the one hand, through the interplay of atypical forms of employment characterised by intermittency which are part of a triangular scheme (the 'short-term employment' model) and, on the other hand, by increasing self-employment at the expense of salaried employment (the 'employment without employer' model).[53]

---

51 F. Kéfer, 'L'avenir du travail: les défis lancés au droit du travail et de la sécurité sociale …', and references, available at http://hdl.handle.net/2268/234206.

52 V. De Stefano, above n. 15.

53 Y. Kravaritou, 'Les nouvelles formes d'embauche et la précarité de l'emploi' [1990] 42(1) *Revue Internationale de Droit Comparé* 129 et seq. See also M. Jamoulle, 'Les transformations du droit belge du travail depuis 1975' [1996] *Contradictions* 118–21.

This destabilisation of the working relationship creates a need for protection of platform workers. They are starting to organise themselves in order to defend their interests. Reactions are beginning to emerge in Parliament.

The legislator – international, European, national – must consider new ways of providing social protection for today's workers, who operate in a highly competitive globalised economy and are subject to new ways of working. This poses a significant challenge and raises complex legal issues related to the feasibility of such reforms. Several factors make the approach complex, in particular the role, more or less opaque, of the platform in the contractual scheme, the diversity of services offered and the adequacy of the economic model with the aspiration of a fraction of the population for flexibility and freedom in the organisation of work.

To bring labour law into the 21st century is to reflect on a legal framework that would be better adapted to contemporary society and the pace at which it evolves. It also implies learning from history in order to avoid the disastrous effects of the complete deregulation of labour in the 19th century.

The solutions to these issues depend not on lawyers, but on the balance of power between trade unions and employers and, ultimately, on the will of the political establishment. It is up to the latter not to kill the dynamism of innovative companies, nor to leave workers on the side of the road without protection or decent working conditions, be it in terms of health and safety at work, job stability or decent pay, for instance. In order to meet these contemporary challenges related to working conditions and work organisation, there is, no doubt, room for the launching of an ambitious political project.

'APP-BASED' WORK

The German Case

Rüdiger KRAUSE*

1. INTRODUCTION

Just as in many other countries, platform work ('app-based work') has also spread in Germany in recent years. This applies to both German and international platform operators. An international survey from 2017 lists 30 labour platforms that are active in Germany, 15 of which are based

* Full Professor of Civil Law and Labour Law at the University of Goettingen, lehrstuhl.krause@jura.uni-goettingen.de.

in Germany itself.[1] Examples include Clickworker, Crowdguru, 99designs, Freelancer, Helpling, Lieferando, Streetspotr and Testbirds.[2] Uber is also present in Germany with various business models, but has already discontinued its most controversial service of arranging rides through unlicensed drivers (UberPop) in 2015 due to a conflict with German public transportation law and a resulting violation of unfair competition law. The emergence of platform work, also referred to as the 'sharing economy' by its proponents, is welcomed by economists on the grounds of increased economic efficiency.[3] For some years now, however, there has been growing discussion in Germany about the social risks posed by the phenomenon of platform work.[4] This debate was initiated by the trade unions in 2012 and 2013,[5] but reached the political level early on[6] and has since been intensively studied in the sociology of work[7] as well as in labour law.[8]

---

1 B. Fabo, M. Beblavý, Z. Kilhoffer and K. Lenaerts, *An overview of European Platforms: Scope and Business Models*, Publications Office of the European Union, Luxembourg 2017, p. 10.

2 Cf. C.B. Baethge, M. Boberach, A. Hoffmann and O. Wintermann, *Plattformarbeit in Deutschland*, Bertelsmann Stiftung, Gütersloh 2019, p. 14.

3 Cf. Monopolkommission, Wettbewerb 2016, Hauptgutachten XXI, pp. 365–08, https://www.monopolkommission.de/images/HG21/HGXXI_Gesamt.pdf.

4 The beginning of a more intensive discourse is marked, as far as can be seen, by the contributions of S. Kawalac and W. Menz, 'Die Verflüssigung von Arbeit. Crowdsourcing als unternehmerische Reorganisationsstrategie – das Beispiel IBM' [2013] 6 *Arbeits- und Industriesoziologische Studien* 5; J.M. Leimeister and S. Zogaj, *Neue Arbeitsorganisation durch Crowdsourcing*, Hans Böckler Stiftung, Dusseldorf 2013.

5 For details see below, section 5.2.

6 Cf. Bundesministerium für Arbeit und Soziales, *Grünbuch Arbeiten 4.0*, Berlin 2015, pp. 15–16 and 66, also available in English: https://www.bmas.de/SharedDocs/Downloads/DE/Publikationen/arbeiten-4-0-green-paper.pdf;jsessionid=00CB0784C78F41A70D13A86A184E861D.delivery2-replication?__blob=publicationFile&v=1; Bundesministerium für Arbeit und Soziales, *Weissbuch Arbeiten 4.0*, Berlin 2016, pp. 6, 9–10, 24, 42, 55–62, 85–86, 100, 128–29, 133, 170–71, 176 and 193, also available in English: https://www.bmas.de/SharedDocs/Downloads/EN/PDF-Publikationen/a883-white-paper.pdf?__blob=publicationFile&v=1.

7 Among the first contributions are: A. Boes, T. Kämpf, B. Langes, T. Lühr and S. Steglich, *Cloudworking und die Arbeit der Zukunft*, Beratungsstelle für Technologiefolgen und Qualifizierung, Kassel 2014; A. Boes, T. Kämpf, B. Langes and T. Lühr, 'Landnahme im Informationsraum. Neukonstituierung gesellschaftlicher Arbeit in der "digitalen Gesellschaft"' [2015] 68 *WSI Mitteilungen* 77. Interdisciplinary approach by I. Hensel, J. Koch, E. Kocher and A. Schwarz, 'Crowdworking als Phänomen der Koordination digitaler Erwerbsarbeit – Eine interdisziplinäre Perspektive' [2016] 23 *Industrielle Beziehungen* 162.

8 Early contributions include: T. Klebe and J. Neugebauer, 'Crowdsourcing: Für eine handvoll Dollar oder Workers of the crowd unite?' [2014] 62 *Arbeit und Recht* 4; W. Däubler and T. Klebe, 'Crowdwork: Die neue Form der Arbeit – Arbeitgeber

However, a legal definition or even regulation of platform work has not yet come about in Germany.

In view of the lack of a binding definition, for the purposes of the following, platform work – as part of the broader concept of the platform economy[9] – is to be understood as any form of organisation of work in which the supply and demand for paid work is matched via an internet platform or a smartphone app, so that its operator, at least at first glance, only assumes the role of an intermediary. Such a definition is admittedly fuzzy at the edges. The more precisely one attempts to define platform work, however, the more complex and less catchy the paraphrases become. This is demonstrated, for example, by Eurofound's attempt at defining the elements of platform work[10] and the U.S. Department of Commerce's criteria for 'digital matching firms'.[11] From a phenomenological point of

auf der Flucht?' [2015] 32 *Neue Zeitschrift für Arbeitsrecht* 1032; S. Lingemann and J. Otte, 'Arbeitsrechtliche Fragen der "economy on demand"' [2015] 32 *Neue Zeitschrift für Arbeitsrecht* 1042; T. Klebe, 'Crowdwork: Faire Arbeit im Netz?' [2016] 64 *Arbeit und Recht* 277; E. Kocher and I. Hensel, 'Herausforderungen des Arbeitsrechts durch digitale Plattformen – ein neuer Koordinationsmodus von Erwerbsarbeit' [2016] 33 *Neue Zeitschrift für Arbeitsrecht* 984; R. Krause, *Digitalisierung der Arbeitswelt – Herausforderungen und Regelungsbedarf – Gutachten B zum 71. Deutschen Juristentag*, C.H.Beck, Munich 2016, pp. 99–108. For an extensive overview on the German and international literature up to 2017, see D. Leist, C. Hießl and M. Schlachter, *Plattformökonomie – Eine Literaturauswertung*, Trier 2017.

9 Cf. Eurofound, *Mapping the contours of the platform economy*, Dublin 2019, pp. 5–18.

10 Eurofound, *Platform work: Types and implications for work and employment – Literature review*, Dublin 2018, p. 2: 'Platform work refers to an employment form that uses a platform to enable organisations or individuals to access other organisations or individuals to solve specific problems or to provide specific services in exchange for payment. Accordingly, the focus of the research is on platforms matching supply and demand for paid labour. The main features of platform work, as it is understood in this project, are: Paid work organised through platforms; Three parties involved: platform, client, worker; Aim is to conduct specific tasks or solve specific problems; Form of outsourcing/contracting out; Break-down of 'jobs' into 'tasks'; On-demand services'.

11 U.S. Department of Commerce, Economics and Statistics Administration, Office of the Chief Economist, *Digital Matching Firms: A New Definition in the "Sharing Economy" Space*, 2016, p. 1: 'Digital matching firms exhibit the following characteristics: 1. They use information technology (IT systems), typically available via web-based platforms, such as mobile "apps" on Internet-enabled devices, to facilitate peer-to-peer transactions. 2. They rely on user-based rating systems for quality control, ensuring a level of trust between consumers and service providers who have not previously met. 3. They offer the workers who provide services via digital matching platforms flexibility in deciding their typical working hours. 4. To the extent that tools and assets are necessary to provide a service, digital matching firms rely on the workers using their own'; https://www.commerce.gov/sites/default/files/migrated/reports/digital-matching-firms-new-definition-sharing-economy-space.pdf.

view, work-related platforms in the German discussion,[12] not unlike in the international debate,[13] are regularly distinguished in principle according to whether they involve a location-based (analogue) 'offline' activity (gig work, on-demand work) or a location-independent (virtual) 'online' activity (crowdwork, cloudwork). In addition, numerous subgroups can be formed in both basic constellations.[14]

This chapter will shed light on platform work in Germany in four steps: in an empirical part (section 2), the first question to be addressed, based on the vast amount of available surveys, is what real significance platform work has in the German labour market and what the central working conditions are. Then, in a legal section (section 3), the classification of this new form of work into the traditional categories will be examined as a prerequisite for the granting of protection under labour law. Further considerations apply to the – albeit restrained – activities on the political level (section 4) as well as the strategies of the various actors of working life to regulate the phenomenon of platform work (section 5).

2. EMPIRICAL DATA ON PLATFORM WORK

Even though there is no doubt about the increase of platform work in Germany in both variants mentioned (location-based and location-independent), the actual prevalence of platform work as well as the income and working hours of platform workers cannot be easily

12 Cf. Bundestags-Drucksache 19/16886 of 29.01.2020; Bundestags-Drucksache 19/22122 of 08.09.2020; S. Kirchner, 'Arbeiten in der Plattformökonomie: Grundlagen und Grenzen von "Cloudwork" und "Gigwork"' [2019] 71 *Kölner Zeitschrift für Soziologie und Sozialpsychologie 3, 4–5.* F.A. Schramm, *Arbeitsmärkte in der Plattformökonomie – Zur Funktionsweise und den Herausforderungen von Crowdwork und Gigwork*, Friedrich-Ebert-Stiftung, Bonn 2016; similar W. Däubler, 'Digitalisierung und Arbeitsrecht' [2016] 6 *Soziales Recht – Special Issue* 2, 7–9.

13 Cf. Eurofound, *Employment and working conditions of selected types of platform work*, Publications Office of the European Union, Luxembourg 2018, p. 6; see also V. De Stefano, *The rise of the "just-in-time workforce": On-demand work, crowdwork and labour protection in the "gig-economy"*, International Labour Office, Geneva 2016, p. 1.

14 Cf. Directorate-General for Internal Policies, *The Social Protection of Workers in the Digital Economy*, Brussels 2017, pp. 28–33; Eurofound, above n. 10, pp. 48–67; Eurofound, above n. 13, pp. 4–6; E. Kaganer, E. Carran, R. Hirschheim and T. Olsen, 'Managing the Human Cloud' [2013] 54(2) *MIT Sloan Management Review* 23, 25–28; J.M. Leimeister, S. Zogaj, D. Durward and I. Blohm, *Systematisierung und Analyse von Crowd-Sourcing-Anbietern und Crowd-Work-Projekten*, Hans Böckler Stiftung, Dusseldorf 2016, pp. 41–53; F.A. Schramm, above n. 12, pp. 5–23.

determined because there are no official statistics on this.[15] There are now a large number of German surveys on the various empirical aspects of platform work.[16] In addition, there are numerous international surveys that also contain data on the situation in Germany.[17] However, the figures published in these studies do not match, but differ considerably in some cases.

According to the comprehensive COLLEEM-I survey of 2018, when asked whether any activity has ever been performed offline or online following a digital matching process between provider and demander, the exceptionally high figure of 10.4% of the total adult population is cited for Germany. When narrowed down to those platform workers who work more than 10 hours per week, the number is reduced to 6.6%, although this is still very substantial. When further narrowed down to those who generate more than 50% of their total income from platform

---

[15] Cf. Bundestags-Drucksache 19/6186 of 28.11.2018, p. 2.

[16] I. Berschtek, J. Ohnemus and S. Viete, *Befragung zum sozioökonomischen Hintergrund und zu den Motiven von Crowdworkern*, Zentrum für Europäische Wirtschaftsforschung, Mannheim 2015; J.M. Leimeister, D. Durward and S. Zogaj, *Crowd Worker in Deutschland*, Hans Böckler Stiftung, Dusseldorf 2016, pp. 31–71; B. Bonin and U. Rinne, *Omnibusbefragung zur Verbesserung der Datenlage neuer Beschäftigungsformen*, IZA Research Report No. 80, Kassel 2017; M.F. Maier and S. Viete, *Plattformbasierte Erwerbsarbeit: Stand der empirischen Forschung*, IZA Research Report No. 81, Mannheim 2017; H.J. Pongratz and S. Bormann, 'Online-Arbeit auf Internet-Plattformen. Empirische Befunde zum "Crowdworking" in Deutschland' [2017] 10 *Arbeits- und Industriesoziologische Studien* 158, 163–72; D. Erdsiek, J. Ohnemus and S. Viete, *Crowdworking in Deutschland 2018: Ergebnisse einer ZEW-Unternehmensbefragung*, Zentrum für Europäische Wirtschaftsforschung, Mannheim 2018; O. Serfling, *Crowdworking Monitor Nr. 1*, Kleve 2018, also available in English: https://www.bmas.de/SharedDocs/Downloads/DE/Meldungen/2018/crowdworking-monitor-englisch.pdf;jsessionid=E6FD5DE9F6920F8AE6E3B2ABB31BD556.delivery1-replication?__blob=publicationFile&v=1; C.B. Baethge, M. Boberach, A. Hoffmann and O. Wintermann, above n. 2; O. Serfling, *Crowdworking Monitor Nr. 2*, Kleve 2019, also available in English: https://www.hochschule-rhein-waal.de/sites/default/files/documents/2019/05/08/discussion_papers_in_behavioural_sciences_and_economics_no5.pdf.

[17] U. Huws, N.H. Spencer, D.S. Syrdal and K. Holts, *Work in the European Gig Economy*, FEPS, UNI Europa, University of Hertfordshire, Brussels 2017; Eurofound, above n. 10, pp. 8–47; European Commission, Directorate-General for Internal Market, *Study to Monitor the Economic Development of the Collaborative Economy at sector level in the 28 EU Member States*, Brussels 2018; A. Pesole, M.C. Urzi Brancati, E. Férnándes-Macias, F. Biagi and I. González Vázquez, *Platform Workers in Europe (COLLEEM-I)*, Publications Office of the European Union, Luxembourg 2018; M.C. Urzi Brancati, A. Pesole and E. Férnándes-Macias, *New evidence on platform workers in Europe (COLLEEM-II)*, Publications Office of the European Union, Luxembourg 2020.

work, the number drops to 2.5%.[18] The 2020 COLLEEM-II survey now differentiates among four groups of platform workers (sporadic, marginal, secondary and main). The group of main platform workers (working hours of more than 20 hours per week or where income from platform work constitutes more than 50% of their total income) amounts to 1.5%. The group of secondary platform workers (working more than 10 hours per week or where income from platform work constitutes more than 25% of their total income) amounts to 4.2% of the total adult population in Germany.[19] A German survey arrives at a comparable figure of around 1.7% of the workforce whose main income is said to be based on platform work.[20] With a total workforce of almost 45 million (based on Q4 2020),[21] this would amount to around 675,000 full-time platform workers. Another international survey provides evidence of more than 1 million workers who generate at least 50% of their income from a platform activity.[22] Other German surveys quote significantly lower figures and assume only a few thousand workers for whom platform work is their main source of income.[23] Another international survey also assumes a low figure (35,000 people) in view of the size of the German labour market as a whole.[24]

There is also a lack of clarity with regard to the wages earned by platform workers. According to a German survey, average hourly wages vary from just under EUR 12/h for the lowest 25% to a median of EUR 30/h and around EUR 70/h for the top 25%.[25] In some cases, these wages are significantly higher than the statutory minimum wage in Germany, which will be EUR 9.50 from 01.01.2021, EUR 9.60 from 01.07.2021, EUR 9.82 from 01.01.2022 and EUR 10.45 from 01.07.2022,[26] although it should

---

18 A. Pesole, M.C. Urzi Brancati, E. Férnándes-Macias, F. Biagi and I. González Vázquez, above n. 17, pp. 14–19.

19 M.C. Urzi Brancati, A. Pesole and E. Férnándes-Macias, above n. 17, pp. 15–16.

20 O. Serfling, above n. 16, pp. 12–13.

21 https://www.destatis.de/DE/Presse/Pressemitteilungen/2021/02/PD21_072_13321.html.

22 U. Huws, N.H. Spencer, D.S. Syrdal and K. Holts, above n. 17, p. 26.

23 B. Bonin and U. Rinne, above n. 16, pp. 9–13, 17–18; H.J. Pongratz and S. Bormann, above n. 16, p. 158, 164; see also M.F. Maier and S. Viete, above n. 16, pp. 14–18; H. Schäfer, 'Crowdwork und Plattformarbeit in Deutschland', [2019] *IW-Kurzbericht* 79.

24 European Commission, Directorate-General for Internal Market, above n. 17, p. 91.

25 O. Serfling, above n. 16, pp. 27–28.

26 Cf. Dritte Verordnung zur Anpassung der Höhe des Mindestlohns (Dritte Mindestlohnanpassungsverordnung–MiLoV3) of 09.11.2020, BGBl. I, p. 2356.

be noted that employees are also subject to social security protection. In contrast, the 2020 COLLEEM-II survey indicates significantly lower average hourly wages, between EUR 6.60 and EUR 23.10, for different types of platform activities, but without differentiating between the Member States surveyed.[27] With regard to a – non-representative – sample of a total of 434 crowdworkers, a German survey concludes that in the area of completing microtasks, the activity is the main source of income for only 6% of workers. However, for 94% of workers, this is only a secondary source of income, with monthly earnings ranging between EUR 150 and EUR 250 and working hours between 7 hours and 17 hours per week. In the area of so-called marketplaces, the share of full-time employees rises to 28%, with this group of people earning an average monthly salary of approximately EUR 1,560 with an average weekly working time of just below 32 hours.[28]

Against the backdrop of these contradictory figures, it is currently difficult to assess the actual significance of the phenomenon of platform work in Germany and, in particular, the factual extent of the social risks as a result of this form of employment.

3. LEGAL STATUS OF PLATFORM WORKERS

One of the most important points of contention in the discussion about platform workers has always been the question of their fundamental legal status, because the applicability of protective regulations under labour law depends on this status. In addition to numerous articles, several dissertations have now been published on this subject, in which the entire range of conceivable classification options under German law is discussed in depth.[29]

---

27 M.C. Urzi Brancati, A. Pesole and E. Férnándes-Macias, above n. 17, pp. 37–38.

28 J.M. Leimeister, D. Durward and S. Zogaj, above n. 16, pp. 48–51.

29 J.A. Gärtner, *Koalitionsfreiheit und Crowdwork*, Duncker & Humblot, Berlin 2020; S. Kress, *Crowdwork*, Duncker & Humblot, Berlin 2021; D. Mayr, *Arbeitsrechtlicher Schutz Soloselbständiger am Beispiel der Plattformarbeit*, Duncker & Humblot, Berlin 2021; J. Pacha, *Crowdwork. Arbeitsrechtlicher Schutz einer neuen Beschäftigungsform*, ZAAR Verlag, Munich 2018; S: Walzer, *Der arbeitsrechtliche Schutz der Crowdworker*, Nomos, Baden-Baden 2019; from an Austrian perspective, see J. Warter, *Crowdwork*, ÖGB-Verlag, Vienna 2016; see also B. Waas, 'Crowdwork in Germany' in B. Waas, W.B. Liebman, A. Lyubarsky and K. Kazuka, *Crowdwork – A Comparative Law Perspective*, Bund-Verlag, Frankfurt 2017, pp. 142–71.

3.1. THE TRIANGULAR RELATIONSHIP OF PLATFORM WORKER, PLATFORM AND CLIENT

In order to qualify an activity, it must first be clear which parties are involved and what the basic content of the contractual relationship is. This question is complicated because the business models of the platform operators ('platforms') – and consequently also the legal relationships – differ in many ways. In any case, there is a framework agreement between the platform and the individual platform worker, which in itself, however, does not contain any duty to act, but only ancillary duties (for example, the duty to update personal data).

Furthermore, there is generally also a framework agreement between the platform and the respective client who wishes to list tasks via the platform in the future. A distinction must be made between this and the contract on the concrete work task. In this respect, direct contractual relationships between the platform worker and the client can arise in various ways. This is the case if the platform acts as the representative of the worker or the client and hereby itself submits or accepts contract offers, or merely transmits contract offers or acceptances of the worker or the client. In this sense in particular, the matching process can take place through individualised offers, as well as through a competitive procedure in which, if necessary, several platform workers carry out the work, but the client only accepts and pays for the best work result. It is not uncommon, however, for the platform to forward the individual offer exclusively in its own name, so that even with regard to the concrete work task, only a contract between the platform and the client, on the one hand, and the platform and the worker, on the other hand, comes into being – that is, there is only an indirect relationship between the client and the worker. In the following sections, rather than analysing all of these different variants, only the question that is practically in the foreground will be examined: whether and under what conditions a legal relationship between the platform and the worker can be assumed that leads to social protection under labour law.

This is not to say that an employment relationship cannot arise in individual cases between a platform worker and a client if, for example, a household-related service (e.g. cleaning activities) is repeatedly provided by the same worker to the same client. If, on the other hand, the client is constantly changing (e.g. driving services for different private individuals), an employment relationship is extremely unlikely. Also, this chapter will not discuss in detail scenarios in which work tasks are advertised on internal company platforms only for company employees ('employer-owned internal platforms').[30] It is true that this form of work organisation can also lead to problems. However, the fundamental status of the workers as employees is not disputed in these cases.

3.2. PLATFORM WORKERS AS EMPLOYEES

The qualification of a platform worker as an employee of the platform is of utmost importance for the scope of social protection, which results from the fact that German labour law basically follows the 'all-or-nothing' approach. According to this approach, the applicability of labour law protection depends initially on whether a worker can be considered an employee. This applies, for example, to the statutory minimum wage, continued payment of wages in the event of illness, protection against fixed-term employment relationships and protection against dismissal. German labour law also recognises the legal concept of employee-like persons. However, this group of persons, which will be discussed in more detail below, enjoys significantly less social protection than employees.

The employment contract as the basis for the employee status of workers is regulated in Section 611a (1) of the German Civil Code (Bürgerliches Gesetzbuch; BGB). This provision was only created in 2017, whereby the legislature did not want to set any new standards, but merely codify the case law of the Federal Labour Court (Bundesarbeitsgericht; BAG), which has been firmly established for decades.[31] According to this case law, the key factor in determining whether a worker is an employee is whether someone is obliged to perform an activity in a state of personal dependence (Section 611a (1) sentence 1 BGB). Personal dependency, in turn, can result from the obligation to follow instructions, as well as from external determination, whereby the details – and, in particular, the significance – of the criterion of integration frequently used in previous case law is disputed. However, it is largely undisputed that simple economic dependency is not sufficient to establish employee status unless personal dependency is also involved. The right to issue instructions may relate to the content, performance, time and place of the activity (Section 611a (1) sentence 2 BGB). The employee is bound by instructions if he or she is

30 Cf. Eurofound, above n. 10, p. 48.

31 Cf. Bundestags-Drucksache 18/9232 of 20.07.2016, p. 31.

not essentially free to organise his or her activities and determine his or her working hours (Section 611a (1) sentence 3 BGB). The question as to whether there is a sufficient degree of personal dependency depends on the nature of the respective activity (Section 611a (1) sentence 4 BGB), whereby an overall consideration of all circumstances must be made (Section 611a (1) sentence 5 BGB). If the actual performance of the contract deviates from the designation in the contract, the circumstances are decisive (Section 611a (1) sentence 6 BGB).

German case law has so far only occasionally had to deal with the legal qualification of platform workers. One case from 2016 involved a programmer who essentially programmed construction projects from home for a company over a longer period of time and carried out additional individual tasks at the request of the company's employees. In its decision, the BAG rejected the existence of an employment relationship, focusing primarily on the fact that the worker was legally free to decide whether and to what extent he worked for the company.[32] A mere de facto pressure to accept work assignments and not to reject them was expressly described as irrelevant. The BAG also did not consider the worker's involvement in the work organisation to be so strong that it could be assumed that the activity was determined by the company.[33]

This decision is in line with the established case law of the BAG, which, particularly in the case of framework agreements, focuses on whether a legal obligation to perform activities has been assumed. If there is no such legal obligation, an employment relationship is denied from the outset.[34] However, this must be distinguished from the individual work assignment, which can certainly lead to the establishment of an employment relationship.[35]

As far as location-based or location-independent platform work in the narrower sense is concerned, different views can be identified in the academic literature. On the one hand, some of the scholarship emphasises the special features of platform activities and focuses on aspects such as

---

32 BAG 14.06.2016–9 AZR 305/15, *NZA* 2016, 1453, paras. 22–25.

33 BAG 14.06.2016–9 AZR 305/15, *NZA* 2016, 1453, para. 27.

34 BAG 31.07.2002–7 AZR 181/01, *AP TzBfG* §12 Nr. 1; BAG 16.04.2003–7 AZR 187/02, *NZA* 2004, 40; BAG 15.02.2012–10 AZR 111/11, *NZA* 2012, 733, para. 15; BAG 16.05.2012–5 AZR 268/11, *NZA* 2012, 974, para. 17; BAG 21.07.2015–9 AZR 484/14, *NZA-RR* 2016, 344, para. 25; BAG 21.05.2019–9 AZR 295/18, *NZA* 2019, 1411, para. 26.

35 Cf. BAG 12.11.2008–7 ABR 73/07, *AP BetrVG 1972* §9 Nr. 13, para. 18.

the pre-programming of work, for example through technical settings, the on-going monitoring of activities (i.e. through screenshots) and the existence of evaluation and reputation systems with associated rewards and sanctions,[36] thus ultimately emphasising 'management by algorithm'.[37] In essence, the argument is that platform work amounts to an 'organisation outside organisations',[38] that is, the respective platform operator seeks to avoid the formal integration of workers as employees in its company, but at the same time structures market relations in such a way that a kind of organisation emerges. The majority of the academic literature, on the other hand, is more cautious and assumes that there is often a lack of the necessary duty to follow instructions or external control and that there is only an economic dependency.[39] In any case, the courts are precluded from developing a new concept of employee specifically for platform

---

36 W. Däubler, above n. 12, 2, 35–37; J. Heuschmid and T. Klebe, 'Erwerbsarbeit in der Plattformökonomie und Schutz des Arbeits- und Sozialrechts?' in U. Faber, K. Feldhoff, K. Nebe, K. Schmidt and U. Wasser, *Gesellschaftliche Bewegungen – Recht unter Beobachtung und in Aktion. Festschrift für Wolfhard Kohte*, Nomos, Baden-Baden 2016, pp. 73, 75–76; E. Kocher and I. Hensel, above n. 8, pp. 984, 987–88; J. Warter, above n. 29, pp. 189–93; J. Wenckebach, 'BAG: Crowdwork ante portas! Von persönlicher Abhängigkeit in der digitalen Arbeitswelt' [2020] 10 *Soziales Recht* 165, 172–73; from an Austrian perspective M. Risak, 'Crowdwork – Erste rechtliche Annäherung an eine neue Arbeitsform' [2015] 50 *Zeitschrift für Arbeits- und Sozialrecht* 11, 16.

37 In detail and differentiated; C. Gerber, 'Crowdworker*innen zwischen Autonomie und Kontrolle' [2020] 73 *WSI Mitteilungen* 182, see also Eurofound, above n. 13, pp. 21–23.

38 Cf. G. Ahrne and N. Brunsson, 'Organization outside organizations: the significance of partial organization' [2011] 18 *Organization* 83.

39 K. Bourazeri, 'Neue Beschäftigungsformen in der digitalen Wirtschaft am Beispiel soloselbstständiger Crowdworker' [2019] 36 *Neue Zeitschrift für Arbeitsrecht* 741, 744; W. Däubler and T. Klebe, above n. 8, 1032, 1035–36; O. Deinert, *Soloselbstständige zwischen Arbeitsrecht und Wirtschaftsrecht*, Nomos, Baden-Baden 2015, pp. 20–23; M. Fuhlrott and S. oltmanns, 'Der Crowdworker – (K)ein Arbeitnehmer?' [2020] 73 *Neue Juristische Wochenschrift* 958, 961–62; J.A. Gärtner, above n. 29, pp. 65–72; S. Kress, above n. 29, pp. 57–75; S. Lingemann and J. Otte, above n. 8, 1042, 1043–45; D. Mayr, above n. 29, pp. 137–215; J. Pacha, above n. 29, pp. 160–94; U. Preis, '§611 a BGB – Potenziale des Arbeitnehmerbegriffes' [2018] 35 *Neue Zeitschrift für Arbeitsrecht* 817, 823; K. Riesenhuber, 'Arbeitnehmer(ähnlicher) Schutz von Crowd-Dienstleistern?' [2021] 52 *Zeitschrift für Arbeitsrecht* 5, 17–25; C. Schubert, 'Neue Beschäftigungsformen in der digitalen Wirtschaft' [2018] 71 *Recht der Arbeit* 200, 203–04; S. Walzer, above n. 29, pp. 139–45; R. Wank, 'Die personelle Reichweite des Arbeitnehmerschutzes aus rechtsdogmatischer und rechtspolitischer Perspektive' [2016] 9 *Europäische Zeitschrift für Arbeitsrecht* 144, 168; G. Wisskirchen and J. Schwindling, 'Crowdworking im Lichte des Arbeitsrechts' [2017] 16 *Zeitschrift für europäisches Sozial- und Arbeitsrecht* 318, 320–25.

workers, detached from Section 611a BGB.[40] Rather, it can only be a matter of applying the statutory criteria appropriately according to the respective organisational structure of the platform work, which amounts to a case-by-case approach.[41]

In the only German case to date concerning the employee status of a crowdworker, the BAG has now partially modified its approach. The underlying case involved a worker who was offered and then able to take on individual assignments via an app, which consisted of checking the proper presentation of branded articles in retail stores or gas stations. The worker carried out this activity for around 14 months and achieved average monthly earnings of EUR 1,750 with a weekly working time of around 20 hours. When the company wanted to terminate the legal relationship, the worker sued it for the existence of an employment relationship. In the second instance, the worker was still unsuccessful before the State Labour Court of Munich, which emphasised that there was no duty to work with regard to the framework agreement.[42] With regard to the individual tasks, the worker had not filed the action for invalidity of a fixed-term employment contract in time, which is required in these cases.[43] In contrast, the BAG ruled in the last instance differently by not considering the framework agreement and the individual assignments separately, but analysing the organisational structure as a whole.[44] According to this, the company had created an incentive system that induced the worker to continuously take on tasks, with the tasks being steered in terms of place, time and content in such a way that it could not essentially be freely designed. The BAG thus takes into account the overall assessment of all circumstances required by Section 611a (1) sentence 5 BGB, as well as the recognition of the actual performance of the contract required by Section 611a (1) sentence 6 BGB, and applies the law in a way that is appropriate to the special organisational structure of platform work. However, the controversial opinions on

---

40 Ebenso LAG Hessen 14.02.2019–10 Ta 350/18, *NZA-RR* 2019, 505, para. 22.

41 Cf. R. Krause, 'Die Share Economy als Herausforderung für Arbeitsmarkt und Arbeitsrecht' in J. Dörr, N. Goldschmidt and F. Schorkopf, *Share Economy*, Mohr Siebeck, Tübingen 2018, pp. 147, 162–63. A detailed analysis is admittedly not required if a platform worker (specifically a rider for a food delivery service) has been expressly hired as an employee, cf. LAG Hessen 12.03.2021-14 Sa 306/20, Juris, paras. 5–6, 24.

42 LAG Munich 04.12.2019–8 Sa 146/19, *NZA* 2020, 314, paras. 121–38.

43 LAG Munich 04.12.2019–8 Sa 146/19, *NZA* 2020, 314, paras. 123–25.

44 BAG 01.12.2020–9 AZR 102/20, *NZA* 2021, 552, paras. 28–54. Agreeing, R. Waltermann, 'Abhängige Beschäftigung in der digitalisierten Arbeitswelt' [2021] 38 *Neue Zeitschrift für Arbeitsrecht* 297, 299; disagreeing, G. Thüsing and G. Hütter-Brungs, 'Crowdworking: Lenkung statt Weisung – Was macht den Arbeitnehmer zum Arbeitnehmer?' [2021] 26 *Neue Zeitschrift für Arbeitsrecht – Rechtsprechungs-Report* 231, 233–236.

the decision of the State Labour Court of Munich[45] clearly show how contentious this issue is in German scholarship.

The application of the general concept of an employment contract under Section 611a (1) BGB ultimately leads to a case-by-case consideration of whether a platform worker qualifies as an employee. At the very least, the concept developed by the BAG makes it easier to overcome the hurdle of a lack of a duty to work, which actually stands in the way of employee status, by focusing on the incentive system that causes the worker to continuously perform his or her work tasks in order to obtain or maintain a positive evaluation and thereby gain financial benefits. On the other hand, there is no evidence that the case law on platform work focuses on the concrete content of the activity. Rather, according to Section 611a BGB, it only depends on how the work is organised, thar is, which freedoms the worker actually has or, conversely, how strongly he or she is bound to the specifications of the platform.

3.3. PLATFORM WORKERS AS EMPLOYEE-LIKE PERSONS

As already indicated, the 'all-or-nothing' approach is mitigated by the legal figure of the employee-like person. According to this protection concept, there is a third category of workers in German law between employees and the genuinely self-employed, to whom certain protective provisions of labour law apply. These include anti-discrimination law, entitlement to the statutory minimum leave, inclusion in the area of occupational health and safety, maternity protection and employee data protection. They also benefit from the limitations of liability developed by case law in favour of employees.[46] In addition, disputes between employee-like persons and their principals are subject to the jurisdiction of the labour courts, which are said to have a greater understanding of social protection issues. In contrast, important protective regulations under labour law are inapplicable to employee-like persons, in particular the statutory minimum wage,[47] as well as protection against fixed-term employment contracts and dismissal.

---

45 See F. Bayreuther, 'Arbeitnehmereigenschaft und die Leistung fremdbestimmter Arbeit am Beispiel des Crowdworkers' [2020] 73 *Recht der Arbeit* 241; C. Schubert, 'Crowdworker – Arbeitnehmer, arbeitnehmerähnliche Personen oder Selbstständiger' [2020] 73 *Recht der Arbeit* 248.

46 Cf. LAG Hessen 02.04.2013–13 Sa 857/12, *BB* 2013, 1726, 1727.

47 Cf. LAG Schleswig-Holstein 11.01.2016–1 Sa 224/15, *NZA-RR* 2016, 291, para. 38.

In contrast to the term 'employee', there is no generally applicable legal definition for the term 'employee-like person'. However, Section 12a (1) of the Collective Bargaining Act (Tarifvertragsgesetz; TVG) provides a definition which, although it only applies to the area of collective bargaining law, is also used by case law as a point of reference beyond this.[48] According to this definition, a person is similar to an employee if, firstly, he or she is economically dependent on another person and, secondly, is in need of social protection comparable to that of an employee. Economic dependence exists if the person is dependent on the income from the activity for the contractual partner to secure his own livelihood, which presupposes a certain permanent relationship.[49] This will mostly constitute cases where the person works for only one client. However, the existence of several clients does not exclude the status of an employee-like person from the outset, provided that the activity for one of the clients predominates and the remuneration earned from it forms the decisive basis of existence.[50] For the comparable need for social protection, the case law depends on whether there is a dependency such as that which generally occurs only in the context of an employment relationship and where the services rendered are comparable to those of an employee in terms of their sociological typology.[51] In all of this, it is not the agreements of the parties involved that are important, but only the factual circumstances.

Based on these criteria, it is again a question of the individual case of whether a platform worker is to be classified as an employee-like person.[52] Economic dependency is most likely to be affirmed in cases where a worker only generates tasks via one or two platforms, as is statistically most frequently the case.[53] Furthermore, the income generated from these tasks must serve to secure one's own livelihood, although this is rather rare for platform workers overall, but it can certainly occur. Finally, the comparable need for the social protection of platform workers results from the fact that they typically do not have their own market access and are dependent on the digital infrastructure of the platform. In addition, the status

48 BAG 17.01.2006–9 AZR 61/05, *NJOZ* 2006, 3821, para. 13.

49 BAG 17.01.2006–9 AZR 61/05, *NJOZ* 2006, 3821, para. 14; BAG 21.02.2007–5 AZB 52/06, *NZA* 2007, 699, para. 11, BAG 21.12.2010–10 AZB 14/10, *NZA* 2011, 309, para. 8.

50 BAG 30.08.2000–5 AZB 12/00, *NZA* 2000, 1359, 1360.

51 BAG 02.10.1990–4 AZR 106/90, *NZA* 1991, 239, 240; BAG 17.01.2006–9 AZR 61/05, *NJOZ* 2006, 3821, para. 14.

52 Detailed analysis by D. Mayr, above n. 29, pp. 254–78.

53 Cf. J.M. Leimeister, D. Durward and S. Zogaj, above n. 16, p. 31.

achieved on a particular platform through the evaluation and reputation systems is not transferable, so that a kind of 'lock-in effect' arises for the platform worker; that is, he or she does not have the 'exit option' typical of independent market actors. If a platform worker is not an employee due to a lack of personal dependency, the requirements for qualification as an employee-like person may therefore still exist.[54] However, the resulting protection under labour law is at a rather low level, as already mentioned.

3.4. PLATFORM WORKERS AS HOMEWORKERS

Finally, whether platform workers can be classified as homeworkers in the sense of the Home Work Act (Heimarbeitsgesetz; HAG) is a contentious issue. However, this is only conceivable for those platform workers who work at home without being tied to a specific location, which is statistically often the case for crowdworkers,[55] while, for example, riders for food delivery companies who work in public spaces are excluded in this respect from the outset. The qualification as a homeworker would result in the application of an independent protection regime that clearly lags behind the general protection under labour law, but is nevertheless more comprehensive than the legal protection afforded to (other) employee-like persons. For example, the HAG contains special provisions on the setting of minimum wages, wage protection, labour protection and (albeit limited) protection against termination. Furthermore, there are special protective provisions on continued payment of wages in the event of illness and provisions on vacation leave. Lastly, homeworkers are included in the scope of the Works Constitution Act (Betriebsverfassungsgesetz; BetrVG) if their primary work is conducted for one establishment.

However, whether platform workers working at home are subject to the statutory application requirements of the HAG is disputed. In the aforementioned case of the construction projects programmer, the BAG affirmed his status as a homeworker,[56] although in this case there was the unique aspect that the company had successively assigned certain tasks to the worker for completion. A minority of scholars also generally assumes that crowdworkers qualify as homeworkers because the provisions of the

54 Ebenso etwa J. Pacha, above n. 29, pp. 198–206.
55 J.M. Leimeister, D. Durward and S. Zogaj, above n. 16, pp. 53–54.
56 BAG 14.06.2016-9 AZR 305/15, *NZA* 2016, 1453, paras. 41–53.

HAG must be interpreted in accordance with the special features of digital work.[57] According to the majority of the literature, however, the HAG is not tailored to the specific work situation of crowdworkers because the specific work tasks to be completed are not assigned to the individual platform worker by the entrepreneur, but rather, the crowdworkers select the tasks that suit them according to the respective digital infrastructure.[58]

3.5. REVIEW OF GENERAL TERMS AND CONDITIONS

Irrespective of the question of the scope of protection under labour law, it should be noted that contracts between platform operators and platform workers can be subject to a judicial review of their content if they are pre-formulated, that is, if they have not been individually negotiated, which is practically always the case. Academic literature cites numerous cases of clauses that are invalid under the relevant rules of civil law (Sections 305 *et seq.* BGB). This applies, for example, to a contractual provision according to which a service provided in full by the crowdworker can be rejected by the platform or the client without giving reasons and accordingly does not have to be paid,[59] although this rarely happens in practice.[60] However, corresponding legal proceedings in which platform workers assert the invalidity of contractual agreements have not yet become known. In addition, an academic article correctly points out the structural distortions that result when the need for the protection of platform workers is addressed exclusively in individual lawsuits and thus a juridification of social conflicts takes place that would be better decided through democratic collective processes.[61]

---

57 In particular J. Pacha, above n. 29, pp. 212–64; similar R. Waltermann, 'Digitalisierung der Arbeitswelt – arbeits- und sozialrechtliche Fragen' in C. Kitaibl, R. Mosler and H. Pačić, *Gedenkschrift Robert Rebhahn*, Manz, Vienna 2019, pp. 635, 647; for a case-to-case approach D. Mayr, above n. 29, pp. 216–54.

58 W. Däubler and T. Klebe, above n. 8, 1032, 1036; O. Deinert, 'Die heutige Bedeutung des Heimarbeitsgesetzes' [2018] 71 *Recht der Arbeit* 359, 363; J.A. Gärtner, above n. 29, pp. 91–95; R. Krause, above n. 8, p. 105; K. Riesenhuber, above n. 39, 5, 40–41; B. Waas, above n. 29, pp. 142, 170–71; G. Wisskirchen and J. Schwindling, above n. 39, 318, 325–26; from an Austrian perspective M. Risak, above n. 36, 11, 16.

59 Cf. W. Däubler and T. Klebe, above n. 8, 1032, 1037–38; B. Waas, above n. 29, pp. 142, 171–76; detailed S. Walzer, above n. 29, pp. 105–23.

60 C. Gerber, above n. 37, 182, 186–87.

61 I. Hensel, 'Die horizontale Regulierung des Crowdworking: Wer bestimmt die Regeln?' in I. Hensel, D. Schönefeld, E. Kocher, A. Schwarz and J. Koch, *Selbstständige Unselbstständigkeit. Crowdworking zwischen Autonomie und Kontrolle*, Nomos, Baden-Baden 2019, pp. 215, 223–24.

3.6. JURISDICTION AND APPLICABLE LAW

Questions of jurisdiction and applicable law in cross-border crowdwork are intensively discussed in the academic literature.[62] However, there have not yet been any legal proceedings in which these aspects have played a role.

4. ACTIVITIES AT THE POLITICAL LEVEL

A study from 2017 analysed the positions and strategies of more than 50 predominantly German political, economic and social actors on the topic of the platform economy and crowdworking, including political parties, ministries, trade unions and numerous associations.[63] In the following analysis, however, not all of these attitudes will be explored. Rather, the focus will be on the question of which actor actually regulates the working conditions of platform workers or seeks to regulate them, and in what way.

The German Federal Ministry of Labour and Social Affairs (Bundesministerium für Arbeit und Soziales; BMAS) took up the phenomenon of platform work at an early stage and addressed it both in the Green Paper 'Working 4.0' from 2015[64] and, primarily, in the subsequent White Paper 'Working 4.0' from 2016.[65] However, there have not yet been any concrete regulatory proposals or even a draft law. At least the BMAS, together with the trade union for food, beverages and catering (Nahrung-Genuss-Gaststätten; NGG), which is responsible for the food delivery companies, published joint policy paper in 2019, which forcefully describe the problematic working conditions in this sector and call for fair working conditions and social protection to also apply in the platform economy.[66] However, it essentially only refers to the current legal situation without announcing any concrete legislative measures.

---

62 W. Däubler, above n. 12, 2, 39–42; W. Däubler and T. Klebe, above n. 8, 1032, 1038–40; J.A. Gärtner, above n. 29, pp. 124–35; S. Kress, above n. 29, pp. 115–31; D. Leist, C. Hiessl and M. Schlachter, above n. 8, pp. 27–31.

63 S. Greef and W. Schroeder, *Plattformökonomie und Crowdworking: Eine Analyse der Strategien und Positionen zentraler Akteure*, Kassel 2017.

64 Cf. Bundesministerium für Arbeit und Soziales, above n. 6, pp. 15–16, 66.

65 Cf. Bundesministerium für Arbeit und Soziales, above n. 6, pp. 6, 9–10, 24, 42, 55–62, 85–86, 100, 128–29, 133, 170–71, 176 and 193.

66 https://www.ngg.net/fileadmin-ngg.net/medien/2019/PDF/190206_Gemeinsames_Papier_NGG_BMAS_final.pdf.

At the end of 2020, the BMAS published a key issues paper in which it advocates fair work in the platform economy, following the deliberations of the 'Denkfabrik Digitale Arbeitsgesellschaft' (Digital Labour Society Think Tank), which is part of the Ministry.[67] Specifically, it calls for, among other things, facilitating the enforcement of employee rights, proposing a burden-of-proof rule in favour of platform workers for this purpose. Insofar as the platform worker presents indications of an employment relationship with the platform operator, the burden of proof for the non-existence of an employment relationship should lie with the platform operator. Furthermore, fair employment conditions are also envisaged for solo self-employed platform workers. This includes minimum notice periods to prevent immediate termination of the employment relationship by the platform operator ('digital cold dismissal'). In addition, regulations on vacation, continued payment of wages in the event of illness and maternity protection are being considered. A joint approach of the BMAS with the German Federal Ministry of Justice and Consumer Protection (Bundesministerium der Justiz und für Verbraucherschutz; BMJV) has also been announced so that general terms and conditions that disadvantage platform workers can be reviewed in court more easily and without complications. In the area of social security law, solo self-employed platform workers are to be included in the statutory pension scheme, and platform operators are to share in the costs of old-age provision. A cost-sharing of the platform operators in the health insurance for solo self-employed platform workers is also to be examined. With regard to location-based platform work (for example, food delivery services), ways to provide protection through statutory accident insurance are to be considered.

All of these considerations in the area of labour and social law are still a long way from being implemented in law, especially since the leading associations on the employer side and the trade unions take opposing positions on the issue of regulating platform work,[68] and the general election in autumn 2021 may lead to a new political situation. Nevertheless, the key issues paper clearly shows which elements a legal regulation of platform work in Germany could contain.

---

67 https://www.denkfabrik-bmas.de/fileadmin/Downloads/eckpunkte-faire-plattformarbeit_1_.pdf.

68 Cf. on the one hand, Bundesvereinigung der Deutschen Arbeitgeberverbände (BDA), *Selbstständigkeit fördern, statt unnötig zu regulieren*, Opinion of 19.11.2020; on the other hand, Deutscher Gewerkschaftsbund (DGB), *DGB-Diskussionspapier zur Plattformarbeit, Regeln für Plattformarbeit*, 2019.

5. ACTIVITIES OF LABOUR MARKET ACTORS

At the level of labour market actors, three groups can essentially be distinguished that have undertaken various activities which are relevant in the present context: firstly the platform operators themselves or the German Crowdsourcing Association acting on their behalf; secondly, the established trade unions; and thirdly, those who are directly affected, that is, the platform workers, insofar as they develop collective forms of action and thereby become self-effective.

5.1. CODE OF CONDUCT OF PLATFORM OPERATORS

A first important step was the creation of a Code of Conduct in 2015 on the initiative of the German platform operator Testbirds, which was further developed in 2017[69] and signed initially by seven German crowdsourcing companies and one British crowdsourcing company active in Germany,[70] as well as supported by the German Crowdsourcing Association.[71] This code provides for various general principles. For example, only legally compliant tasks are to be assigned, information about the legal situation is to be provided, and respectful interaction is to be cultivated. With regard to payment, a price calculation according to the best knowledge and conscience of the platform operator is promised, as well as a number of individual modalities for the payment of remuneration (at least once a month). There is also talk of a user-friendly working environment, opportunities for further training, clear task definition, constructive feedback, a regulated acceptance process, including the basic granting of an opportunity for reworking, and respect for the privacy of crowdworkers.

The fundamental shortcomings of codes of conduct have long been known. Firstly, they are merely unilateral regulations and not contractual agreements with representatives of the crowdworkers concerned. Secondly, they are soft law, so it is at least doubtful whether a crowdworker would be able to invoke these principles in a court case. Thirdly, and lastly, many of these principles are vaguely formulated. Nevertheless, this first step

---

69 http://crowdsourcing-code.com/.

70 Testbirds, Clickworker, Content, Crowdguru, Streetspotr, AppJobber, ShopScout and Bugfinders.

71 Currently, the Code of Conduct has been signed by Testbirds, Clickworker, Content, Crowdguru, Streetspotr, AppJobber, Digivante as well as (since 2019) Jovoto and Textbroker.

should not be underestimated, as these principles attempt to constructively address the main problems in the working conditions of crowdworkers and to provide tried and tested solutions.

5.2. INITIATIVES OF ESTABLISHED TRADE UNIONS

As mentioned at the outset, the German trade unions were quick to recognise the risks that the spread of platform work could pose for workers by substituting regular jobs with poorly paid and insecure jobs.[72] As early as 2012, the trade union for service workers (Vereinte Dienstleistungsgewerkschaft; ver.di) published a position paper on the subject entitled 'Crowdsourcing and cloudworking: dangers for society and employees'.[73] One trigger for the trade union debate was the introduction of the 'Generation Open' programme by IBM, in which, as far as can be seen, internal and external crowdworking was practiced on a large scale for the first time in Germany, which prompted the trade union for metal workers (IG Metall) in 2013 to draw attention to this novel phenomenon and to develop counterstrategies.[74] In addition to the two trade unions ver. di and IG Metall, the aforementioned trade union NGG is also active in the area of platform work. It is no coincidence that these three trade unions, which are united under the umbrella of the German Confederation of Trade Unions (Deutscher Gewerkschaftsbund; DGB), have turned their attention to platform work, as the organisational areas of IG Metall, ver.di and NGG are the ones most affected by this new phenomenon.

A major response to this new development is the amendment of the trade union statutes. For example, IG Metall expanded its statutes in 2015 to the effect that since 2016, not only employees, but also self-employed persons, can become trade union members.[75] This includes platform workers who are not employees, but also extends considerably further. The same applies to the ver.di trade union,[76] the NGG trade union[77] and the trade union

[72] Concise summary of the specific risks of platform work by B. Keller and H. Seifert, 'Atypische Beschäftigungsverhältnisse in der digitalisierten Arbeitswelt' [2018] 71 *WSI Mitteilungen* 278, 282.

[73] https://innovation-gute-arbeit.verdi.de/++file++557583e5aa698e5a58000e47/download/verdi-Positionspapier_Cloudworking-Crowdsourcing.pdf.

[74] https://www.igmetall.de/download/docs_0195804_IGM_Crowdsourcing_Web_ec8e869de1e912d44199c2db810c5585eec9ce57.pdf.

[75] See Section 3 No. 1 para. 5 statutes of IG Metall.

[76] See Section 6 No. 1 lit. b statutes of ver.di.

[77] See Section 4 No. 1 para. 2 statutes of NGG.

for building, agriculture and environment (IG Bauen-Agrar-Umwelt; IG BAU).[78]

The most comprehensive activities in the field of platform work have so far been developed by IG Metall, which is probably due primarily to the personal commitment of authoritative trade union executives, but also to the considerable resources available to this largest and most powerful German trade union. For example, IG Metall had already launched the 'Crowdsourcing Project' in 2015, which aims to improve working conditions on digital platforms. A milestone is the so-called 'Frankfurt Paper on Platform-based Work' from 2016, which was developed by IG Metall in collaboration with the Austrian Chamber of Labour (Arbeiterkammer), the Austrian Trade Union Federation (ÖGB), the Danish Union of Commercial and Clerical Workers (HK) and the Swedish trade union Unionen, as well as the U.S./Canadian trade unions International Brotherhood of Teamsters Local 117 and Service Employees International Union.[79] This declaration outlines numerous demands relating to respect for national law and international principles, clarification of the employment relationship, the right of association, pay, social security, issues of arbitration and transparency and the on-going optimisation of regulation.

One important fruit of this initiative is the participation in the revision of the aforementioned code of conduct of platform operators in its 2017 version. By contrast, a collective agreement between IG Metall and individual platform operators or the German Crowdsourcing Association has not yet come about, although it is not known for what reasons this is the case, or whether legal concerns from the perspective of anti-trust law may have played a role. That this problem is familiar to the trade unions is shown by the 'Frankfurt Paper on Platform-based Work', which addresses this issue with the wording that: 'Laws that prohibit platform-based workers classified as independent contractors from organising and negotiating collective agreements with platform operators should be reassessed.'[80] Of course, the authoritative decision of the ECJ in the FNV Kunsten case[81] has been discussed extensively in Germany, with differing assessments in the academic literature as to whether collective agreements

78 See Section 4 No. 2 sentence 2 lit. c statutes of IG BAU.

79 https://www.igmetall.de/download/20161214_Frankfurt_Paper_on_Platform_Based_Work_EN_b939ef89f7e5f3a639cd6a1a930feffd8f55cecb.pdf.

80 Cf. IG Metall et al., 'Frankfurt Paper on Platform-based Work', above n. 79, p. 5.

81 Case C-413/13, *FNV Kunsten Informatie en Media v. Staat der Nederlanden*, ECLI:EU:C:2014:2411.

of employee-like persons or solo self-employed persons are compatible with European anti-trust law according to Article 101 TFEU.[82] Although there are good reasons to believe that at least economically weak platform workers, regardless of their status, can invoke the freedom of association guaranteed under German constitutional law in accordance with Article 9 para. 3 of the Basic Law (Grundgesetz; GG),[83] conversely, there is no doubt that the question of the admissibility of collective agreements can only be bindingly decided by the ECJ.

A second result is the development of the dedicated platform 'Fair Crowd Work', which went online in 2017 and whose primary goal is to break down the isolation of individual crowdworkers and enable them to effectively safeguard their own work-related interests.[84] A central instrument for this is the creation of transparency across the various platforms by giving platform workers the opportunity to evaluate the platform operators in turn, so that in this way a reverse rating is created, as it were.[85] Currently, there are 12 ratings of platforms on the 'Fair Crowd Work' website, ranging from comprehensively positive to predominantly negative.[86] This is intended to create an incentive for platform operators to continuously improve their working conditions in order to obtain a more positive rating and, if necessary, to prevent the migration of qualified platform workers in particular to better-evaluated competing platforms. In terms of model theory, this works if platform operators are interested in a positive reputation or even have to seriously reckon with platform workers choosing the exit option in larger numbers to continue working on another platform in the event of a negative rating, because this reduces the labour pool, which in turn can reduce the number of crowdsourcers and, above all, the number of profitable matching processes.

---

82 Instead of many see R. Krause, 'Kollektivverträge für soloselbstständige Plattformbeschäftigte?' in O. Deinert, T. Klebe, R. Pieper, M. Schmidt and S. Wankel, *Festschrift für Michael Kittner zum 80. Geburtstag*, Bund-Verlag, Frankfurt 2021, pp. 239–46; C. Schubert, 'Tarifverträge zum Schutz von Crowdworkern trotz Kartellverbot?' in O. Deinert, J. Heuschmid, M. Kittner and M. Schmidt, *Demokratisierung der Wirtschaft durch Arbeitsrecht. Festschrift für Thomas Klebe zum 70. Geburtstag*, Bund-Verlag, Frankfurt 2018, pp. 351–62, each with further references.

83 Comprehensive argumentation by J.A. Gärtner, above n. 29, pp. 136–214.

84 http://faircrowd.work/de/.

85 This is also in line with the approach of the 'Fairwork' initiative, cf. Fairwork, *Fairwork Germany Ratings 2020: Arbeitsstandards in der Plattformökonomie*, Berlin, Oxford 2020, pp. 11–14, 22–26, available also in English: https://fair.work/wp-content/uploads/sites/131/2020/11/Germany-English-report-1.pdf.

86 http://faircrowd.work/de/platform-reviews/.

Whether this mechanism, which relies on market forces, actually has an effect has not yet been empirically investigated, however. Provided that the number of labour providers is sufficiently large to ensure a constant supply of labour from the perspective of the platform operators, regardless of their reputation and the prevailing working conditions, evaluation on the part of the platform workers plays no role from a purely economic perspective and therefore remains largely inconsequential. The fact that a number of German platform operators have signed the code of conduct even without economic or even legal compulsion demonstrates, however, that at least a number of actors on the company side are interested in a positive image and smooth labour relations.

The third element to be mentioned is the creation of an Ombuds Office for the settlement of individual disputes between crowdworkers and those platform operators who have signed the aforementioned code of conduct. The Ombuds Office, which began its activities in 2017, consists of five persons:[87] a neutral chair (currently a judge from the local labour court in Frankfurt); a representative of the German Crowdsourcing Association; a representative of the DGB or a member of a trade union; a representative from one of the platform operators that have signed the code of conduct; and a crowdworker registered on one of the platforms. This composition of the Ombuds Office is intended to take into account the different interests and horizons of experience in the settlement of disputes. The regularly published annual reports show that the Ombuds Office is definitely being used. Thus, in 2017, a total of seven cases, in 2018, a total of 23 cases[88] and in 2019, a total of 14 cases[89] were brought to the Ombuds Office, including for the first time two cases in English. Most disputes were settled amicably. In individual cases, however, the Ombuds Office also expressed its views on the interpretation of the code of conduct or on the other rights and obligations of the parties involved, concerning questions such as when remuneration is earned and under what conditions a contractual relationship may be terminated by the platform operator due to an expression of opinion or the disclosure of trade secrets by a platform worker. Hence, the creation of an Ombuds Office serves as a mechanism

87 Cf. Section 3 Crowdsourcing Code of Conduct, Ombuds Office, Rules (updated 21.09.2018), https://ombudsstelle.crowdwork-igmetall.de/rules.html.

88 https://ombudsstelle.crowdwork-igmetall.de/pdf/Ombuds_Office_for_paid_Crowdsourcing_Report_2017_2018_EN.pdf.

89 https://ombudsstelle.crowdwork-igmetall.de/pdf/Ombuds_Office_for_paid_Crowdsourcing_Report_2019_EN.pdf.

for resolving individual disputes, but at the same time contributes to the development of some kind of a 'platform law'.

The fourth element to be mentioned, IG Metall and the YouTubers Union, an Internet movement founded in 2018 and now with more than 15,000 members, agreed to cooperate in 2019 under the title 'FairTube' in order to achieve better working conditions in this field as well. Then, at the end of 2020, the association FairTube e.V. was founded, whose main goal is to promote fairness, transparency, accountability, dialogue, freedom from discrimination and democratic participation for all platform workers. FairTube e.V. began its online operation in February 2021.[90]

Furthermore, the trade union ver.di has established an independent organisational unit for individual counselling of self-employed members, with its own budget, which serves a total of around 30,000 self-employed members, although no information is available on the extent to which this service is used by platform workers in particular. In addition, ver.di is holding talks with some platform operators in Germany with the long-term goal of reaching binding regulations on the working conditions of platform workers.[91] Some report that collective agreements have already been concluded between platform operators and platform workers with the participation of ver.di as well as other German trade unions,[92] but there is no reliable information on this.

5.3. SELF-EMPOWERMENT OF PLATFORM WORKERS

In addition to the activities of the established trade unions, there have also been independent actions by platform workers in the area of food delivery ('riders'), some of whom also network across companies and internationally via social media (Facebook, WhatsApp). In this respect, the first issue is the establishment of works councils in accordance with the provisions of the BetrVG, which, however, is only effective under current law if the workers are employees or homeworkers, working mainly for the establishment (Section 5 para. 1 sentence 2 BetrVG). For example, a works council was set up at Deliveroo's Cologne site in spring 2018 with the support of the trade union NGG, but it eventually had to cease

90 https://fairtube.info/.

91 T. Haipeter and F. Hoose, 'Interessenvertretung bei Crowd- und Gigwork' [2019] *IAQ-Report 05*, pp. 11–13.

92 Eurofound, above n. 13, p. 54.

its activities because the management did not extend the fixed-term employment contracts of the works council members.[93] At Foodora, on the other hand, the riders were apparently more successful with regard to the establishment of a works council at the Cologne site,[94] while it recently became known that attempts are being made at Lieferando to disrupt the establishment of a works council independent of the employer, also at the Cologne site.[95] Furthermore, at Delivery Hero, which is also active in the field of food delivery, parity co-determination has even been established on the supervisory board following a decision by the Berlin Regional Court[96] applying the German Co-Determination Act due to the large number of employees hired as workers. Following the conversion of the company into a European Company (SE), this consists of six members, three of whom are from the employee side, which originally included a rider.[97] However, according to Delivery Hero SE's Corporate Governance Annual Report 2019, the person in question was only a member of the Supervisory Board from July 2018 to March 2019.[98]

Incidentally, Deliveroo and Foodora riders at the Berlin site did not turn to the established trade union ver.di, but to the grassroots association Free Workers' Union (FAU) to represent their interests.[99] This has resulted in negotiations with Foodora as well as labour-struggle-like actions by riders, but not in any kind of collective agreement.[100] Whether the FAU is a trade union under German labour law at all and could therefore conclude an effective collective agreement is, however, doubtful and has been denied by the regional labour court (on the occasion of an earlier labour dispute).[101] Moreover, at the German food delivery company Gorillas, the riders at the Berlin site organised themselves independently in a 'Gorillas Workers Collective' and in the summer of 2021 waged such a fierce struggle against

---

93 I. Zander, 'Naturtalent der Mitbestimmung' [2018] 3 *Mitbestimmung* 16, 17–18.

94 T. Haipeter and F. Hoose, above n. 91, 18.

95 https://taz.de/Lieferando-torpediert-Betriebsratswahl/!5676689/.

96 LG Berlin 09.03.2018–102 O 72/17 AktG, *ZIP* 2018, 1692.

97 G. Hinck, 'Rider Captain unterwegs in den Aufsichtsrat' [2018] 3 *Mitbestimmung* 19, 20–22.

98 Delivery Hero SE, *Corporate Governance-Geschäftsbericht 2019*, p. 45, https://ir.deliveryhero.com/download/companies/delivery/cgreport/Delivery_Hero_Corporate_Governance_Bericht_2019_de.pdf.

99 G. Palmer, 'Foodora & Co.: Die Revolte der neuen Dienstbotenklasse' [2017] 62(7) *Blätter für deutsche und internationale Politik* 32.

100 Cf. A. Degner and E. Kocher, 'Arbeitskämpfe in der "Gig-Economy"?' [2018] 51 *Kritische Justiz* 247, 248–53.

101 LAG Berlin-Brandenburg 16.02.2010–19 SaGa 2480/09, *BeckRS* 2010, 68201.

the platform operator that even the Federal Minister of Labour and Social Affairs got involved in the dispute.[102]

All this shows that the food delivery platform workers, who belong to the type of on-location, platform-determined work according to Eurofound's categorisation, are most keen to collectivising their interests, while this is the case to a lesser extent for the platform workers belonging to the types of on-location, worker-initiated work and online contest work.[103] This difference can probably be attributed to the fact that the riders meet directly more often in public traffic areas or in certain other places than isolated platform workers and, due to the uniformly precarious working conditions, there is more of a feeling of solidarity and a will to improve one's own working situation through joint action.

6. CONCLUSION

Platform work has gained a foothold in Germany in recent years, although the actual spread of this new form of work organisation remains unclear, and estimates range from a mere niche existence to the assumption of a significant share of the German labour market. So far, case law has only had to deal with questions of platform employment in very small number of cases, affirming employee status according to the circumstances of the individual case, which then leads in principle to the applicability of the entire protection under labour law. In a number of cases, however, platform workers will ultimately only have the status of solo self-employed persons. In these cases in particular, it will therefore be important to determine whether new statutory regulations can create a minimum level of protection. Corresponding considerations are being discussed at the political level. However, their implementation is currently uncertain and will depend to a large extent on the general political development in Germany. The activities of the trade unions, above all IG Metall, are at least as important for improving the working conditions of platform workers. In this respect, working towards an appropriate code of conduct for platform operators, the creation of the 'Fair Crowd Work' website, the establishment of an Ombuds Office to settle disputes between platform operators and

---

102 https://www.tagesspiegel.de/berlin/streiks-bei-berliner-lieferdienst-arbeitsminister-heil-schaltet-sich-in-gorillas-streit-ein/27419858.html.

103 Cf. Eurofound, above n. 13, p. 33.

crowdworkers and cooperation with the YouTubers Union are innovative activities with which IG Metall is breaking new ground in order to take into account the specifics of platform work, especially in purely online activities. All this is still a long way from the traditional protection of workers' interests through collective agreements and worker participation, but they are important first steps toward developing relevant protections in a rapidly changing world of work.

CASE LAW APPROACHES AND REGULATORY CHOICES ON PLATFORM WORK

The Italian Case

Maria Teresa Carinci*

1. THE IMPORTANCE OF THE PHENOMENON: QUANTITATIVE AND QUALITATIVE DATA

It is difficult in Italy to quantify the exact number of 'platform workers', meaning by that the people who perform work, generally of brief or very brief duration (a gig task or gig work) for a beneficiary 'via'[1] digital

* Full Professor of Labour Law at University of Milan, mariateresa.carinci@unimi.it.

1 This broad expression can theoretically include three situations: a) the case where the platform directs the worker for its own benefit, thus behaving like a true employer; b) the case where the platform directs the worker, but for the customer's benefit, thus behaving like a temporary staffing agency; c) the case where the platform merely

infrastructures consisting of a website or an app on a mobile device (typically a smartphone).

The broad category of platform workers thus includes all those people who, after interacting with the beneficiary of the service through the platform, provide their work – either entirely online ('gig workers', who also include crowdworkers, the most typical example of which is the Turkers of Amazon Mechanical Turk)[2] or in the physical world ('workers via app', such as riders on food delivery platforms)[3] – with some 'interference' during the performance by the platform, which thus does not act as a mere intermediary since it is still somewhat involved in the performance of the task.

In Italy, at present, not only have there been only a limited number of surveys that attempt to determine the number of platform workers, but they are also far from being exhaustive. This is due to obvious reasons: firstly, it is well known that in most cases, the platforms classify platform workers as self-employed workers. As a result, because self-employed workers do not need to be registered with the public entities that regulate the labour market,[4] their number cannot be determined through public registers, so mere estimates must be made. Secondly, there is no generally agreed-upon 'work platform' category, and thus the area to be investigated is also open to dispute and depends upon the choices underlying each survey project.

As a result, the surveys conducted to date – which, for the most part, rely on interviews of the workers – address the qualitative profile of this segment of the labour market in an attempt to outline the profile of workers who operate via platform.

---

puts the worker and customer together, engaging in pure mediation. This last case, however, is outside of the scope of this discussion, as highlighted in the text.

2 For a description of the characteristics of crowdworking, see International Labour Organisation, *Digital labour platforms and the future of work. Towards decent work in the online world*, Geneva 2018, p. 3 et seq. in https://www.ilo.org/wcmsp5/groups/public/---dgreports/---dcomm/---publ/documents/publication/wcms_645337.pdf.

3 The classification adopted herein thus excludes 'asset rental' platforms for the leasing and hiring of property (like AirBnB) and 'sharing' platforms, namely, the sharing of owned property (like BlaBlaCar), in which the providing of labour, if any, is secondary to the use of the property.
For a first attempt to classify the platforms, see International Labour Organisation, above n. 2. See, previously, Florian A. Schmidt, *Digital Labour Markets in the Platform Economy: Mapping the Political Challenges of Crowd Work and Gig Work*, 2017, in https://www.researchgate.net/publication/314719905_Digital_Labour_Markets_in_the_Platform_Economy_Mapping_the_Political_Challenges_of_Crowd_Workand_Gig_Work.

4 That obligation pertains only to employed workers and certain types of 'weak' self-employed workers.

However, it is undisputed that the labour market segment in question is growing rapidly.

In a study published in December 2018,[5] after examining a sample of 26 labour platforms[6] with registered offices in Italy, the Bank of Italy showed that from 2012 to 2017, the total revenue of these companies went from a few million euros to almost 50 million euros per year as a result of both the increase in their number (from one to 24 platforms in six years) and the increase in their size.

The first surveys, published in 2018, estimated that taking into account workers via app and crowdworkers (although it is more difficult to estimate the latter), between 550,000 and 750,000 workers operate in the sector, including around 10,000 food delivery riders.[7]

However, a subsequent survey, published in 2019,[8] estimates that the number of gig workers in Italy is smaller (around 213,000 persons).

Regardless of the exact numbers, there can be no doubt that platform work is destined to increase, due to the competitive advantages that it currently ensures (as a result of the platforms classifying the workers in most cases as self-employed, as well as the lack of ad hoc rules).[9]

Moreover, the emergency caused by the COVID-19 outbreak has further increased the diffusion of this type of labour as well as work via the Internet in general (and thus also the work via the Internet performed by employees of the beneficiary of the work, known as 'remote working').

But who is the gig economy worker?

The qualitative data revealed by the surveys is interesting.[10] Above all, it[11] shows that most of the workers are located in the central-northern areas of

---

5 See Bank of Italy, *Il lavoro nella gig economy. Evidenze dal mercato del food delivery in Italia*, in *Questioni di economia e finanza*, n. 472/2018, on www.bancaditalia.it.

6 The investigation examines only labour-based platforms, thus excluding true asset rental and sharing platforms.

7 See Italian National Social Security Authority (*Inps*), *Rapporto annuale 2018*, 2018, p. 102 on www.inps.it. See also Fondazione Debenedetti, *Rapporto 2018* (not available on the Internet) presented at the Economics Festival of Trento in June 2018: see *La Repubblica* 2 June 2018 and *IlSole24ore* 2 June 2018 in the previously cited research.

8 See Italian National Public Policy Analysis Institute (*Inapp*), *Rapporto sul futuro del lavoro. Le dinamiche del lavoro non standard in Italia*, 2019, p. 54 at https://inapp.org/it/ProgettiCompetitivi/MOSPI/documentazione.

9 Italian law currently only covers riders in the delivery sector (see section 4).

10 Regarding the profile of riders in the food delivery sector, see Italian National Social Security Authority, above n. 7, p. 93 et seq.

11 Here reference is made to the data from the research by Italian National Public Policy Analysis Institute, above n. 8, p. 53 et seq. See also, however, the results of the

the country and are male, with higher than average education levels than most employed persons. All age groups are represented, but among those who engage in this activity as their only job, the youngest (in the 18–29 age range) and the oldest (in the 50–64 range of age) are the most common.[12]

The surveys also reveal some rather worrying additional information: a low percentage of gig workers also have another job, while most of them are looking for work, are inactive or are students.[13] Moreover, a high percentage of gig workers rely heavily on the income from this kind of work, which they consider essential to satisfy their primary needs, and many say that they had to delay unexpected expenses in the past year for financial reasons.[14] Lastly, a not insignificant percentage of gig workers report that they have done this kind of work for more than three years (13%) or more than one and a half years (15%).[15]

In addition, since most of those interviewed work in the informal economy (i.e. they have signed no labour contract and thus work 'under the table'), the qualitative investigations reveal a profile of a very fragile worker – from both an economic and a contractual perspective – who risks being permanently segregated in a marginal labour market.

2. THE LEGAL FRAMEWORK FOR WORKERS IN THE GIG ECONOMY: RESPONSES OF THE COURTS

The courts were the first to question the rules applicable to platform workers' labour relationships. The answer to this question, in Italy as in other countries, in the absence of an ad hoc law that specifically governs this form of work,[16] it depends on whether the labour contract between worker and platform is classified as employment (*lavoro subordinato*) or self-employment (*lavoro autonomo*).

The Italian labour law system is entirely built around two fundamental contractual forms: the employment contract, which guarantees the worker

---

investigation conducted by Italian Labour Union Research Centre (*Osservatorio UIL)* on the gig economy that was published in 2019, at https://sindacato-networkers.it/2019/09/osservatorio-sulla-gig-economy-in-italia-i-risultati-del-2019/.

12 See Italian National Social Security Authority, above n. 7, p. 104.

13 E.g. Italian National Public Policy Analysis, above n. 8; see also Italian National Social Security Authority, above n. 7, p. 102 et seq.

14 E.g. Italian National Public Policy Analysis, above n. 8.

15 See Italian National Social Security Authority, above n. 7, p. 106.

16 But see section 4 for the specific rules applicable to riders in the delivery sector.

significant protections enshrined in law and which cannot be waived by the individual labour contract (regarding, e.g. working time, vacations and leave, protection in the event of illness, termination, etc.); and the self-employment contract, in which the opposite principle prevails, namely, that the parties are free to determine the terms of the exchange and that it essentially has no safeguards for the worker. Over time, however, the law has intervened by identifying, within the self-employment area, two sub-categories: on the one hand, 'weak' self-employment ('coordinated and continuous' work [*lavoro coordinato e continuativo*]; and on the other hand, 'hetero-organised' work [*lavoro eterorganizzato*]). The law gave them certain specific protections for the worker's benefit, although very few protections have been envisaged for 'coordinated and continuous' work, while very broad protections are granted for 'hetero-organised' work. However, the latter situation can be changed by the national collective agreement if it has been signed by certain labour union organisations (see section 4).

Herein, it is important to emphasise that Italian courts, which so far have been asked to resolve the issue of classifying the labour relationship of riders working on delivery platforms (thus, a case of labour via app),[17] have taken different positions.

According to the first ruling in the area (Court of Turin, 7 May 2018),[18] the Foodora riders – who had signed 'coordinated and continuous' self-employment labour contracts with the platform (see section 3) – must essentially be considered self-employed workers because the platform merely coordinates them (as required by the contractual form that was chosen), but it does not direct them insofar as it does not exercise directive power over them (as, however, is required by an employment contract). Specifically, according to the Court of Turin, the riders were free to accept or not accept the job from time to time and to determine the delivery route. Moreover, the platform exercised no disciplinary power over the workers who did not perform the job properly; in fact, the ranking system used by the platform was not intended to punish nonperforming workers, merely to reward good workers.

---

17 Italian case law has, for the time being, addressed the problem of classifying the labour relationship of workers via app, but no rulings regarding crowdworkers have been handed down.

18 See Court of Turin, 7 May 2018, n. 778, with a note by P. Ichino, 'Subordinazione, autonomia e protezione del lavoro nella *gig-economy*' [2018] 2 *Rivista Italiana di Diritto del Lavoro* 283 et seq.

However, if we take a position in this regard, this first ruling pertained only to a cursory examination of how the ranking system really works. As indicated by the most recent case law[19] and as many surveys have now revealed,[20] the ranking systems used by the platforms and, in particular, the delivery platforms, which have been the most closely investigated, are based on constant remote control of the worker's activity (through the geolocation allowed by the apps downloaded on the smartphone). A sanctioning system is associated to this remote control for all practical purposes (the worker is penalised in the assignment of hourly slots, his/her account may be suspended and, in the most serious cases, deactivated). Furthermore, this remote control involves a far-reaching directive power that is largely 'automated' based on the operation of the algorithm. Using the algorithm, the ranking system influences the choice of hourly slots, allowing workers with higher scores to choose the best hourly slots before the other workers. The platform, by setting the algorithm, tells the worker through the app the best routes to follow to make the deliveries and the times to adhere to, among other factors.

Shortly thereafter, a second lower court ruling (Court of Milan, 10 September 2018)[21] – relating to Glovo riders – essentially took the same position.

However, the Court of Appeal of Turin, in the appeal proceeding of the Foodora case (Court of Appeal of Turin, 4 February 2019)[22] came to

---

19 See Court of Milan, prevention measures autonomous section, 27 May 2020 (decree), with a note by R. Galardi, 'Uber Italy commissariata dal Tribunale di Milano per l'ipotesi di reato di intermediazione illecita e sfruttamento del lavoro' [2020] *Labor. Il lavoro nel diritto online* at https://www.rivistalabor.it/uber-italy-commissariata-dal-tribunale-milano-lipotesi-reato-intermediazione-illecita-sfruttamento-del-lavoro/.

20 See, for all, the investigation by the television programme *Report* broadcast on RAI 3 on 11 November 2019, *Easy Rider: la dura vita dei fattorini*, available at http://www.rai.it/programmi/report/inchieste/easy-riders-deef2e44-3027-46be-ac54-e2e401013f9e.html.

21 See Court of Milan, 10 September 2018, n. 1853, with a note by E. Dagnino, 'Ancora ostacoli sulla "via giurisprudenziale" alla protezione dei lavoratori della gig economy in Italia' [2019] 1 *Argomenti di Diritto del lavoro* 151 et seq., which held that the rider is not subject to the platform's directive, organisational and disciplinary power: 'the fact that riders may, at their discretion, decide from week to week what days and hours to work – and also not to work at all – fundamentally precludes any such constraints'; the worker also was not non-hetero-organised during the performance of the work, nor were there 'subsidiary indices' that would lead to a finding of employment (workers used their own work tools – the bicycle – and did not receive fixed, but rather variable, compensation).

22 Court of Appeal of Turin, 4 February 2019, n. 26 with a note by A. Recchia 'Contrordine! I riders sono collaboratori eterorganizzati' [2019] 4 *Il Lavoro nella Giurisprudenza* 398 *et seq*.

a different conclusion, ruling that the riders are indeed self-employed, but must be included in the new category of 'hetero-organised' work introduced by the Jobs Act in 2015.[23]

This is not an insignificant decision.

The new classification of the riders is important for two reasons. Firstly, and most significantly, it recognises that these workers are in no way totally free to decide whether, how or when to work, as the lower court held, to the contrary, that they are subject to significant constraints when they are performing the work ('hetero-organisation'). Secondly, it provides the first interpretation of the characteristics of the new notion of 'hetero-organised' work introduced by the Jobs Act in 2015.

Turning to this first aspect, according to the Court of Appeal of Turin, contrary to the ruling of the lower court, the riders are not free to perform the work according to their preferences because they are de facto constrained to conform their work[24] to the organisation created by Foodora (namely, without the platform exercising true directive power over them). For example, the riders are not free to determine their working time, but must choose one of the hourly slots made available by the platform, and the riders are not free to determine the delivery route, but must choose the shortest route to meet the timeframe imposed by the platform, among other constraints. If workers do not conform their work to Foodora's strictures, they cannot properly perform the obligation they took on. As will be discussed below, that 'de facto adaptation' is the 'core' of the new form of the 'hetero-organised' work introduced by the Jobs Act.

Having thus classified the labour relationship of Foodora's riders, the Court of Appeal should have, as required by the Jobs Act,[25] applied to them all the protections provided in the employment situation. In truth, the ruling is ambiguous on this point: it seems to be inclined – in conflict with the law – to selectively extend employment protections to 'hetero-organised' work.

However, the Italian Supreme Court (Italian Supreme Court N. 1663 of 24 February 2020),[26] which was subsequently called upon to rule in the

---

23 Specifically, by Article 2 of Italian Legislative Decree No. 81/2015.

24 From an overall perspective and also in relation to each hourly slot.

25 Article 2 of Italian Legislative Decree No. 81/2015 (the Jobs Act) requires application of all employment protections, except where the national collective bargaining agreement excludes all or some of them. However, no collective bargaining agreements have done so in the case under discussion here.

26 Italian Supreme Court 24 January 2020, n. 1663 with a note by A. Recchia 'La Cassazione "consegna" ai riders la collaborazione eterorganizzata' [2020] 3

final instance on the same Foodora case, firstly confirmed the classification of the riders' labour relationship as 'hetero-organised' work (as previously held by the Court of Appeal of Turin) and secondly, explicitly ruled that all the employment protections must be applied to 'hetero-organised' work.[27]

Lastly, to provide a complete picture, two additional rulings must be noted: the first by the Criminal Court of Milan; and the second by the Tribunal of Palermo.

In its decision, the Criminal Court of Milan (Court of Milan, prevention measures autonomous section, decree, 27 May 2020)[28] ordered that prevention measures should be applied to Uber Italy for having facilitated the commission by third-party companies (to whom it had contracted the delivery of goods) of the crimes of unlawful intermediation and exploitation of labour (Article 603-*bis* of the Italian Criminal Code) to the detriment of the riders. This latter ruling was not handed down by the Labour Court but by the Criminal Court when applying the prevention measures laid down by law to prevent the commission of serious crimes (specifically, unlawful intermediation and exploitation of labour). However, the decision is very interesting for our purposes because of the careful factual reconstruction of the case: the ruling shows very clearly that the riders (often non-EU workers with temporary residence permits for humanitarian reasons) were: a) recruited by the companies hired by Uber Italy to perform the deliveries on its behalf without any formal labour contract;[29] b) subjected to on-going and very specific directives from the employer companies and Uber Italy's managers; and c) subjected to far-reaching sanctions and also severely exploited (with low compensation, backbreaking hours, sanctions imposed outside of any legal rules, harassment of all kinds, etc.).

The same position was subsequently taken by the Tribunal of Palermo (Tribunal of Palermo, 24 November 2020, n. 3570) which, again on the basis of a careful investigation, recognised that there is a subordinate nature in the relationship between the rider and the platform and that it was due to that decisive reason that the rider – beyond appearances – lacked any

Il lavoro nella giurisprudenza 239. See recently Tribunal of Milano, 28 March 2021, which recognised shoppers as 'hetero-organised' workers.

27 Unless the national collective agreement excludes some protections.

28 See Court of Milan, prevention measures autonomous section, 27 May 2020 (decree), above n. 19.

29 With consequent complete evasion of social security contributions.

substantial freedom to choose whether and when to work. It was, instead, the organisational system put in place by the platform (and incorporated into the algorithm designed to allocate the tasks) that determined whether and when the worker had to make deliveries (making the ranking system a decisive factor in the procedure).

The latter ruling is particularly interesting because it recognises the rider's subordinate position by both applying the 'classic' notion of subordination (understood as hetero-direction) and by resorting to the notion of subordination as 'dual alienation', which was previously affirmed by a well-known 1996 ruling by the Constitutional Court,[30] but hardly ever used in case law. According to the latter approach, subordination exists if there are two conditions: alienation – meaning that the end result of the assignment is for the sole use of others; and alienation of the production organisation that renders the service (hetero-organisation). It is clear that if we take the notion of subordination as dual alienation – therefore changing the focus of the investigation – then the notion of subordination embraces a wider area than the traditional one: it is no longer crucial to ascertain that the employer has directive power, but only titleship of the organisation for which the work is rendered.

However, it is too early to say whether this broader nation of subordination will be accepted in the Italian system.

What is certain, however, is that the recent Italian court decisions have thus brought to light that platform work – which is often presented as an exciting innovation that allows the worker to organise their time and work flexibly – is not at all, in itself, a guarantee of freedom to choose whether or how to work. Instead, platform work can conceal very traditional forms of subordinate work (if not outright exploitation) behind the screen of technology.

The novelty of work via[31] platform does not consist, therefore, of the absence of the directive power, which is a characteristic of the employment (or the 'hetero-organisation' characteristic of 'hetero-organised' work), since the platform, by definition, *organises* the workers' work more or less intensively.

---

30 Constitutional Court, 12 February 1996, n. 30.

31 The platforms being considered here, by definition, interfere to a greater or lesser extent in the organisation of the work; as demonstrated by the facts, see the decision of the Court of Milan, prevention measures autonomous section, 27 May 2020 (decree), cited above n. 19, and Tribunal of Palermo, 24 November 2020, N. 3570 and the investigation by television, cited above n. 20.

Instead, the novelty of the aforesaid work consists of the following: since the algorithm can very rapidly connect the activities of a large number of workers by coordinating those activities among them in real time, the platform makes it possible to significantly fragment the tasks given from time to time to each worker (gig tasks), reducing them to jobs of brief or very brief duration.

Therefore, the platform's main work characteristic is the compartmentalisation (and hence the brevity) of the tasks that triggers excessive competition among workers.

If it is true that historically, the aim of labour law has been to combat competition among workers, today platform work requires specific intervention by the legislator to reach this goal.

3. DIFFERENCES, ACCORDING TO CASE LAW, AMONG THE FORMS OF WORK IN THE ITALIAN SYSTEM

As previously stated, the Italian labour law system is based on a fundamental dichotomy between the employment contract (Article 2094 of the Italian Civil Code) and the self-employment contract (Article 2222 of the Italian Civil Code).[32] As said before, the law thus has introduced, in the self-employment arena, two additional 'weak' forms of self-employment: 'coordinated and continuous' work (Article 409, no. 3 of the Italian Code of Civil Procedure, added to the Italian Code of Civil Procedure by Italian Law 533/1973); and 'hetero-organised' work (Article 2 of Italian Legislative Decree 81/2015). The legislation has given them specific protections.

It is thus based on this framework that Italian courts have classified platform work.

The question is now to identify which characteristics, according to the prevailing case law, distinguish each notion described above.

Starting with the employment contract, it is a widely agreed view in case law that in an employment contract, the worker undertakes to personally perform work subject to the employer's directive power. The employment contract is thus distinguished by the fact that the employer

32 Actually, Article 2222 of the Italian Civil Code delineates the prototype-concept of self-employment – the service contract – which is accompanied by many other specific self-employment contracts which are always contemplated by the Italian Civil Code (transport contract, mandate-contract, etc.) that have the same characteristics as the prototype-concept.

has directive power (i.e. the worker is 'hetero-directed'). According to a first 'classical' notion of employment, directive power consisted of the power to provide specific and precise directives regarding how, where and when to work. However, subsequently, court decisions have appended to a second 'expanded' notion of employment, in which there is directive power even if directives of a general nature are given (e.g. that relate to goals to be achieved or that relate only to the time and place where the work is to be performed, but not its substance). This second 'expanded' notion of employment – aimed at also including within the scope of employment highly qualified workers (managers, journalists, doctors, etc.) in addition to those workers that perform unskilled, repetitive tasks – is, by now, widely accepted and, according to established case law, exists alongside the 'classical' notion cited above.

Conversely, the notion of subordination as 'dual alienation' affirmed in the ruling of February 12, 1996, n. 30 of the Constitutional Court has been accepted so far only in a few isolated cases of case law.

The notion of a self-employment contract mirrors that of the employment contract: according to court decisions, a labour contract is a self-employment contract if the worker undertakes to perform primarily personal work without being subject to the other party's directive power. Obviously, as the scope of employment expands, the perimeter of self-employment shrinks.

As mentioned, the foregoing fundamental distinction was then enhanced (and complicated) by the addition, in 1973, to the Italian Code of Civil Procedure (Article 409, n. 3) of the concept of 'coordinated and continuous' work (or 'quasi-employment' [*lavoro parasubordinato*]). 'Coordinated and continuous' work does not technically constitute a contractual type in and of itself, but rather, a notion that cuts across all self-employment contracts in the system.[33] The aspects that distinguish it do not relate to the agreement between the parties, but the actual manner in which the workers perform their work.

The objective of the legislative intervention regarding 'quasi-employment' was to give certain[34] employment protections to a segment of true

33 See note 32, above.

34 E.g., rules on waivers, settlements and automatic inflation adjustment of work receivables. In addition, those workers enjoy a form of mandatory social security protection; they must be enrolled in the mandatory occupational injury and illness insurance managed by INPS and be afforded maternity and unemployment benefits. The employment court has jurisdiction over disputes (see Article 409, n. 3 of the Italian Code of Civil Procedure).

self-employed workers[35] who are particularly vulnerable, because they do not have enough market power to negotiate the terms of the exchange on an equal footing with their counterparties.

To that end, the law has defined the characteristics that distinguish 'coordinated and continuous' work: a) the prevailing personal nature of the work, meaning that the worker's labour must be more significant than the use of capital, equipment and the contribution of any staff; b) the continuous nature of the work, meaning that the work de facto continues over time for the benefit of a beneficiary (pursuant to a single contract or multiple sequential contracts); and c) the coordination of the work, meaning a functional connection between the worker's activity and the principal's organisation.

If these three requirements are met, the law presumes that the self-employed worker is in a position of substantial weakness compared to the counterparty, into whose organisation the worker is de facto 'inserted' in a long-term manner.

However, the manner of the worker's 'insertion' into the principal's organisation has given rise to much discussion and conflicts in case law, as the law did not clarify what exactly was meant by 'coordination'. Specifically, some decisions have held that 'coordination' was just a form of directive power, albeit milder than that in the employment situation. However, it is apparent that in that way, 'coordinated and continuous' work ended up constituting a segment of employment, restricting the notion of employment.

Lastly, in 2017 the law intervened on the point – with an amendment to the original law (Article 409, N. 3 of the Italian Code of Civil Procedure) – to provide explicitly that coordination exists when the parties, by mutual agreement, state in the contract the manner of the connection between the worker's activity and the principal's organisation (e.g. stating in the contract the times, places and manner in which the work must be performed). It was thus clarified that 'coordinated and continuous' work – as a sub-category of self-employment – is not compatible with the exercise of directive power in any form.

However, because of the ambiguity of the concept of 'coordination' mentioned earlier, or the gradual spread across businesses of technologies that have made it ever easier and faster to link the internal and external facets of a company (email, internet, etc.), 'coordinated and continuous' work, especially starting in the 1990s, has often been used by employers for evasive purposes; namely, to conceal work relationships under the guise

35 As such, therefore, they are not subjected to the directive power of the other party.

of 'coordinated and continuous' self-employment which were, in fact, employment relationships, and thus evade the relevant protections (and the associated costs).

Specifically to obviate this situation and, at the same time, increase protections for weak self-employment (this was the declared intent), in 2015[36] the law again intervened by introducing the new concept of 'hetero-organised' work (which was added to, but did not do away with, 'coordinated and continuous' work).

'Hetero-organised' work, which, like 'coordinated and continuous' work, is not a contract, but a notion that cuts across all self-employment contracts in the system,[37] is present if the worker's activity has the following characteristics: a) it is solely personal; b) it is continuous (using the same meaning explained above for 'coordinated and continuous' work); and c) is 'hetero-organised'.

The 'hetero-organisation' is the core of this new form of work, which, according to case law, applies if the worker, when performing the work, is de facto forced to conform his activity to the principal's changing organisation. The manner of this connection, thus, is not specified in the contract, as required for 'coordinated and continuous' work, nor is it set by the employer from time to time by exercising directive power, as required for employment.

Thus, workers are 'hetero-organised' when they are not free, while working, to independently decide[38] how the work will be done but, to the contrary, are forced to unilaterally change the timing, places and/or manner of performing the job in the midst of the work, in order to integrate it into the principal's organisation, which changes over time.

Consider, just as an example, the computer expert who – having a self-employment contract that requires weekly upgrading of the computer accounting programs used at a company – is then required to go to the company's offices to satisfy their obligation during the (changing) time slots when individual computers are not being used by employees.

Platform workers also find themselves in a very similar situation in all cases where they are de facto forced to work in the hourly slots and in the space/time manner imposed by the platforms' organisation.

---

36 After the attempt made with the introduction of 'project work' (*lavoro a progetto*) by Italian Legislative Decree 276/2003 (the 'Biagi Decree'), which was subsequently made more restrictive by Italian Law 92/2012 (the 'Fornero Law'), the provisions relating to 'project work' were repealed by Italian Legislative Decree 81/2015 (the 'Jobs Act').

37 See above n. 20 and n. 31.

38 Within the limits set forth from the outset in the contract.

Clearly, 'hetero-organised' work can conceal – under the guise of the autonomy that must distinguish it – the exercise of true directive power by the alleged principal (as the Criminal Court of Milan and the Tribunal of Palermo held in their 2020 decisions, see paragraph 2). However, that form of work nonetheless offers the worker an advantage in terms of the burden of proof: the worker does not need to demonstrate that directive power actually exists, but merely that he/she de facto conformed his/her performance to the changing organisation of the principal. In that case, the worker can obtain significant protections.

What, then, are the protections applicable to this form of work?

It is, in principle, much more protected than 'coordinated and continuous' work: in fact, the law extends to 'hetero-organised' work all the protections applicable to the employment. However, at the same time, it allows collective agreements signed by the labour associations which are 'comparatively most representative at the national level' to change or exclude some of those protections, or even all of them (sector by sector).[39] The result is that the considerable protection guaranteed to the worker in theory can then be significantly reduced or eliminated by the collective agreement. In that regard, it is notable that the first national collective agreement for 'hetero-organised' riders took effect on 16 September 2020 (see section 4).

At the same time, it is clear that categorising platform work as 'hetero-organised' work does not answer the two fundamental questions that this form of work poses: how to ensure a sufficient income flow to the worker given the excessive fragmentation of the jobs (gig tasks); and who is responsible for the obligations created by the work relationship, since two parties (both platform and user) can simultaneously, although to varying extents, organise the work. Only an ad hoc law can answer these questions.

4. THE LEGISLATIVE REGULATION OF PLATFORM WORK CARRIED OUT BY SELF-EMPLOYED RIDERS

In 2019, a new law was enacted (Italian Decree Law 101/2019, converted, with amendments, into Italian Law 128/2019) dedicated specifically

39 Moreover, the prevailing view is that there is no limit on the collective agreement's ability to change the protections provided by law. A different approach is taken, however, by Court of Rome, 6 May 2019, n. 4243, with a note by E. Fiorelli, 'Collaborazioni etero-organizzate: l'esistenza di un Accordo collettivo nazionale esclude l'applicazione della disciplina del lavoro subordinato' [2019] 6 *Labor* 699.

to the work relationship of the riders, self-employed workers, with the delivery platforms (which, however, did not amend the legal framework just described). On the one hand, the law in question explicitly confirmed that as a general rule, where the characteristics are satisfied, platform workers (whether riders or another type of worker), must be classified as performing 'hetero-organised' work. On the other hand, it introduced ad hoc rules only for self-employed riders who operate via platform 'work to deliver goods in an urban environment with the use of bicycles or motor vehicles'.

Thus, practically speaking, the 2019 law is essentially useless, because: a) it merely confirms existing case law rulings (according to which work via platform is a type of 'hetero-organised' work); and b) its scope of application is overly restricted, because it governs only the work relationship of riders who operate via platform who perform their work in a fully independent manner (and thus must be considered 'coordinated and continuous' workers or 'simple' self-employed workers).

Considering the current organisation of the delivery platforms – as was previously discussed – this is a rare situation in the real world.

Furthermore, a law that merely addresses the single case of self-employed riders and ignores other types of relationships that present similar problems (as in the case of cleaners/housekeepers, baby-sitters, home repair, etc.) in all likelihood violates the principle of reasonableness of the law imposed by Article 3 of the Italian Constitution.[40]

As to its substance, the 2019 law imposes certain rules – which cannot be weakened by an individual or collective agreement – relating to certain essential aspects of the contract and the riders' self-employment relationship: a) the contract must be in writing for evidentiary purposes [*ad probationem*];[41] and b) compensation cannot be on a piecemeal basis, and the worker must be guaranteed a minimum hourly compensation based on the amount set forth in the national collective agreement for similar industries. This provision (which took effect 12 months after the approval of the law, i.e. 5 September 2020) can be waived by collective

40 Or, which is the same thing, the 'principle of unavailability of the type', as held many times by the Italian Constitutional Court, see Italian Constitutional Court, 25 March 1993, n. 121; Italian Constitutional Court, 23 March 1994, n. 115; Italian Constitutional Court, 15 April 2015, n. 76.

41 Noncompliance with the written form results not only in the imposition of administrative sanctions but also an obligation to pay compensation to the worker and may be evaluated by the Court for purposes of determining the terms to actually apply to the work relationship.

agreements only if signed by the labour and employer organisations that are 'comparatively most representative at the national level'. Furthermore, the worker must be paid increases for work at night, on holidays or in adverse weather conditions; and c) discrimination in any stage of the relationship is prohibited, and the dignity of the worker is protected according to the rules of the Italian Workers' Statute applicable to employment (to the extent applicable). Moreover, d) workers may not be disconnected from the account by the platform and penalised for refusing a job; e) the EU regulation on personal data protection (GDPR 679/2016) applies; f) workers benefit from the mandatory occupational injury and illness insurance managed by INAIL[42] (the responsible public entity) and the insurance premium payable is particularly high because, pursuant to law, it is associated with one day of work; and lastly, g) the end user is responsible for the safety obligations imposed on the employer in an employment relationship for the benefit of the worker (based on the 'utmost technologically possible safety' principle).[43]

Taking a closer look, some of these rules, originally conceived for the employment contract, are ineffectual in a true self-employment contract (consider, e.g. the rules regarding prohibitions on discrimination which impose limits on employers' powers that, by definition, are not present in a self-employment relationship).

What, then, is the true impact of the new law?

The purpose of the 2019 law was to set a threshold of minimum rules that cannot be waived by a contract (either an individual or a collective one) for all the riders on the platforms, regardless of their work relationship.

Consequently, any future collective agreements that apply to the work of 'hetero-organised' riders may not waive those minimum mandatory rules.

However, the 2019 law, as aforementioned, contains a significant exception to this principle: the rule regarding time-based compensation may be changed to piecemeal compensation, albeit only by collective agreements signed between labour and employer organisations that are 'comparatively most representative at the national level'. Therefore, significantly, the threshold of minimum protections provided on paper

---

42 Italian National Institute for Insurance against Accidents at Work (*Istituto Nazionale per l'Assicurazione contro gli Infortuni sul Lavoro*).

43 Under Article 2087 of the Italian Civil Code, the employer must guarantee to the worker the 'utmost safety technologically possible' by using devices and organising the work in the most appropriate manner to safeguard health.

to benefit all self-employed riders can be further reduced in practice by certain collective agreements.[44]

That said, we must point out, again, that the rules set forth in Italian law are largely insufficient. This is true from the standpoint of the substance insofar as they fail to address the two crucial problems of: a) identifying the party who is liable to the worker; and b) the excessive fragmentation of the relationship (and the compensation). This is also true from the point of view of its application, because it fails to address many other types of platform work that present similar problems.

5. COLLECTIVE BARGAINING AGREEMENTS FOR EMPLOYED OR SELF-EMPLOYED RIDERS

In Italy, until recently, only two national collective agreements had been signed, neither relating to platform work as a whole, but solely to the work relationships characteristic to riders on delivery platforms. The former involves riders who are employees, and the latter involves self-employed riders (whether 'hetero-organised', 'coordinated and continuous' or 'simple' self-employed workers). On 29 March 2021, an important corporate collective agreement was signed by Just Eat and the major collective unions.

By way of introduction, it must be borne in mind that because of trade union pluralism,[45] multiple labour organisations can exist, operate and sign collective agreements in every sector in Italy. In the absence of a trade union law, none of those collective agreements applies to everyone, and thus in theory each applies only to the parties (employer and worker) who are members of the trade organisations that signed it.

However, based on settled court rulings, the collective agreement applies if the employer is a member of the signatory trade union.[46] As to the workers, however, it is sufficient that they do not object to its application. If those conditions are met, the collective agreement must be applied to the individual work relationship.

---

44 See the Collective Agreements signed by Assodelivery and UGL on 16 September 2020, para 5.

45 Based on the principle of trade union freedom set forth in the Italian Constitution (Article 39 of the Italian Constitution) and the absence of a trade union law on trade union representation and the effectiveness of the collective agreement.

46 According to case law, it is sufficient that the employer, even if it is not a member of the signing trade union, de facto manifests an intent to adhere to it and actually applies the collective agreement to all of its employees.

The first collective agreement covering delivery platform riders was signed on 18 July 2018 by the main employer and worker organisations in the transport and logistics sector (particularly, CGIL,[47] CISL[48] and UIL[49] representing the workers), as an addendum to the national collective agreement for the sector. This addendum specifically governs the relationship of employed riders who distribute merchandise 'including through the use of innovative technologies (platforms, handhelds, etc.)'.

It must, however, be pointed out that the delivery platforms are not members of the employer organisations that signed that collective agreement. The main platforms in the industry have created a specific national association, Assodelivery, which is not a party to that agreement. However, the riders have created local trade organisations (often within a city, such as Milan, Bologna, Turin, etc.) that are coordinated at a national level (the name of the network is 'Riders for Rights'). At the same time, some riders are also members of the three main Italian trade unions (CGIL, CISL and UIL).

With regard to the collective agreement in question, there is thus a problem of effectiveness, since the platforms (not represented by the signatory trade unions) are not bound by it (and, in fact, do not apply it). In addition, the 2018 collective agreement covers riders who are employees, but it has already been pointed out that for the most part, riders sign self-employment contracts with the platforms. The collective agreement could thus be applied only if a court, when asked to rule on a specific individual contract, categorised it as an employment contract.

The substance of the addendum to the 2018 Logistics and Transport Collective Agreement deals only with certain fundamental aspects of the riders' employment relationship, leaving other matters for second-level bargaining. For example, it places the workers on the classification scale and sets their compensation level;[50] it sets the upper and lower hourly limits for a full-time work arrangement;[51] it envisages the possibility of

---

47 Italian General Confederation of Labour (*Confederazione Generale Italiana del Lavoro*).

48 Italian Workers' Trade Unions Confederation (*Confederazione Italiana Sindacati Lavoratori*).

49 Italian Labour Union (*Unione Italiana del Lavoro*).

50 The national collective agreement classifies riders in a professional area and assigns an increasing compensation parameter to them based on the means of transport used (bicycles, motorcycles or scooters) and makes the travel allowance inapplicable.

51 For full-time work, the agreement sets the normal and maximum hourly duration (39 and 48 hours per week, respectively), and a minimum daily duration (not fewer than two hours).

part-time work (with a minimum of 10 hours per week and two hours per day); and allows the company and workers to negotiate flexible clauses in writing regarding the timeframe and length of the service, thus giving the platforms broad margins of flexibility.

These rules seem, however, quite 'traditional' and have no effect on the real issues that negatively impact the riders' extremely fragmented work relationships.

From the standpoint of protecting the platform worker, two clauses of that collective agreement stand out from the others.

The first concerns how work shifts are distributed. The employer, with notice that is 'normally' weekly, may inform riders of shifts 'also using multimedia platforms', but those shifts 'can in no way be organised or given (...) to the worker based on the reputational ranking criterion generated by algorithms or otherwise'. The second clause relates to remote control by global positional system (GPS): the information and data recorded 'may not be used in any way for disciplinary purposes'.

These provisions constitute a first, timid, attempt to limit the powers (both legal and de facto) of the platforms that result from the reprocessing – through the algorithm – of the data originating from the workers themselves.

It is clear, however, that the final objective for the workers' labour organisations must be full transparency and the creation, jointly with the platforms, of the algorithm that manages the work relationships. Only in that manner will it be possible in the future to truly protect the worker.

On 16 September 2020, while the Italian Ministry of Labour was holding a contracting table with the participation of the organisations representing the industry (the 'Riders for Rights' National Coordination and CGIL, CISL and UIL), the second collective agreement covering riders was signed, as a surprise – this time between Assodelivery (the association representing the delivery platforms) and a national trade union (UGL).[52] This trade union (a right-wing-leaning labour union) had long been present in Italy but had never shown any involvement in this sector. In fact, it is unknown whether delivery persons are indeed members of this union.[53] This is an extremely significant factor, as will be discussed below.

The main objective of the collective agreement between Assodelivery and UGL is to uniformly regulate the work relationship of all self-employed

52 Italian Workers Union (*Unione Generale del Lavoro).*

53 Actually, P. Ichino, '*Contratto per i riders: è davvero pirata?*' [2020] *Lavoce.info*, writes that an association, which has enrolled 1,000 riders, recently joined UGL.

riders, whether they are 'hetero-organised' workers (under the Jobs Act), 'coordinated and continuous' workers (pursuant to Article 409, N. 3 of the Italian Code of Civil Procedure) or 'simple' self-employed workers (under Article 2222 of the Italian Civil Code). In so doing, this collective agreement weakened the rules imposed by the Jobs Act for 'hetero-organised' work (limited to the riders' work relationship).

The collective agreement of 16 September 2020 derogates from the rules provided by the 2019 law for self-employed riders. In particular, it provides that these workers will be compensated on a piecemeal rather than a time-based basis.

It is thus apparent that the purpose of this collective agreement is to exploit all the loopholes of the law to reduce the protection for all riders (self-employed workers) to the minimum level afforded by the mandatory rules under the 2019 law.

But can this collective agreement do that?

Both the Jobs Act (for 'hetero-organised' work) and the 2019 law (for time-based compensation) provide that national collective agreements (only if signed by the relevant trade unions) can weaken the rules. Thus, the law authorises only the trade union (or the group of trade unions) that represent most of the workers and the companies in the sector to sign a collective agreement that detracts from the general rules. This is the meaning to be given to the term 'comparatively most representative' trade union.

However, it is debatable whether the UGL – although long active in the labour movement – can be said to be the 'comparatively most representative' trade union among those defending the interests of the riders in the delivery sector. That trade union has brought no actions to date to protect riders, nor is it known whether or how many riders are members of it.

We must therefore conclude that this collective agreement will not have the proposed effect of modifying the rules. The Italian Ministry of Labour noted as much in a memorandum of 16 September 2020. Recently the Court of Bologna (Court of Bologna decree, 30 June 2021) decided in this same sense.

That said, it is worth briefly reviewing the rules set forth in that collective agreement, focusing on those that weaken the law's rules.

As to, above all, compensation, the collective agreement provides that riders will be paid on a piecemeal basis stemming from the time estimated by the platform to perform each delivery (based on 10 euros gross per hour). Only when the delivery service is launched in new cities or centres does the platform ensure that the worker receives, for a four-month period, minimum compensation of 7 euros per hour, which is guaranteed even if the worker must remain inactive or the volume of deliveries actually performed does not reach 7 euros. Under certain conditions (in accordance with the 2019 law), certain increases must be added to the base compensation,[54] which the collective agreement nonetheless attempts to limit as much as possible in certain cases, almost to the point of removing them.[55] A bonus is paid to extremely productive workers (600 euros every 2,000 deliveries within a calendar year, up to a maximum of 1,500 euros per platform).[56]

With regard to the rules on health and safety, the collective agreement provides that the rules for self-employment (which consist of obligations to disclose the risks specific to the work environment) are applicable. It adds two additional minimum provisions: the platform must provide each rider with a reflective jacket and (but only for riders using bicycles) a helmet. The platforms make e-learning courses on traffic safety and food preservation available to workers. However, the 2019 law provides mandatorily that self-employed riders are covered by the safety rules for employees, which require the employer to adopt all safety measures (personal protective equipment or organisational measures) to best protect workers' health. These mandatory provisions cannot be modified by collective agreements.

Regarding the management of jobs and the ranking of workers – this time consistently with the provisions of the 2019 law – the 2020 collective agreement prohibits platforms from using discriminatory automated systems and requires them to ensure transparency of the ranking system. It also gives workers the ability to object to circumstances that had a negative impact on their evaluation in a dialogue with the platform. It also specifies – again, in accordance with the 2019 law – that a rider's refusal of a job shall have no impact on the distribution of job opportunities. A joint commission envisioned by the collective agreement will monitor the platforms' compliance with their undertakings regarding the design and operation of the algorithm.

54 Which amount to 10%, 15% or 20% of base compensation depending on whether one, two or three of the conditions indicated are present.

55 Night work (from midnight to 7 a.m.), work performed during certain holidays (such as during Christmas, Easter, New Year's Day, etc.) or work performed in adverse weather conditions (at least 2 mm of rain per hour or snow). In conditions of 'objective danger', the platforms shall stop their activities.

56 However, if the platform is present in fewer than 12 provinces, the bonus is cut by 50 per cent.

It is apparent that if the trade unions truly monitor the operation of the algorithm and can influence its functioning, this would result in a true leap in quality in the protection of these workers. But significant concerns remain in this regard.[57]

6. CONCLUSION

Based on the discussion above, it seems clear that the Italian legal system has not yet succeeded in providing a satisfactory response to the need for protection of platform workers.

This form of work has grown rapidly in recent years, especially in the urban centres in the northern part of the country, and it employs a workforce that is weak from both social and contractual standpoints, and thus needs protection.

Case law has attempted to provide an initial response to the demand for protections coming from the workers (the delivery platform riders) using the work categories already existing in the system (specifically, 'hetero-organised' work). Despite that, however, the courts' response has not been and cannot be fully effective because the existing rules do not address or resolve the two main issues presented by platform work: a) the brevity of the jobs associated with fragmentation of the tasks, which leads to occupational (and income) uncertainty and induces excessive competition among workers; and b) the detection of the party liable to the worker.

The lawmaker has proven to be quite timid up to now. Firstly, even though the general rules on 'hetero-organised' work (the form of work that court decisions have made reference to) are in principle highly protective for the worker, they can be weakened by national collective agreements signed by the 'comparatively most representative' trade unions. Secondly, the only specific law on platform work, enacted in 2019, only applies to a very specific area (riders on delivery platforms) and it only adds minimum

57 Trade union representatives receive more favourable treatment than mere riders. More specifically, trade union representatives who are members of the Joint Commission are entitled 'to daily compensation of EUR 70.00 per member for each day of work plus reimbursement of travel expenses for those coming from their city of residence'. However, for riders that 'serve as trade union managers, designated by the Trade Union Organisation that is a party to this Agreement, Assodelivery will pay for a maximum annual number of 1,500 hours, to be calculated lump-sum as EUR 12.00, for serving in the role and trade union prerogatives'.

rules, some critical parts of which (i.e. compensation) can be weakened by national collective agreements signed by the relevant trade unions.

The 'comparatively most representative' trade unions, at least until recently, have not managed to exert sufficient force to effectively regulate this sector.

This conclusion must be revised at least in part because, as aforementioned, on 29 March 2021, Just Eat and the major Italian trade unions signed the first company collective employment agreement governing the employment relationship of riders as subordinate workers. The autonomous union of riders ('RidersXiDiritti': 'Riders for Rights'), which took an active role in the negotiations, also signed up to this contract by way of a separate protocol.

The Just Eat company collective agreement is important because the company explicitly undertakes to hire riders under an employment contract. It is thus evident – if there ever was any doubt – that the platforms can easily adapt their organisational model, without giving up their profit, while awarding the rights and protections of subordination to riders (with the limits and costs that this entails for the employer).[58] Indeed, adoption of a work organisation model that respects workers' rights (according to the paradigm of sustainable development) can even benefit the company in terms of earnings: this is demonstrated by the crash, on 30 March 2021, in the price of the shares of Deliveroo, which stands firm, unlike Just Eat, in rejecting the claims of riders.

At the same time, however, the Just Eat contract contains a series of provisions aimed at making the employment rules as 'elastic' as possible in order to adapt this form of labour to the needs of the platform. It does so either by providing for the use, as a 'common form of subordinate employment contract in the company', of the vertical and horizontal part-time employment contract for a shorter number of hours (which is variable depending on the individual employment contract, from 10 to 20 to 30 hours per week), or by providing for the use of other flexible forms of

---

58 The Just Eat collective agreement grants riders the same kind of workplace health and safety protection that subordinate work does; in addition to the coverage guaranteed by insurance and social security institutions, it provides for: private life insurance, civil liability insurance for damage to third parties; work breaks, holidays, leave and weekly rest; a precise definition of working hours (which includes all the time the worker is waiting for orders at the designated hub); the guarantee that each work shift will last at least 2 hours, remuneration calculated on the basis of working time, which is higher in the case of night work, extra work and overtime; severance pay; and reimbursement of expenses per kilometre, etc.

contractual relationship, such as staffing contracts or fixed-term contracts (without quantitative limits for the first nine months).

As far as the part-time employment contract is concerned, the minimum hours provided for in the individual contracts will be spread over the week according to a schedule agreed upon between the worker and the company every seven days, but which is subject to changes at the unilateral decision of the employer, without any additional costs and at a minimum of two days' notice. It is also envisaged that the company may offer employees so-called 'open shifts', that is, open time slots that the worker can decide to accept or not accept (at least this is the provision on paper).

In any case, the worker is guaranteed minimum continuity of the activity: each time slot must have a minimum duration of at least 2 hours.

The enormous adaptability of this form of individual part-time employment contract to the needs of the platform is clear.

It should also be noted that the collective agreement does not set out what criteria the platform will apply in allocating shifts among the workers. What is certain is that the rider, as an employee, must in any case receive the wage for the minimum number of hours planned for the week even if the employer does not engage the worker for all of them.

That said, one crucial question remains: will the platform continue to monitor the workers and assign them to one or the other time slot according to their performance (thereby creating a ranking based on the time taken, for example)? Or will they use monitoring to allocate extra work or overtime?

The collective employment contract is not at all clear on this point. It contains a clause that provides, on the one hand, that the app installed on the worker's smartphone be equipped with a GPS system, defined as an 'indispensable work tool for carrying out the work,'[59] and, one the other hand, that the data collected (apart from, obviously, having to be processed in compliance with the provisions of the GDPR pertaining to the protection of personal data) 'will not be used for disciplinary purposes'.

The latter provision thus makes it clear that on the one hand, data will indeed be collected and, on the other hand, it does not rule out at all that the data can be collected and processed in order to monitor the productivity of the worker, to extend their working hours by favouring one

[59] When 'work tools' – and not control tools – are taken into consideration, art. 4 of the Workers Statute rules out any need for trade union authorisation. But the notion of 'work tool' is defined by law and is not disputable by the contractual parties.

or the other, for example, in the allocation of extra work or overtime, or in offering them the so-called 'open shifts'.

In short, considering the foregoing analysis, the Just Eat collective contract is, for the workers, an important step forward in their protection. By providing for the hiring of riders under a subordinate employment contract, albeit by way of a very flexible part-time contract, it reduces the fragmentation of tasks and ensures the worker a certain degree of employment and income stability; it also identifies who in the platform is responsible toward the worker.

At the same time, however, the collective contract in question fails to 'unveil the algorithm' – that is, to make the employer's exercising of directive power and control transparent. Thus, intervention of the law remains indispensable. The law should impose on the platforms – perhaps along the lines of the provisions on workplace health and safety with the creation of an ad hoc worker representative – the requirement to provide adequate information on the automated management of employment relationships; in short, on how the algorithm works.

THE BATTLE BETWEEN THE LEGISLATOR AND JUDGES OVER PLATFORM WORKER ACCOUNTABILITY

The French Case

Barbara GOMES and Tatiana SACHS*

1. INTRODUCTION

Just as platforms operate globally, so the controversy surrounding the status of platform workers is also globalised. In this regard, France is no exception.[1] At the time of writing, the debate is far from over. In order to provide the best possible account of the state of French law, two clarifications are needed. Firstly, a mapping of the various types of work needs to be prepared. Using the same tool (i.e. a digital application)

* Assistant Professor in Labour Law, Polytechnic University of Hauts-de-France, barbara-gomes@live.fr; Assistant Professor in Labour Law, Paris Nanterre University, tatiana.sachs@parisnanterre.fr. The writing of this chapter was completed by the end of March 2021 and is up-to-date until this point.

1 About the situation of platorm workers in France, S. ABDELNOUR and D. MEDA, *Les nouveaux travailleurs des applis*, coll. 'La vie des idées', PUF, Paris 2019.

could lead to a uniform consideration of all the platforms. Doctrinal work,[2] as well as that of state bodies, has been undertaken in this respect.[3] Some platforms, known as collaborative platforms, facilitate disinterested exchanges between individuals (scientific exchange platforms or voluntary work platforms). Other platforms allow for the exchange of goods and services in return for a payment (sale of old furniture, carpooling, etc.). Among these platforms, some offer non-standardised services (e.g. Malt) and act as intermediaries between clients and service providers, such as entrepreneurs, craftsmen and artists, with the latter using the platform to increase their clientele. Other platforms, which pose certain problems regarding the status of workers, offer, thanks to digital tools, a service provided by workers whose activities are supervised. This chapter will focus here on the latter category, that is, work platforms.

The second clarification touches upon a social inventory of fixtures. Given the diversity of activities that can be organised numerically, as well as platforms and employee statuses, it is difficult to produce figures.[4] However, it is estimated that 0.8% of the population in active employment and 7% of self-employed individuals use platforms in the exercise of their functions. This percentage is increasing. Between May 2016 and April 2020, the supply and demand for work on freelancing platforms increased by about 60%. The popularity of work platforms, on the one hand, and the deteriorating situation of platform workers, on the other, and which has been made even more visible due to the Covid-19 pandemic, has made the need for regulation even more urgent.

Initially political and doctrinal, the controversy over the status of workers on work platforms has had a judicial and legislative dimension. Since the *Loi Travail* of 8 August 2016,[5] a battle has been waging between

---

2 The term work platform does not mean a non-collaborative platform, i.e. one that allows exchanges on a non-profit basis, but market platforms that develop an economic and commercial activity requiring the use of people who carry out this activity, and with whom contracts are therefore concluded for their labour force in order to do so.

3 N. Amar and L.-C. Viossat, *Les plateformes collaboratives, l'emploi et la protection sociale rapport de l'Inspection Générale des Affaires Sociales*, 2015, https://www.igas.gouv.fr/spip.php?article551 (with an English summary); Conseil National du Numérique, *Travail à l'ère des plateformes. Mise à jour requise*, report July 2020, https://cnnumerique.fr/publication-du-rapport-travail-lere-des-plateformes-mise-jour-requise-en-presence-de-cedric-o.

4 All of the following figures can be found in J.Y. Frouin, *Report – Réguler les plateformes numériques de travail*, December 2020, https://www.gouvernement.fr/partage/11921-rapport-reguler-les-plateformes-numeriques-de-travail.

5 Loi n° 2016-1088 du 8 août 2016 relative au travail, à la modernisation du dialogue social et à la sécurisation des parcours professionnels.

the legislature and the judiciary. Thus, on the one hand, the government is trying to legitimise the economic model of the work platforms[6] by guaranteeing the legal independence of workers, while on the other hand judges are bringing them back to the salaried sector by reclassifying service provision contracts as employment contracts.[7] It is the chronology of this battle that this chapter retraces first. This shall then be analysed and finally, in the third section, the prospects for the status of platform workers are discussed.

2. CHRONOLOGY OF A DUEL[8]

2.1. THE *LOI TRAVAIL* (2016)[9]

In France, it was the legislature who first took legal action on the status of platform workers. Thus, the Law of 8 August 2016, known as the *Loi Travail*, in response to strike action by drivers, introduced into the Labour Code provisions applicable to 'workers using an electronic networking platform', including the right to strike, the freedom to join a trade union and the provision of coverage against accidents at work (which gives preference to 'private' insurers over affiliation to the general scheme).[10] From this first legislative intervention, it appears that the legislature wanted to maintain the organisational model defended by the platforms in several respects. Firstly, the terminology endorses the platforms' ambition to be mere players in connecting service supply and demand of services. While the European Union has disqualified this way of qualifying the activity of certain platforms, the French legislature has given it a place.

---

6 This goal is obvious in the mission given to the commission instituted in March 2020 to reflect on this matter (Y. Frouin, *Report – Réguler les plateformes numériques de travail*, December 2020, p. 109).

7 B. Gomes, 'Employees or self-employed: what legal protection for platform workers?' [25.09.2019] 265 *Open* 1.

8 A. Fabre, 'Les travailleurs des plateformes sont-ils des salariés, Revue de droit du travail' [2018] *Droit Social* 547; T. Pasquier, 'Sens et limites de la qualification de contrat de travail. De l'arrêt Formacad aux travailleurs "ubérisés"' [2017] *Revue de Droit du Travail* 95; A. Jeammaud, 'Le régime des travailleurs des plateformes: une œuvre tripartite' [2020] *Droit Ouvrier* 181.

9 Loi n° 2016-1088 du 8 août 2016 relative au travail, à la modernisation du dialogue social et à la sécurisation des parcours professionnels.

10 Articles L. 7342-2 et seq. of the Code du travail (https://www.legifrance.gouv.fr/codes/section_lc/LEGITEXT000006072050/LEGISCTA000033013014/#LEGISCTA000033013014).

Secondly, while the legislature does not impose a qualification on the relationship between the provider and the platform, the wording chosen seems to suggest that the organisational model that is chosen places workers on the side of independence. Article L. 7341-1 of the Labour Code, which defines the scope of application of the provisions reserved for platform workers, outlines the legal organisational model desired by the platforms. Finally, in this law, the legislature outlines the construction of a specific status for platform workers, which consists of rights grouped under the title 'social responsibility of platforms'.[11] In this respect, in an initial interpretation, one could detect an Italian or Spanish inspiration, countries in which economic dependence has given rise to the development of appropriate protections.

2.2. JUDGES' RESISTANCE: THE TAKE EAT EASY (2018) AND UBER (2020) JUDGMENTS

French judges, and in particular the social chamber of the Court of Cassation, refused to follow the path traced out by the legislature. Seized by platform workers with requests for requalification of their service contracts to employment contracts, the judges relied on two principles: the unavailability of the qualification of employment contracts and the necessity to take into account the real conditions of the contracts that must guide them in the operation of requalification. Thus, they consider that the contracts binding the workers to the platforms are employment contracts. The approach that was used bases workers on the concrete conditions of the work relationship. The 'veil' has a triple thickness: a) a contractual veil, that is, the contract between the worker and the platform is a civil and commercial contract; b) a technological veil, that is, technology makes the figure of the employer disappear, who, although a legal person, is often embodied in one or more natural persons; and c) an organisational veil, that is, the activity generated by the platform appears as a market in which the supply and demand for a service meet.[12] In the first case, handed down on 28 November 2018, the judges used the most classic criterion for identifying the employment contract: the existence of a power of direction and sanction. The judges did not hesitate in dissecting the digital tools

---

11 I. Desbarats, 'Quel statut social pour les travailleurs des plateformes? La RSE (CSR) en renfort de la loi' [2017] *Droit Social* 97.

12 M. Julien and E. Mazuyer, 'Le droit du travail à l'épreuve des plates-formes numériques' [2018] *Revue de Droit du Travail* 189.

used by the platforms to characterise manifestations of power. Thus, it was noted that 'the application was equipped with a geolocation system enabling the company to monitor the courier's position in real time and to record the total number of kilometres travelled by them and, on the other hand, that Take Eat Easy had the power to sanction the courier'.[13]

While welcomed by some, this decision has nevertheless been the subject of criticism, which is primarily aimed in two directions. Firstly, the solution has been criticised in particular because of its repercussions on the economic model of the platforms.[14] Secondly, certain commentators have pointed out that the use of evidence of leadership and sanctioning power gave the jurisprudential solution a low range. Indeed, the platforms may use tools that make these manifestations more diffuse and thus escape requalification. Although subsequent decisions have adopted the same solution, the criteria used by judges have changed significantly. Thus, in the Uber judgments of the Paris Court of Appeal and the Court of Cassation, the judges used other indices, which should be specified. The Paris Court of Appeal noted elements characterising a kind of economic dependence: the impossibility for the driver to build their own clientele, or to decide the routes of the rides or the fares. One author suggested that ultimately, the judges, without fully assuming it, characterised the economic dependence of the workers. Ruling along the same lines, the Court of Cassation, however, put forward other indications that could characterise integration into an organised service. In its ruling of 4 March 2020,[15] the Court of Cassation noted:

> that this driver had joined a transport service created and entirely organised by this company, a service which exists only thanks to this platform, through

---

[13] Cour de cassation, chambre sociale, 28 November 18, pourvoi n° 17- 20.079, https://www.courdecassation.fr/jurisprudence_2/chambre_sociale_576/1737_28_40778.html. See comments by C. Courcol-Bouchard and T. Pasquier, 'Le livreur, la plateforme et la qualification du contrat', [2018] *Revue de Droit du Travail* 812; B. Gomes, 'Semaine sociale Lamy' [2018] 1841 *Actualités du Droit* 6.

[14] G. Loiseau, 'Menace sur le modèle économique des plateformes de mise en relation en ligne' [2020] 4 *Communication Commerce Électronique*.

[15] Cour de cassation, chambre sociale, 4 March 2020, n° 19-13.316 (for the English version, https://www.courdecassation.fr/IMG/20200304_arret_uber_english.pdf). For comments, see T. Pasquier, 'L'arrêt Uber – une décision a-disruptive' [2020] *Actualités juridiques contrat* 227; L. Willocx, 'L'arrêt Uber, une conception mixte de la subordination' [2020] 5 *Revue de Droit du Travail*; P. Prépin, 'De l'illusion de l'ubérisation à la réalité du salarié' [2020] 62 *Revue des droits et libertés fondamentaux* (http://www.revuedlf.com/droit-social/de-lillusion-de-luberisation-a-la-realite-du-salarie-commentaire-sous-cass-soc-4-mars-2020-n-19-13-316/).

> the use of which he does not constitute his own clientele, does not freely set his rates nor the conditions of exercise of his transport service.

Furthermore, the Court insists on the lack of control by the driver over the fares and routes. Finally, the judges point out that the platform has the 'faculty to temporarily disconnect the driver from its application as of three refusals of journeys and that the driver may lose access to his account in case of exceeding a rate of cancellation of orders or reports of "problematic behaviour"', which characterises the existence of a link of authority. As can be seen, the judges' criteria have somewhat evolved, making it possible to bring more platform configurations within the employee category.

2.3. THE *LOI D'ORIENTATION DES MOBILITÉS* (2019)[16]

As decisions are made, judges enrich their analyses of the platforms and repeatedly reject the path paved by the legislature. The 4 March 2020 ruling is all the more remarkable since it was handed down after the adoption of the Mobility Act (known as the 'LOM') on 24 December 2019, in which the legislature once again changed the legal framework of digital platforms. After an initial failure in 2018,[17] the legislature once again intervened, through Article 44 of the LOM, on the issue of the status of platform workers, and more specifically, of platforms 'for the electronic linking of platforms operating in the sectors of driving a chauffeur-driven transport vehicle (VTC) and the delivery of goods by means of a two- or three-wheeled vehicle'. The system creates the possibility of drawing up so-called 'social responsibility' charters (known as 'social charters'), which are supposed to provide a series of 'guarantees' for the workers of these platforms. According to the law, 'the platform may draw up a charter determining the conditions and procedures for exercising their

16 Loi n° 2019-1428 du 24 décembre 2019 d'orientation des mobilités.

17 In September 2018, during the examination of the so-called "professional future" bill, an amendment provided for the establishment of "charters" by the platforms, *'determining the conditions and modalities for exercising its social responsibility, defining its rights and obligations and those of the workers with whom it is in relation'*. It was thus a question of "securing" the platforms against the (proven) risk of requalification, as the elements and compliance with the charter could not constitute indications of subordination. For formal reason, the Constitutional Council cancelled this measure (Decision no. 2018-769 DC of 4 September 2018; B. Gomes, 'Employees or self-employed: what legal protection for platform workers?').

social responsibility, defining their rights and obligations and those of the workers with whom they are in contact'. This charter specifies in particular:

> 1° The conditions for exercising the professional activity of the workers with whom the platform is in relation, in particular the rules according to which they are put in relation with its users as well as the rules that may be implemented to regulate the number of simultaneous connections of workers in order to respond, if necessary, to a low demand for benefits by users. These rules guarantee the non-exclusive nature of the relationship between workers and the platform and the freedom for workers to use the platform and to connect or disconnect, without imposing time slots; 2° The modalities aimed at enabling workers to obtain a decent price for their services; 3° The modalities for developing professional skills and securing career paths; 4° The measures aimed in particular at: a) Improving working conditions; b) Preventing occupational risks to which workers may be exposed as a result of their activity and damage caused to third parties; 5° Arrangements for information sharing and dialogue between the platform and workers on the conditions under which they carry out their professional activity; 6° The quality of service expected, the methods of control by the platform of the activity and its performance and the circumstances that may lead to a breakdown in the commercial relations between the platform and the worker meeting the requirements of Art. L. 442-1 of the Commercial Code, as well as the guarantees which the employee enjoys in such cases.

It is useful to highlight the precise content of the charter.[18] This content reveals the ambivalence of the approach of the legislature: the legislature takes note of the exercise of power of the platform over the worker (does not the logic of accountability flow from this recognition?) and at the same time provides legal support to this power. Indeed, the exercise of this power is encouraged and guided. Aware of this ambivalence, the legislature wanted to temper the possible extensions of this ambivalence through the introduction of a reinforced presumption of independence.[19] Thus, Article 44 adopted by the legislature provided that the charter cannot be

---

18 The procedures for submitting and approving the charter were set out in a decree published on 23 October 2020 (Decree No. 2020–1284 of 22 October 2020 on the procedures for applying the social responsibility of electronic networking platforms, etc.).

19 The 'Madelin law' of 11.02.1994 already established a presumption of non-salaried employment, not changing much in practice but expressing the preference given by the legislator to self-employment as a form of employment to be encouraged. On the 'Madelin law', see M. Véricel, 'Des incidences en droit social de la loi Madelin sur la qualification de salarié' [1995] *ALD* 54.

used to justify the requalification of contracts for the provision of services as employment contracts. The aim was to 'secure' the platforms establishing such 'social charters' against the (proven) 'risk' of requalification.[20] Sixty deputies and 60 senators referred the matter to the Constitutional Council, under the conditions provided for in Article 61 of the constitution. Among the many grievances invoked were the lack of normative scope of the charter (due to its optional nature). The legislators challenged the legal scope of the approved charter, and more particularly its 'sacralisation' with regard to the judges: its 'mere existence [could] not, in itself and independently of its content, characterise a link of legal subordination between the platform and the worker'.[21] In other words, the judges would not have been allowed to take it into account in disputes concerning the reclassification of a contract for the provision of services concluded between an employee and a platform. In view of the scope of these charters and the impossibility for judges to rely on their existence and content to question the qualification of the relations between platforms and workers, the aim of the text was such as to prevent judicial actions. In other words, far from offering an opportunity to grant rights to the self-employed, the charter and its 'social guarantees' tended to substitute the possible, much more protective application of social legislation by guarantees that are unilaterally defined by the platforms.[22] Consequently, did the mechanism proposed by the LOM not lead to the creation of a 'legal regime that can only be fixed by law'? In doing so, the legislature would not have made full use of its competence defined in Article 34 of the Constitution to establish 'the fundamental principles of labour law',[23] as well as the 'fundamental principles of civil and commercial obligations'.[24] Being sensitive to the

---

20 The Court of Cassation ruled on the question of the nature of the contractual relationship between a work platform, particularly one operating in the sector of delivery of goods on two wheels (Take Eat Easy), and one of the deliverymen working for it (whose situation is not different from that of other deliverymen working for the same platform). Therefore, through its intervention, the legislator probably intends to change the emerging trend in case law and affirm, if not impose, the self-employed status of the workers of these platforms.

21 Cons. const. 20 Dec. 2019, No. 2019-794 DC, para. 29.

22 In this sense, and everything else being equal, a parallel can be drawn with Proposition 22 in California. Voted in last November, this law was written and put to the vote by the driver and delivery platforms in reaction to the AB5 law, which re-qualified the relationship between these platforms and their workers as salaried employees.

23 Art. 34 of the Constitution: 'the law determines the fundamental principles of labour law, trade union law and social security'.

24 Cons. const. 11 Apr. 2014, No. 2014-388 QPC, consid. 5.

criticisms expressed, the Constitutional Council censured the securing of the platforms against the risk of requalification that Article 44 intended to operate. However, it does not censor the very concept of the charters.[25] The Council considers that the legislature may allow private operators to define commitments whose themes are (simply) listed by the law, insofar as it is only a question of bringing together (genuinely) independent workers.

The Constitutional Council sat on the fence: on the one hand, it does not question the qualification of the platforms as intermediary companies between service providers and service seekers, companies whose social responsibility must be enriched. On the other hand, it intends to preserve the possible path of requalification as an employment contract. In French law, the legal situation of platform workers is thus at a crossroads.

3. LESSONS FROM THE BATTLE

Although the battle between legislators and judges remains unresolved, the controversy over the status of platform workers has already revealed a triptych: the worker, the power and the company.

Clearly, the controversy brought back to the forefront the discussion on the characteristics of the employment relationship that are necessary for the worker to benefit from the protections offered by labour law.[26] On this point, one question is obvious, and its relevance extends well beyond France: does the worker have control over the means of production to enable him or her to act on the market as a self-employed person? To employ the expressions used in English law, does he have the means to conduct his own business? Already present in French case law,[27] this way of analysing work situations has never been so explicit. This is probably due to the ambition of platforms to be mere intermediaries in a market. Ultimately, tackling this question is a way of taking this ambition literally: are the platforms just creating the conditions for a market in which the worker has the means to organise himself? Or, on the contrary, do the

---

25 Decision no. 2019-794 DC, prec. About this decision, see B. Gomes, 'Constitutionnalité de la "charte sociale" des plateformes de "mise en relation": censure subtil, effets majeurs', [2020] 1 *Revue de Droit du Travail* 42.

26 This chapter deliberately tries to avoid these trapped terms of subordination or economic dependence, because, depending on the legal system, these categories encompass very different situations.

27 A. Jeammaud, 'L'avenir sauvegardé de la qualification de contrat de travail, à propos de l'arrêt Labbane' [2001] *Droit Social* 22.

platforms integrate the worker within an organisation where they control the nuts and bolts?

An analysis of French rulings on this matter shows that judges are moving away from one conception of power to another.[28] The characterisation of an inter-individual relationship of power between employer and employee over the content of the service is replaced by that of a power that has control over an organisation, and therefore over the conditions of performance of the service.[29] Judges wants to characterise the existence of an undertaking into which the employee is integrated and whose organisation is beyond his control. Here lies one of the main bones of contention on the platforms: the emergence, in court rulings, of a legal representation of the company.

By confirming that the platforms do not just play a simple role of intermediation, the judges put the spotlight on the company as an activity, that of producer of a transport service. The rulings of the Social Chamber of the Court of Cassation also emphasise another dimension of the company: the company as an organisation.

The analysis of the company as an organisation is not easy. The difficulty lies in the chosen modalities of coordination of activities within the platform. If the enterprise is a blind spot in many social science disciplines, heterodox, institutionalist economists have put forward a characteristic feature of the enterprise: it presents itself as an anti-market (the market being, on its part, the form of coordination that has caught the attention of economists).[30] The term 'anti-market' needs clarification. Modes of coordination in the firm are different from modes of coordination in the market. In the market, coordination occurs through competition mechanisms and around one value, that is, the price. Market players are capable of assigning values to things and determine their behaviour on the basis of this assessment. In the company, coordination is based on various mechanisms, including the exercise of hierarchical power. Hierarchical power implies that the employee is removed from market pressure, at least directly. Schematically, enterprise and market could be schematised in the following manner. The market is a primarily horizontal form of organisation in which coordination takes place through a variable (i.e. the price). The firm, on the other hand, is a form of organisation within which coordination is based on a vertical logic. This is why the

---

28 Without abandoning the other.

29 T. Pasquier, 'L'arrêt Uber – une décision a-disruptive' [2020] *Actualités Juridiques Contrat* 227.

30 O. Favereau, 'Marchés internes, marchés externes' [1989] 40(2) *Revue Économique* 291.

company can be considered as an anti-market. Clearly, platforms disrupt this opposition between the vertical and horizontal logic of coordination. Digital innovations flatten this verticality and lead to more horizontal modes of coordination within the organisation. This phenomenon is very important in work platforms. They organise the internal functioning of the organisation on the model of a market. The role of a platform is to not cushion the market pressure. By doing so, platforms give the illusion of a company without power – a company without an employer. Upon closer observation, this illusion is mainly produced by the atomisation of the power to evaluate work performance. While evaluation is one of the dimensions of people's managerial power, it is devolved to the customers. In such a context, the work of the judges is indeed that of demystification: shining a light on the existence of a power that creates the conditions for the worker's exposure to market risk, by means of the parameters of the algorithm and the client rating systems, among other factors. The judges' task is to reach a demystification: to uncover the existence of a power that creates the conditions for the worker's exposure to market risk, by means of the parameters of the algorithm and client rating systems, among others.

4. PERSPECTIVES

There have been numerous legal setbacks for the business model of digital work platforms. The decisions of the Constitutional Council which detracted all interest from the 'Social Charter' and of the Court of Cassation's Uber ruling of 4 March 2020 have clearly dispelled the illusion created by the platforms: that is, to reduce them to an intermediation role. The Uber ruling leaves no room for doubt: the French conception of subordination, which is a condition for the status of employees, encompasses the situation of platform workers reduced to fictitious self-employed individuals.[31] The unparalleled publicity given to this judgment testifies to the conviction of the judges on this point.[32]

Dissatisfied with the inflection given by the judges, the legislature continues their search for legal instruments that would 'secure' the economic model of work platforms. Thus, on March 5, 2020 and following the publication of the Uber ruling, the government set up a working group

31 See above, section 2.2.

32 Advertisement including a press release and a translation in two languages available the same day (a new approach by this chamber).

to reflect on the status of platform workers.[33] The perseverance, bordering on obstinacy, of the government is all the more remarkable since, so far, the court decisions have had no effect on the practice of the work platforms: they pay those who have had their contracts re-qualified by the courts the low compensation they owe them, without changing their economic model.[34] Perhaps it is the fear of large-scale intervention by the agency that collects social security contributions (URSAFF) that motivates the government.[35] In any case, while the working group's terms of reference emphasised the need to develop a framework for the collective representation of platform workers, the report focused on the need to 'secure' the status of platform workers. The objective of securing the status of platform workers is to put in place a legal framework that protects the platforms against a judicial challenge of their model. Indeed, protecting platforms from judges is the credo of the report. In order to do so, the report recommends that the worker become accountable for a 'security obligation:' they must become an employee of a third company, which subleases the employee to the platforms. According to the promoters of such a system, it deserves credit

---

33 This is the orientation of the "Frouin" commission. The site of the National Digital Council states that 'in a letter dated 5 June 2020, the Prime Minister asked Jean-Yves Frouin, Chairman of the information mission on the representation of platform workers, to work on the legal security of workers and platforms, the strengthening of their social protection and, finally, to continue work on the institution of social dialogue between workers and platforms. The idea of an intermediate status between salaried employment and independence is thus evoked, even though it was rejected by a report of the Senate Social Affairs Committee a few days earlier', Report on labour in the age of the platforms submitted on 1 July 2020 in the presence of Cédric O, https://cnnumerique.fr/remise-du-rapport-sur-le-travail-lere-des-plateformes-le-1er-juillet-2020-en-presence-de-cedric-o. See also, F. Mehrez, 'La délicate sécurisation juridique de la relation des plateformes et de leurs travailleurs' [2020] ActuEL RH.

34 Essentially brought before the industrial tribunals, the main purpose of this procedure is for workers, through requalification, to obtain compensation for paid holidays, damages for breach of the employment contract without real and serious cause, compensation in lieu of notice or compensation for concealed work.

35 Urssaf d'Île-de-France had initiated a recovery action in this regard for an amount of around €5 million. However, it was invalidated by the Paris Social Security Court (TASS) due to the irregularity of the recovery procedure and the nullity of the letter of formal notice sent to Uber France in February 2016. TASS, 19.12.2016, 16-03915. Since then, no further information has been made public. It should be noted that in France, the recovery proceedings initiated by URSSAF are not publicised. It is therefore difficult to know the extent to which action has already been taken, and the scale of such action. However, intervention on the scale of an entire platform, and not on a few individual cases, would have led to a legal challenge by the platform concerned, particularly in view of the financial stakes involved. Therefore, it is highly likely that this did not happen.

for offering workers the advantages of salaried employment, particularly in terms of social protection, while guaranteeing them a certain degree of autonomy toward the platforms. However, this model has numerous pitfalls. Firstly, it risks making workers bear the cost of intermediation. Certainly, a sharing of the costs of intermediation is proposed. However, it is still surprising that the worker has to pay for the protection that they deserve if the conditions for employment are met. In actuality, the worker will pay an additional cost in place of the 'normal' debtor, that is, the platforms, to protect them from the risk of becoming an employer. Then, if the intervention of this intermediary employer allows the workers to benefit from social protection rights, this scheme ratifies a renunciation: to determine a responsible employer. As a two-sided figure, the employer remains difficult to grasp, as in any labour supply operation, as there is, on the one hand, the legal employer (i.e. the intermediary company) and, on the other, the platform (i.e. the user company). Despite having prerogatives in terms of work organisation, the platforms escape all responsibility, which are the counterpart of these prerogatives.

As is evident, this project has no other ambition than to protect the economy of the platforms. And if rights are granted to workers, it is to make the demand for the requalification of collaboration contracts into employment contracts less desirable. New directions of reforms should therefore be considered: reforms that are based on an understanding, not a denial, of the power relations and responsibilities at work within the platforms.

THE 'APP-BASED' EMPLOYMENT RELATIONSHIP

The Spanish Case

Fernando Fita Ortega*

1. IMPORTANCE OF THE PHENOMENON

There are no official statistics regarding the gig economy in Spain. However, at least three different documents can be consulted in relation

---

* Associate Professor of Labour and Social Security Law, University of Valencia, Fernando.Fita@uv.es. This chapter is a result of the research carried out in the framework of the project DER2017-83488-C4-3-R "Los derechos fundamentales ante el cambio del trabajo subordinado en la era digital" supported by the Ministerio de Ciencia, Innovación y Universidades, the Agencia Estatal de Investigación and FEDER.

to this phenomenon and its impact in Spain.[1] All three works underline the high participation in gig economy in Spain. According *Digital Labour Platforms in Europe*, the UK has the largest proportion of platform workers who do it as their main job (3.6%), followed by the Netherlands (2.8%) and Spain (2.7%). Nevertheless, adjusted estimates (adjusted for high frequency Internet use) show that Spain leads the range (12.5% in Spain). There is a fourth report, but only referred to Catalonia,[2] interesting as it also confirms the data of the previously mentioned ones and adds some relevant information.

Some remarkable figures can be drawn from the *Huella Digital* research. The first is related to gender, as it shows that women are less involved in platform work (22.4% compared to 32.5% men out of the global working age population), but women are more likely to have a platform job as their only source of income (11.5%) than men (8.1%). The second is related to the age of platform workers. Platform workers can be found in any age group (the report only takes into account people from 16 to 65 years of age), but the percentage of platform workers is higher among young people: 21.5% between 16 and 24 years of age; 25.7% between 25 and 34 years of age; 22.7% between 35 and 44 years of age; 17.7% between 45 and 54 years of age; and 12.5% between 55 and 65 years of age.

Finally, the data this report offers related to the activities carried out throughout platform apps is interesting, showing that platform workers generally do more than one activity through apps, as well as the wide range

---

1 a) C. Urzì Brancati, A. Pesole, and E. Fernández-Macías, *Digital Labour Platforms in Europe: Numbers, Profiles, and Employment Status of Platform Workers*, EUR 29810 EN, Publications Office of the European Union, Luxembourg 2019. Available at https://op.europa.eu/en/publication-detail/-/publication/14e150fe-adbf-11e9-9d01-01aa75ed71a1/language-en/format-PDF/source-101693069.

b) Unidad De Servicios Estadísticos Y Consultoría (SSCU), Universidad de Hertfordshire & Ipsos MORI, in association with Fundación de Estudios Progresistas Europeos (FEPS), UNI Europa and Fundación Felipe González, published 29 March 2019. Available at https://www.fundacionfelipegonzalez.org/pdf/huella-digital-la-plataformizacion-del-trabajo-en-europa/.

c) A. Cañiguerał, Fundación COTEC para. la innovación. Executive summary in English available at https://cotec.es/media/COTEC_PIA_Ouishare_WorkerTech_EN_ExecutiveSummary.pdf.

2 *La dimensió de l'economia de plataforma a Catalunya*. Comisiones Obreras, 18 June 2018, available at https://www.ccoo.cat/pdf_documents/2018/informe_economia_plataforma_catalunya.pdf.

of activities performed by platform workers who provide services at least once a week:

- 40.4%: office work (short tasks, click-work)
- 35.4%: more qualified tasks (design, edition, software development, translation)
- 33.9%: routine tasks in the office in somebody's else premises
- 31.4% some occasional jobs in private houses (plumbers, electricians, etc.)
- 30.5%: regular task in private houses (cleaning, gardening, etc.)
- 34%: professional services (i.e. accountant or juridical)
- 28.6%: transport of persons (Uber, cabify, etc.)
- 27.8% personal services (hairdresser, physiotherapy, etc.)
- 28.2% delivering food by car or van
- 27.5% delivering food by bicycle
- 26.6%: delivering other products by car
- 26.8% delivering goods by bicycle, motorcycle, scooter

In relation to their status, the report shows that 48.3% of platform workers said they did it on a full-time basis; 10.7% part-time; 6.4% self-employed; 4.2% full-time parents; 3.7% retired individuals; and 10.6% students. The remaining platform workers were classified as unemployed; suffering from long-term illnesses; or handicapped. The report *La dimensió de l'economia de plataforma a Catalunya* shows that 55% of platform workers have a university degree; that platform work as a source of income is more frequent among foreigners; and that platform work is mainly carried out from the worker's place of residence.

2. THE QUALIFICATION OF THE ACTIVITY CARRIED OUT BY PLATFORM WORKERS

2.1. DIFFERENT LEGAL STATUS FOR PLATFORM WORKERS IN SPAIN

The question of qualification of the nature of the activity is essential in order to determine the rights of those who perform activities under these conditions. In the case of Spanish legal system, there are three different options: a) consider them as self-employed; b) consider them as self-employed with economic dependence (TRADE); and lastly,

c) recognise them the condition of employees. In all three cases, the Spanish regulations provide some rights for workers, with those rights being broader in the latter case and narrower in scope in the former case.

However, before noting the different rights that can emerge in different situation, it is important to remark that there are two further intermediate 'categories': a) the special labour relationship;[3] and b) self-employed – not necessarily TRADE – with some typical 'labour' rights.[4] Self-employed individuals are considered those who are not subject to the managerial decisions of anybody else, so that they autonomously organise their work and fully bear the risks of their activity. *Ley 20/2007 del Estatuto del Trabajo Autónomo* (LETA) delegates a number of rights to them, some of those emerging straight forwards from the Spanish Constitution (CE), and others recognised by the infra-constitutional law.

These include: a) the right to work and the free choice of profession and trade (art. 35 CE and 4.2.a LETA); b) the freedom of economic initiative and freedom of competence (38 CE and 4.2.b); c) the right to copyright and industrial property regarding his/her works or services (art. 4.2.c LETA); and d) the respect to his/her fundamental rights and non-discrimination (art. 14 CE, art. 4.3 and art. 5 of LETA), respect of privacy and dignity. They also constitute e) the right to adequate protection in cases of sexual harassment or harassment on grounds of gender or any other circumstance or personal or social condition (art. 4.4 LETA, 10 CE and 18 CE); f) the right

---

3 Is the case of sales representatives, their legal status can be included either in the common employment relationship, in a special employment relationship or, finally, in a self-employment relationship. The differential factor is the degree of submission to the "employer's" organisational power (*dependencia*). When the activity is carried out inside the employer's premises, so that there is the possibility of displaying maximum control on to employers' activity, the relation would be considered as an employment relationship with full application of the Workers' Statute. When the activity is carried out the employer's premises but it is still him/her who organises it (what areas to cover, the working time or working schedule, etc.), then the activity is considered employment relationship but with special regulations adapted to the peculiarity of the conditions in which activity is performed. When the activity is fully organised by the agent, then it does not exist an employment relationship (art. 2.f Workers' Statute and art. 1 *Real Decreto* 1438/1985, 1 August), but a civil contract (so-called contract of Sales Agent).

4 Is the case of Sales Agents, Ley 12/1992, related to Sales Agents, affords some contractual rights to the Sales Agents which are typical from employment law (regular payment of retribution; duration of the contract; extinction of the contract of employment, right to be informed about the commissions, etc.) and which are much more detailed and extended than in the Civil Code.

to training and professional re-adaptation (art. 4.2.d. LETA and 40.2 CE); g) the right to physical integrity and health protection (art. 4.2.e LETA, 15 CE and 43 CE); h) the right to punctual payment of the retribution agreed (art. 4.2.f LETA); i) the right to work-life balance, including the right to leave in cases of birth, new-born care, risk during pregnancy, risk during breastfeeding, adoption and similar issues regulated by the Civil Code (art. 4.2.g LETA); j) the right to have assistance and minimum social benefits in cases of need (included unemployment, since Ley 32/2010, 5th of August 2010 – art. 4.2.h LETA); and k) the right to claim before courts and use alternative dispute resolution mechanisms (art. 4.2.i and j LETA and art. 24 CE).

Most of these rights do not have a specific regulation, and thus they are only listed in the law. However, the law regulates some of them (such as discrimination) and set some specific rights for self-employed workers. That arises in issues such as form and durability of the contracts (art. 7 LETA); health and safety regulations (art. 8 LETA and *Ley 31/1995, 8 November; de Prevención de Riesgos Laborales);* protection of minors (art. 9 LETA); and the guarantee of economic rights (art. 10 LETA), which includes the right to sue the main company when the self-employed individual works for a contractor in cases of outsourcing.

In relation to collective rights, self-employed workers who hire subordinate employees have the right of association (but not to create trade unions), as employers, in order to defend their professional interest. Self-employed workers who do not hire subordinate employees can affiliate to trade unions and create specific associations for self-employed workers (art. 19 LETA; art. 1 *Ley Orgánica 11/1985 Libertad Sindical*, 8 August; *Ley* 19/1977, 1 April regarding the right of freedom of association, and *Ley Orgánica* 1/2002, 22 March regarding the right of association).

Legislation (art. 11 LETA) considers TRADE to consist of those self-employed individuals who pursue an economic or professional activity in exchange for money, habitually, personally, directly and predominantly for one individual or legal entity, known as the client, on which they depend economically because they receive from that client at least 75% of their income obtained from the work performed and from economic or professional activities. In any case, certain conditions must be ascertained in order to achieve recognition as TRADE: a) neither hiring employees nor contracting with third parties the whole or part of their activity; b) not executing their activity in an undifferentiated way in relation to those who do any kind of activity for the client under a contract of employment; c) having a productive infrastructure in order to perform their activity;

d) carrying out their activity according their own organisational criteria; e) perceiving a retribution assuming the risk of the activity. The lawmaker opted to add such requirements in order to distinguish TRADE from self-employed individuals and employees.

The lawmaker allocates more rights to TRADE in comparison to self-employed individuals who cannot be considered TRADE. Firstly, the law gives them certain collective rights, such as the right to specific collective bargainin[5] (agreements of professional interests in which the regulation of weekly rest, maximum working time and its distribution can be regulated) or to exercise the collective activity in defence of their professional interests (arts. 13 and 19 LETA). Moreover, legislation recognises several individual rights to them: 18 days of annual holidays; overtime only on voluntary basis; and the right to reorganisation of the working schedule when the TRADE is a female victim of gender violence, among others (arts. 14, 15 and 16 LETA).

The condition of employee is attributed to those who perform their activity under the sphere of control of the employer (*dependencia*) and assume the risk of the activity (*ajenidad*). In order to identify the presence of both elements, Spanish courts use a 'clue system' (similar to that which is used in other countries) wherein the existence of *dependencia* can be drawn from different factors. These factors include: a) the regulation of working time (working days, work schedule not decided by the employee, etc.); b) the company's power to control the activity and the resulting existence of disciplinary measures taken by the employer; c) the obligation to use clothes or items with the logo of the company; and d) the organisation of work being under the control of the company.

To summarise, the evidence shows that an employee works under the company's control such that the organisation of the activity is decided by the employer. On the other hand, *ajenidad* is analysed from different perspectives: the property of productive tools; the property of the result of work (*fructus separati*); the risk of the activity performed (guaranteed salary); and the relation with the market in which the employee works (employees do not work directly in that market, as a third person is interposed).

---

5 The agreements reached do not have, in any case, *erga omnes* effect. They only display effects on those who are represented by the negotiators and only to TRADE workers who expressly accept it.

2.2. THE CLUE SYSTEM AND ITS SUITABILITY FOR PLATFORM WORK

The clue system is still relevant and critical – even in platform work – in order to ascertain if a specific relationship is under the rules of employment law. Thus, new technologies have not called into question the clues used for the qualification of an employment relationship, as they are flexible and their capability to adapt to new productive realities has been demonstrated throughout the decades in which they have been used.[6]

Nevertheless, because of the specific characteristics of platform work, the juridical nature of such activity has been discussed. This is because, firstly, Spain currently finds itself in one such 'grey zone', that is to say, an area in which there are contradictory clues depending on the focus.[7] Secondly, owners of platforms attempted distance themselves from the contract of employment when initial demands of recognition of the condition of employees were raised. Thus, they not only forbade the use of some terms, such as salary, uniform and work schedule,[8] that recall a subordinate relationship, but they also have introduced changes in the work organisation, jeopardising even more the juridical qualification of the relationship. Whereas in the former case it is possible to perceive an attempt to mask a real contract of employment (bogus self-employment fraud), in the latter, the strategy of platform companies is to move the conditions in which the activity is carried out away from the employment relationship.

In both cases, platform companies are trying to avoid the presence of those clues pointing to subordination. However, their serious attempts to achieve that goal have not been successful. The semblance of workers' freedom to decide their working time or to refuse to undertake jobs, which is usually claimed by platform companies in order to deny the existence of an employment contract, is not a consequence of workers' autonomy, but instead, of the organisational possibilities that such a system guarantees for the employer. Crowdsourcing is based on a wide range of manpower, such

---

6 J. Gorelli Hernández, 'Indicios de laboralidad en el trabajo a través de plataformas (Crowdsourcing offline)' [2019] 86 *Revista de Derecho Social* 42–47.

7 M. Agis Dasilva, 'Una revisita a los contornos de lo laboral. Algunas reflexiones' (to be published in the collective book *Os impactos das novas tecnologias no direito do trabalho*).

8 See Judgment nº 193/2019 of Juzgado de lo Social nº 31 Barcelona, of 11 June 2019.

that it is easy to substitute a particular worker. This can be promptly done thanks to the technology that platforms use.[9]

However, it is possible to conclude that whether the legal status of platform workers is that of TRADE or employees, they need protection, as they bear all the risk due to being the weak counterpart in the contractual relationship. Therefore, the emerging problem is to determine what legislation gives better protection to such workers. Todolí Signes holds the opinion that none of the existing legal status is suitable for platform workers. TRADE legislation is a specific form of self-employed work, and the terms of the conflict centre around platforms as mere intermediaries between those who do the service and those who use it, or subordinated employees who obey their entrepreneur's instructions. This is a common employment relationship because many of the implications of treating such workers as employees do not fit with the characteristics of this work (i.e. significant flexibility on working time for the employees; rotation of the workforce, etc.). Hence, Signes proposes to create a new special employment relation that is specific to platform workers.[10] Other Spanish colleagues also support the idea of a new special employment relationship, including in it those who are outside of the subordinated relationship and cannot be considered self-employed, because the requisite of continuity is not present in their activity.[11]

Other scholars are in favour of recognising all platform workers in a unique and new statute, whatever the juridical qualification of their contractual relationship with the platform could be; that is to say, creating a kind of professional statute. In such a sense, digital platforms claim a new category inside TRADE (Digital TRADE), aiming to definitively settle all platform workers within TRADE regulations but offering to extend some social benefits, following the French example with *Loi n° 2016-1920 du 29 décembre 2016 relative à la régulation, à la responsabilisation et à la simplification dans le secteur du transport public particulier de personnes.*[12] Such a proposal seems to face the same constitutional problems and limitations as the exclusion from the sphere of application of employment

---

9 J. Gorelli Hernández, 'Indicios de laboralidad en el trabajo a través de plataformas (Crowdsourcing offline)' [2019] 86 *Revista de Derecho Social* 59–60.

10 A. Todolí Signes, 'El trabajador en la "Uber economy": ni dependiente ni autónomo, sino todo lo contrario' [2016] 25 *Trabajo y Derecho* 43–60.

11 S. González Ortega, 'Trabajo asalariado y trabajo autónomo en las actividades profesionales a través de plataformas informáticas' [2017] 138 *Temas Laborales* 123.

12 This is the case of *Asociación Española de la Economía Digital* (Adigital) in his *Propuesta normativa en materia de trabajo en plataformas digitales.*

law encountered by certain transport actors in 1999 (STC 47/1999, 22 March).

Certain academics agree on a similar scope of achieving a uniformed regime of platform work, but, contrary to the aforementioned example, these scholars suggest creating an employment status for platform workers.[13] These options recreate the debates held in the 1980s about employment law, which attempted to ascertain what it is useful for and to whom it must be addressed,[14] in an endeavour to extend the protection of employment law, underlining the aspect of the weak counterpart in the relationship. One such argument is that the Directive (EU) 2019/1152 of 20 June 2019 on transparent and predictable working conditions in the European Union notes in its first paragraph that the definition of worker has to take into consideration the case law of the Court of Justice. In this sense, the *Tribunal Superior de Justicia* of Asturias, in its sentence of 25 July 2019 (n°. 1818/2019), has suggested the latter idea, referring to the case law regarding freedom of movement of workers (Case C-66/85, *Lawrie Blum*).

Regarding this question, it is important to note that recently (10 March 2021), the Spanish *Ministra del Trabajo* has reached an agreement with the major trade unions (UGT and CCOO) and the employers' organisations (CEOE. and CEPYME) declaring that riders – and all those delivering goods – working with digital platforms are not self-employed workers, and that the workers' representatives must be informed about how artificial intelligence systems can affect the working conditions of such employees, including the access and maintenance of the employment and the creation of personal profiles.[15]

2.3. CRITERIA OF SPANISH LABOUR COURTS: EMPLOYMENT STATUS OF PLATFORM WORKERS

Spanish labour courts have issued a variety of diverse decisions on the nature of platform workers. However, the majority of decisions of *Juzgados*

---

13 Similar to the idea proposed by M. Freeland 'From the contract of employment to the Personal Work Nexus', [2006] 35 *Industrial Law Journal* 1.

14 M. Agis Dasilva, 'Una revisita a los contornos de lo laboral. Algunas reflexiones' (to be published in the collective book *Os impactos das novas tecnologias no direito do trabalho*).

15 That agreement has lead to the pubication of the Royal Decree-law 9/2021, 11th of May.

de lo Social (the primary judicial instance in number in employment procedures, in terms of number of cases) have been, up to now, in favour of recognising an employment relationship between the owner of the platform and the worker.[16] This tendency is even more clear in appeal judgments where, using the criteria for identifying subordination, the vast majority of the appeal sentences have decided that the activity that riders perform for platform companies is an employment relationship.[17] This is also the case of the only decision (thus far) of the Spanish Supreme Court (*Tribunal Supremo*) of 25 September 2020 (Judgment nº 805/2020), which invalidated Judgment nº. 715/2019 of *Tribunal Superior de Justicia* Madrid of 19 September 2019, which considered the relationship to be a real TRADE relationship. All of them affect companies such as Glovo and Deliveroo, and the majority respond to individual claims for dismissals.[18]

It is remarkable that in most of the cases that have arrived before the courts demanding recognition of an employment relationship, the employer typically began their relationship with no contract at all, or merely a contract for services with a self-employed individual, and latter recognising a contract of TRADE. That shows the key elements present in platform work: black economy and bogus self-employment, perhaps coexisting with real self-employment. It also highlights the problem of establishing different borders for regulating human work, that is to say, the multiplier effect that different borders have in the difficulties in deciding activity classifications.[19]

What are the criteria that judges are using in order to decide whether there is a real TRADE relationship, or whether it conceals what is truly

---

16 Existing judgments related to off-line platform activities only affect riders of Glovo and Deliveroo.

17 Judgment of Tribunal Superior de Justicia (Asturias) nº. 1818/2019, of 25 July; judgments of Tribunal Superior de Justicia (Madrid) nº 1155/2019 27 November, nº. 40/2020 of 17 January, nº. 68/2020 of 3 February, nº 1223/2019 of 18 December; judgments of Tribunal Superior de Justicia (Cataluña) nº, 1034/2020 of 21 February, nº 1432/2020 of 7 May, nº 1449/2020 of 12 May, nº. 2557/2020 of 16 June, nº. 4021/2020 of 22 September; judgment of Tribunal Superior de Justicia (Galicia) appeal nº 1188/2020 of 18 November; judgment of Tribunal Superior de Justicia (Castilla y León/ Valladolid) nº. 291/2020 of 17 February.

18 Some others, as the judgment of *Tribunal Superior de Justicia (Madrid)*, nº. 40/2020 of 17 January, arise from the activity of the Labour Inspectorate, who claims the social contributions due to the Social Security System, considering the relationship is, by nature, subordinated. Therefore, this judgment affects the whole plaintiff of the platform company.

19 J. Cruz Villalón, 'El concepto de trabajador subordinado frente a las nuevas formas de empleo' [2018] 83 *Revista de Derecho Social* 19–20.

an employment contract? These criteria are the traditional ones, given the continuity in the interpretation of law that courts have followed for analysing new forms of work:[20]

Firstly, there is the irrelevancy of *nomen iuris* (or the principle of reality).[21] The nature of the contract emerges from the material aspects in which the rights and duties are performed, and it is irrelevant that the parties have declared it to be something else. This criterion avoids the issue that the parties engaged in the contract could decide what legislation is of application, and thus it makes material aspects of the relationship prevail above formal ones. In other words, the parties' own expressed wishes or intentions may not be a factor in determining the nature of the contract and thus in determining on whom the statutory duty is to rest.

The irrelevancy of *nomen iuris* not only applies to the name the parties give to their relationship, but also to other different formal aspects of the relationship, such as the regime of social security or taxation that the parties apply. These regimes are not an option for them, but a consequence of the real nature of their relationship, and an incorrect regime might lead to responsibility in those areas and can determine the nature of their relationship.

Surprisingly, Appeal Judgment of Tribunal Superior de Justicia of Madrid nº 715/2019, of 19 September 2019, confirming in the first instance Judgment nº 284/2018 of *Juzgado de lo Social* nº 39 of Madrid (recognising a real TRADE), does not seem to take into account this criterion, although the judgment refers to it.[22] Considering that the analysis of this judgment is more complex, we can now observe that the appeal judgment focuses, among other aspects, on the fact that in the case the rider asked the company (Glovo) to sign a TRADE contract and considers that it was not proved that the activity did not respect the terms of the contract of employment. This fact is denounced in the dissenting opinion of Judge Mr. Enrique Juanes Fraga, who recalls the non-disposability of labour rights according to article 3.5 of Spanish *Estatuto de los Trabajadores* (ET).

Secondly, there is the character *intuitu personae* (personal perfomance) of the contract. Considering *intuitu personae* contracts as those contracts

---

20 Ibid. p. 14.

21 A. Ojeda Avilés, 'Los trabajos periféricos y el esfuerzo por unificar su regulación' [2009] 47 *Revista de Derecho Social* 46.

22 The STSJ Madrid nº 715/2019, fixed the facts taking into account what conditions the contract established, disregarding how the activity was performed, as the rider could not prove they were different. Sometimes the reality that the judgment reflects does not seem to be accurate.

in which 'the personality of one party is regarded as essential from the perspective of its particular aptitudes', including competencies and qualities of the party that recommend it to become a contractual partner,[23] among the qualification criteria with which courts evaluate the possibility of substitution of the worker.

However, the criterion of substitution has many nuances, it must not operate sporadically[24] and there has to be a real possibility and not a mere or desirable clause in the contract, which is difficult to implement with no prejudice for the employee.[25] In those cases when it does not have effective relevance in the execution of the contract, the clause can be considered as an element inserted in what is essentially an employment relationship in order to camouflage it (Judgments of Supreme Court nº 263 of 26 February 1986 or 22 December 1992, appeal nº 2654/1991).

Thirdly, there is the 'clue system'. Clues for individuating subordination are, as said above, still valid. They offer the possibility to approach new ways of performing activities and decide about their nature. Courts distinguish between clues of subordination (*dependencia*) and clues that show the person does not run his/her own business and does not assume the risk of such a business (*ajenidad*).

The clues of *dependencia* relate to the main aspect leading to recognition of the existence of a real TRADE individual, which is that of the workers' freedom to decide their working time or to refuse to undertake jobs. Nevertheless, as STSJ Asturias nº. 1818 of 25 July 2019[26] states, it must be borne in mind that such freedom of choice has to be exercised inside the regime the platform applies, which can lead to a penalisation of those riders who choose to refuse orders. That is considered a kind of soft control carried out by means of a programme which allows for permanent control of employees, as those occupying the highest positions in the ranking can choose the best periods for work, and those refusing to undertake a job run the risk of not been offered a job again.

In such a context, the freedom to decide whether to undertake a job, or when to be disposable, does not offer any power to the rider that

---

23 D. Deaconu-Dascălu, 'The scope of the assignment of contract' *Public Administration & Regional Studies* 7th Year, No. 2 /2014 Galati University Press, p. 99.

24 Judgment nº 193/2019 of Juzgado de lo Social nº 31 Barcelona, of 11 June 2019.

25 This is the same criterion followed in the judgment of Central London Employment Tribunal of November 2016 Ms. M. Dewhurst (Case No:2202512/2016).

26 In the same sense, Judgment of *Tribunal Superior de Justicia* (Madrid) nº 1155 of 27 November 2019.

would afford any influence in the development of the activity. Ultimately, platform companies decide the riders' working days, zones and schedules, and availability of riders is essential for the service they provide. Such a situation means that platform companies can easily find a person to undertake the job and thus that riders lose any power for bargaining – rendering them in need of protection of employment law.

Other clues of *dependencia* include when employees work exclusively for one company. Therefore, not working exclusively for one company is a clue of autonomous work. This clue was used – among others – in the Judgment nº 284/2018 of *Juzgado de lo Social* nº 39 of Madrid in order to confirm the relationship within TRADE work. This judgment uses it in spite of the fact that the court noted that the freedom of the worker to contract with third parties the performance of any kind of activity had the limit of respecting the percentage of their income from the company to continue showing TRADE status (which requires that at least 75 per cent of the worker's income comes from the company). Nevertheless, as Judgment nº 193/2019 of *Juzgado de lo Social* nº 31 Barcelona, of 11 June 2019, affirms:

> ... jurisprudence already admitted the presence of an employment contract in cases of multiple employment, insertion in the business organisation and the absence of an autonomous business organisation by the worker and assistance to a workplace) as before the advancement of the Supreme Court doctrine has been adapted to the reality of the socio-labour context.

Platform companies exercise a certain control over the quality of the activity and the performance of riders, which can, in some circumstances, result in their exclusion. This control is exercised by means of the evaluation that clients complete, so that, in order to guarantee a high standard of services, the companies rely on them instead of giving instructions and thereby directly controlling the activity. Platform companies also require riders to pass two interviews before being allowed to work as a rider. In these interviews, the companies give instructions about how the service must be performed.

Other clues include whether riders limit their activity to get the job order through the app and follow the instructions the company provides. The platform company demands certain behaviours both with the restaurant and the customer, and they also provide health and safety instructions for handling the food they deliver. The app is able to keep both the customers and the platform company informed about where the rider is using the geolocation device. GPS is more than a tool to control distance, as companies also use it for deciding which rider to call according to the criterion of the efficient running of the business. It also allows for companies to control the route that the riders follow, as well as where are they during their working time. In relation to uniforms, despite the fact that the companies do not allow the rider to wear apparel with the name of the platform company, they use the boxes provided by the company with their logo, which constitutes the visible face of the company in the general public. Platform companies keep the disciplinary faculty and normally add many more justified causes to end the contract than those regulated by the legislation governing self-employed workers. They are closer to the justified causes regulated in *Estatuto de los Trabajadores* for employees.

Clues of *ajenidad* are related to when the employee does not own the main tools needed for performing the activity. Certainly, riders do use their own bikes or scooters, but they are not the essential tool for performing the activity, which is the platform itself. The ownership of the transport that couriers use in order to do their activity does not allow one to conclude that they are running a business, as the cost of the bikes and their maintenance shows that they are a secondary element of the personal activity (criterion already established by STS of 26 February 1986, regarding messengers who performed their activity with bikes or scooters). Another such clue is found when platform work is carried out throughout apps: companies provide an application without which the activity cannot be performed, and they exercise decisive influence over the conditions under which that service is provided. Users have to install these apps on their mobile phones in order to obtain the instructions necessary to complete the job.

It is this app which organises the services and offers jobs to those who are online at the moment and location chosen by the rider, so that it is the platform's technology that renders possible the contact between the rider and the customer. Hence, algorithms are responsible for the decision, but behind them exists a corporate owner of the digital media through which an economic activity is developed. In addition, the platform keeps the contacts of both restaurants and customers (clients of these restaurants).

In other words, it is impossible to argue that riders could perform their activity as self-employed workers without the app. Platform companies base their success in the technological equipment of their property, which is used by riders. Furthermore, Platform companies get in touch with restaurants and determine the commercial conditions and the prices which are paid to riders by the client. The rider does not intervene either in establishing the price nor in the payment itself, which is made through the app. Riders do not even know which restaurants are in collaboration with the platform. Moreover, platform companies conduct the necessary publicity of their services. The only contact riders have with the market in which they perform their activity is precisely when they do the activity. In case of cancellation of the service once a rider has undertaken it, or when the final customer is not at the address provided, the rider has the right to the basic tariff of the service. Riders perceive their remuneration from the platform company with the periodicity established by the platform company and in accordance with an invoice provided by the company.

The fact that the rider is responsible before the customer for damages or loss of product during the delivery is compatible with an employment relationship, as it represents a manifestation of employment duties emerging from the contract of employment. The final clue is the existence of a presumption of an employment relationship (art. 8.1 ET). Courts also refer to the provision of art. 8.1 ET which establishes that a contract of employment must be presumed to exist between anyone rendering a service on behalf of and within the scope of the organisation and management of another, and the person receiving it in exchange for compensation paid to the former. However, this legal presumption has only very weak force, as it recalls the two basic aspects that certify the existence of a contract of employment: *dependencia* and *ajenidad*. The Royal Decree-law 9/2021 of the 11th of May (the so-called 'Riders' Law') has reinforced this presumption, as it has amended the *Estatuto de los Trabajadores* introducing a new paragraph which reads:

> In application of art. 8.1 ET, it is presumed included in the scope of this law the activity of people who provide paid services consisting of the delivery or distribution of any consumer product or merchandise, by employers who exercise the business powers of organization, management and control directly, indirect or implicit, through the algorithmic management of the service or working conditions, through a digital platform. (author's own translation)

Despite the ambiguous reading of the norm (which is probably due to the fact that the Royal Decree-law is the result of social dialogue and the consensus reached in that procedure), the new paragraph is most likely to be used by the courts in order to decide about the nature of those working relationships.[27]

---

[27] The Riders' Law consists in two articles. The second one refers to the right of workers' representatives to be informed by the company of the parameters, rules and instructions upon which the algorithms or artificial intelligence systems are based which affect decision-making regarding working conditions, access and maintenance of employment, including profiling. This "transparency right" tries to prevent

Applying these clues, the Judgment nº. 805, 25 September 2020, of the Spanish Supreme Court arrived at the conclusion that the relation between Glovo and its riders is, under the conditions examined in the case, a subordinated relationship and that the claimant had to be considered as an employee.[28] The sentence ignores the petition of submitting the question asking for a preliminary ruling to the European Court of Justice, remembering that the national court is not under such an obligation when it finds that the question raised is irrelevant, that the provision of EU law in question has already been interpreted by the Court of Justice or that the correct application of EU law is so obvious as to leave no scope for any reasonable doubt.

The judgment refers to the Order of the Court in case C-692/19 *Yodel Delivery Network*, 22 April 2020, where the European Court of Justice settled that the Directive 2003/88/CE, concerning certain aspects of the organisation of working time, must be interpreted as precluding a person engaged by his putative employer under a services agreement which stipulates that he is a self-employed independent contractor from being classified as a 'worker' for the purposes of that directive, where that person is afforded discretion:

1) to use subcontractors or substitutes to perform the service which he has undertaken to provide;
2) to accept or not accept the various tasks offered by his putative employer, or unilaterally set the maximum number of those tasks;
3) to provide his services to any third party, including direct competitors of the putative employer; and
4) to fix his own hours of 'work' within certain parameters and to tailor his time to suit his personal convenience rather than solely the interests of the putative employer,

   provided that, first, the independence of that person does not appear to be fictitious and, second, it is not possible to establish the existence of a relationship of subordination between that person and his putative employer.

---

discrimination in the use of artificial intelligence in the employment relationship, a measure addressed in the same direction that the proposal for a regulation of the European Parliament and of the Council laying down harmonised rules on artificial intelligence (Artificial Intelligence Act) and amending certain union legislative acts (COM/2021/206 final).

28 Following that decision, the Supreme Court has ruled in the same sense about Deliveroo riders (Auto Tribunal Supremo of 15 May 2021, appeal nº 1618/2020).

In his judgment, the Spanish Supreme Court refers to the evolution of the concept of subordination and underlines the importance of evaluating to what extent the person who provides the service has autonomy. Mentioning the criteria settled in the preliminary rulings of the ECJ in cases C-256/01 (*Allonby*) 13 January 2004, and C-434/15, (*Asociación Profesional Élite Taxi*) 20 December 2017, the Court concludes that Glovo in not a mere intermediary among restaurants, consumers and riders. The Court argues that Glovo is a company whose activity consists in delivering goods, fixing the essential conditions for providing this service and owning the main assets for carrying out that activity. On the other hand, the court concludes that riders do not run a business, but they perform their activity within the organisational power of the company, under its direction, as their autonomy is very limited, affecting only secondary aspects, such as the transport to use and the route to take.

3. COLLECTIVE RIGHTS OF PLATFORM WORKERS

Full collective rights (right of association; right to collective bargaining and right to strike) are only recognised to employees. TRADE individuals have been afford the right to affiliate to trade unions (but not create one); the right to create a specific organisation for self-employed workers; the right to bargain agreements of professional interest (*acuerdos de interés* professional); and the right to adopt conflict measures for defending their professional rights. Self-employed individuals (hiring dependent employees) have only the right to create employers' associations, to bargain collective agreements as an employer (thus not regulating their working conditions, but those of individuals who work for them) and the right to lockout as a defensive measure before illegal or abusive strikes. Self-employed individuals, whenever they do not have employees, can join a trade union regardless of whether they can be qualified as TRADE.

3.1. RIGHT TO STRIKE

The main theoretical question that has arisen in relation to the collective rights of TRADE is related to the right to adopt measures of conflict in order to defend their professional interest. The right to strike and the right to adopt collective conflictive measures do not have the same protection in the Spanish Constitution. As the decision of the Constitutional Court 11/1981, of 8 April 1981, declares, the systematic placement of both rights in the constitution (the right to strike is part of section 1 of Chapter Two which addresses rights and freedoms, whereas the right to adopt measures concerning collective conflict is in section 2 of Chapter Two, which simply mentions citizens' rights):

> has obvious consequences in respect of the future legal system of each right, that of strike in art. 28 and the adoption of measures of collective conflict in art. 37. Thus ... constitutional lawmaker considered strikes to be a fundamental right whereas the right to take measures of collective conflict was seen as a right which is not accorded that category.

Hence, the attempts to establish a parallel between both practices by conceiving of the lockout as a strike of employers, have been disregarded.

The Spanish Constitutional Court differentiates between each practice:

> The first difference refers to freedom of work. Strikers are salaried individuals who have freely decided to take part in a protest movement or, if it is preferred, what may be termed a situation of conflict. Opposed to this, the decision to carry out a lockout affects not only conflictive personnel but also peaceful personnel whose rights and freedoms are seriously infringed. Against the comparison between strike and employer's lockout it may be said that the parallel corresponds to the era in which these practices were prohibited. It is true that both are forms of coercion; however, there is no functional identification of both terms. Lockout is not an "employer's strike". Its practice only has collective significance in terms of the plurality of the workers affected. There is no protest in a lockout, simply defence. The differences are also very marked in respect of the basis of each practice. As has correctly been stated, strikes are a counterweight designed to permit persons in a situation of wage dependency to establish a new relation of forces in a manner which is more favourable to them. It tends to re-establish the balance between parties with unequal economic power. In contrast, lockout is a greater complement of power granted to a person who already held power beforehand.

In this context, it does not seem that an eventual recognition of a right to 'strike' of – at least – economically dependent self-employed workers could break this conceptual scheme. In the case of economically dependent workers (TRADE), it is possible to appreciate the existence of a counterpart to put under pressure in order to bargain for working conditions. Indeed, the economic dependence of these workers puts them in a situation of weakness with regard to their contractual counterpart. The situation is somewhat comparable to that of the subjects to whom the first labour rules were addressed. For this reason, the regulations applicable to these personnel do recognise a certain right to negotiate, as a guarantee mechanism for these workers by virtue of their situation of economic dependence.

Thus, it is possible to speak of a *tertium genus*, located between the right to strike and the right to lockout which are legally recognised, respectively, in arts. 28.2 and 37.2 CE. Despite the regulation, self-employed workers may not receive the same legal treatment as the right to strike, it could dodge eventual liabilities for failure to comply with the obligations contracted, although it may enter into conflict with interests and rights – even fundamental rights – of third parties.

Article 19.1.c of Law 20/2007 could set a legal basis for this conclusion as it regulates the right of autonomous workers to exercise collective activity for safeguarding their professional interests, which has a clear conflictual resonance that goes beyond mere representation, which, although it cannot legally equate to the strike, eliminates contractual liability for non-compliance with its customers, although it may conflict with interests and rights – even fundamental – of third parties.[29] However, this is not unanimously accepted,[30] as some authors argue that TRADE's conflict actions are only tolerated as a civil right (in the same way that demonstrations are recognised), but the resulting breach of contract could have civil consequences.[31] In this sense, decision TC 11/1981 (adopted before TRADE workers were regulated) said:

> A strike is characterised by the deliberate wish of strikers to place themselves provisionally outside the framework of the work contract. The constitutional right to strike is granted so that the holders of the right may temporarily disassociate themselves from their legal and contractual obligations. Here there is an important difference which separates the strike constitutionally protected by art. 28 and that which at some point may be termed independent workers' strike, of self-employed or professionals who although in the broad sense are workers, are not employed workers bound by a salaried work contract.

---

29 M. F. Fernández López, 'Los derechos fundamentales de los trabajadores autónomos económicamente dependientes' [2008] 42 *Revista de Derecho Social* 2–29. The idea of 'collective' has a clear conflictual resonance that goes beyond the mere representation, which, although it cannot legally equate to the strike, eliminates contractual liability for non-compliance with its customers, although it may conflict with interests and rights – even fundamental – of third parties.

30 M. T. Alameda Castillo, 'Un nuevo reto para. el derecho de conflictos: el paro profesional reivindicativo' [2018] 84 *Revista de Derecho Social* 187.

31 This is the case, for example, of R. Roqueta Buj, 'Los derechos colectivos de los trabajadores autónomos. Los acuerdos de interés profesional' [2012] 114 *Temas Laborales* 43.

> Cessation of this type of persons' activities, if the business or professional activity is free may take place without the need for any norm to grant them any right, although without prejudice to the consequences entailed by the disruptions this may produce.

In any case, there would be the obligation for respecting the limits imposed by public security or social order, in a similar way to what happens with the constitutional clause of maintenance of the essential services of the community (present both in art. 28.2 CE as in art. 37.2 CE). In the 'strike' of TRADE workers this final remark is of special interest since it is not dealing with a strike with constitutional support.[32]

In addition to the above considerations, it is important to consider that the exercise of the right to strike by the employees (in a subordinated relationship) of the digital platforms presents significant difficulties. This is because of the lack of adaptation of the regulations and jurisprudence to the productive context characterised by digitalisation. Despite the fact that strikes can be decided by the employees themselves – meaning the difficulties to obtain employee representatives is not a problem – the process of the decision-making presents several obstacles. In cases where the strike is decided by the employees directly, their support is required – by simple majority – through a secret ballot (art. 3.2.b *Real Decreto Ley de Relaciones de Trabajo*). The absence of a physical space shared by the employees renders it difficult to discuss the need to adopt the measure and carry out the balloting. There is no legal recognition of a purely virtually organised assembly for the sake of balloting. Hence, a mobilisation organised through a mobile application, such as WhatsApp, without any previous agreement to support it, must necessarily be declared illegal, and the dismissal of the worker who actively participates in it (urging the strike or contributing, with his attitude, to maintaining it) could not be declared null and void.[33]

On the other hand, the effectiveness of the strike is also compromised in these cases by the characteristics of work on platforms. The activity organised through platforms is characterised by the existence of a vast plurality of potential workers providing the service in a competitive

---

32 J. García Murcia, 'Los derechos colectivos del trabajador autónomo' [2009] 9 *Actualidad Laboral* 5.

33 Judgment nº 53/2019 of *Juzgado de lo Social* nº 33 of Madrid of 11 February 2019 (sentence nº. 53/2019) does not consider legal the dismissal of an employee who, using WhatsApp, promoted a strike without respecting the legally enforceable rules. The judgment considers that his comments were mere opinions in relation to the stoppage so that it cannot be interpreted as an incitement to support the strike. The judgment concludes that his comments were protected by the freedom of expression.

regime, which fosters an individualistic spirit. Thus, given a call for a strike, it will be easier for the digital entrepreneur to fill the job position of the strikers. In such cases it is difficult to argue that the employer is illegally substituting the strikers, as it should be analysed from the perspective of workers' right not to strike.

In short, work through platforms has an organisational advantage, which afford the employer an army of workers willing to accept a temporary provision of services, which, by the way, affects the price of their services as they have to compete among themselves. On the other hand, the interpretation of the Spanish courts regarding the absence of technological illegal substitution of strikers reinforces this conclusion, facilitating the argument of 'technological asepsis' in order to untangle the consequences of those decisions from the company's will.[34]

In relation to strike pickets, in the absence of a well-defined geographical work space, their performance would be almost impossible or, at least, of little efficacy, as an eventual boycott of the app could not be considered a legal action. It is likely that this boycott would be considered an illegal action because this kind of action would cause disproportionate damage to the company and would affect the right to work of those who did not wish to join in.[35] A different conclusion could be drawn in cases where the employee voluntarily decides – by his own decision or legitimately pressured by the pickets – to disconnect his application, an option that also encounters obstacles in practice, given the difficulties in effectively protecting the exercise of the right to strike before possible retaliations.[36] In fact, given the criteria often used for offering services, it can be difficult to demonstrate possible retaliations for taking part in a strike. It is important to note that platform companies adopted such an attitude during the first digital workers' mobilisations in demand of better working conditions.[37] The 'reputational' systems for assessing the activity

---

34 Judgment nº 193/2019 of Juzgado de lo Social nº 31 of Barcelona, of 11 June 2019.

35 As the company alleged in the letter of dismissal in the case of Judgment nº 53/2019, of *Juzgado de lo Social* of Madrid of 11 February 2019.

36 This is the case of Judgment nº 193/2019 of Juzgado de lo Social nº 31 of Barcelona, of 11 June 2019.

37 Following the strike calls in 2017, those distributors who decided to go on strike in defense of better working conditions were dismissed/disconnected. In the case of Deliveroo, some five riders were disconnected in Madrid. In Barcelona, more than fifteen were dismissed/disconnected, linked to the RidersxRights organization. In a similar action, Glovo disconnected one courier. This is a perfect picture of what platform companies think about the collective organization of riders and their right to strike (data extracted from AA.VV., *El trabajo en las plataformas digitales de reparto, cit.*, pp. 80–81).

of the riders contribute to the problematic accreditation of the imposition of sanctions for participating in strikes, as that valuation can be affected by the exercise of collective rights and, thus, implies an indirect sanction for the legitimate exercise of a fundamental right.[38]

3.2. RIGHT TO COLLECTIVE BARGAINING

Spanish legislation affords TRADE workers a right to collective bargaining, as it is possible to regard them as the weakest party in the relationship because of their economic dependence. Thus, TRADE workers can bargain the so-called *acuerdos de interés professional*, even though this is not an obstacle for the principle of autonomy of will to exercise authority, as a general rule, over the relations between them and their respective clients. The recognition of agreements of professional interest does not imply transferring to collective bargaining the task for establishing the working conditions. This only recognises the possibility of an agreement that transcends the mere individual contract, but with limited personal effectiveness, since it only affects their signatories.

In the case of *acuerdos de interés professional*, the conflict arises between the right to influence the working conditions and the competition law. For collective bargaining of employees, the freedom to negotiate is recognised (art. 85 ET). Art. 13 of Law 20/2007 applicable to TRADE workers circumscribes the negotiation, exclusively, to the working conditions with the limit of the competition law. This reference to the protection of competition, which is not mentioned in the labour regulations,[39] seems to

---

38 V. De Stefano, 'La "gig economy" y los cambios en el empleo y la protección social' [2016] 27 *Gaceta Sindical: reflexión y debate* 158. V. Cordero Gordillo, 'La huelga y otras medidas de acción colectiva en el ámbito de las plataformas digitales' in *El futuro del trabajo: cien años de la O.I.T. XXIX Congreso Anual de la Asociación Española de Derecho del Trabajo y de la Seguridad Social*, Ministerio de Trabajo, Migraciones y Seguridad Social, Colección Informes y Estudios. Serie General nº. 23, Madrid 2019, p. 1341.

39 However, this does not mean that collective bargaining is not affected by competition law. Numerous conflicts between the right to collective bargaining and the right to competition have arisen in Spanish labour case law. In any case, it is possible to conclude that the trend exemption from the application of the antitrust rules to collective bargaining is not necessarily applied in the same way in cases where the collective determination of working conditions affects autonomous workers. José María Goerlich Peset and Adoración Guamán Hernández, 'Los escenarios del conflicto' in AA.VV. *Libertades económicas, mercado de trabajo y derecho de la competencia. Un estudio de las relaciones entre el ordenamiento laboral y la disciplina del mercado*, C.E.S., Madrid 2011, p. 271.

be explained by the position that TRADE workers occupy in the economic system, as they intervene in the market of goods and services in the same conditions in which employers act, unlike subordinate workers, who do so in the labour market.[40]

On the other hand, collective bargaining (which can conclude in collective agreements with *erga omnes* effect) for employees of those who work through digital platforms also faces important problems. The first such problem is the non-recognition of riders as employees by the platform companies they work for. The only experience of the collective bargaining agreement of platform employees is the recent modification (Official Journal – *Boletin Oficial del Estado* – of March 29, 2019) of the V *Acuerdo Laboral de ámbito estatal para. el sector de Hostelería.* This is a frame agreement aiming to set the structure of collective bargaining in the sector of hostelry. As result of the modification, the functional sphere of application of the collective agreement is wider as it includes the activity of delivering of food and beverages performed through digital platforms. The agreement was signed, representing employees, by the majority of representatives of trade unions at the national level (*Comisiones Obreras* and *Unión General de Trabajadores*) and *Confederación Intersindical Galega* (a trade union which is recognised as the most representative of the autonomous community of Galicia). Employers were represented by the *Confederación Empresarial de Hostelería de España* and the *Confederación Española de Hoteles y Alojamientos Turísticos.*

The union's legitimacy to include employees in the hostelry sector that operate through platforms does not pose any problems, since the signatories are representative unions, who are granted this power by virtue of their greater representativeness (art. 87.2 ET). Neither does the fact that no specific representation of hostelry entrepreneurs who operate through platforms are involved in the signature impede the legitimacy of the agreement, because what legitimises an organisation to sign an *erga omnes* collective agreement constitutes a certain representativeness in relation to the affected sector, not the means through which it is organised (the digital platform, in this case).

The only objection to the inclusion of riders in this collective agreement regards the functional sphere of application of the collective agreement, as it would be much more reasonable to include them in the transport sector rather than that of hostelry.

---

40 Ibid., p. 271.

It would be more complicated to reach a collective agreement by union or non-union workers' representatives in the company. In the case of agreements signed by non-union workers' representatives (*Comités de Empresa* and *Delegados de Personal*), the promotion of internal union elections will encounter numerous obstacles, impeding the mere existence of such a representation. In the case of trade union representatives, their constitution in accordance with the legal rules is still in its early stages. This situation might be counterproductive for the platform companies who perhaps will desire to avoid the application of the agreement applicable for the sector (of which there is only one thus far), since they will need to find a valid interlocutor with whom to negotiate a company agreement.

3.3. RIGHT TO UNIONISM AND REPRESENTATION

The double channel of the representation of workers within the company that characterises the Spanish model encounters difficulties in its implementation in the gig economy from both a legal and sociological perspective. The legal difficulty arises because the model of unitary representation, of the elective base, is designed for those who share the same geographical and temporal space. From this coexistence arises the community of interests on which the model of unitary representation (*Delegados de Personal* and *Comités de Empresa*) is based, as it allows a direct contact between electors and eligible employees. The principle of immediacy between representative bodies and represented constitutes one of the axes of the regulations on workers' representatives, which justifies the fact that the electoral district is constituted by the workplace and not by the company, since the workplace best guarantees the proximity between electors and elected.

In order to reach this aim, electoral legislation does not allow employees who have been hired for less than one month to take part in the balloting. Legislation also impedes the eligibility of those who have not been hired for at least six months (art. 69 ET). Such requirements render arduous the presence of non-unionised representatives in the digital platform sector, as it is characterised by short-term work and a huge rotation of workers,[41]

---

[41] M. L. Molero Marañón, 'La representación de los trabajadores en los procesos de subcontratación' in AA.VV., *La representación de los trabajadores en las nuevas organizaciones de empresa*, Ministerio de Trabajo e Inmigración, Madrid 2010, p. 75.

as well as workers who labour independently, dispersed over geographically expansive areas and in direct competition with one another.[42]

In such conditions it is difficult to establish the solidarity among workers needed for collective organisation. But if such solidarity is established, it would be complicated to proceed with the balloting as it requires identification of the workplace that constitutes the electoral circumscription. This is a relevant question, as it determines who are eligible electors, the employees in charge of controlling the balloting and where to install the ballot box, among other issues.

This fact will also cause prejudice to trade unions. They are interested in promoting elections to works councils, and taking part in them, as a result of the criterion for asserting the representativeness in Spain, as for trade unions – as well as for independent candidates – it will be difficult to reach the electors. This is feasible if they attend to the traditional means of trade union action in the company, as they are now regulated in labour regulations (right to a meeting room and a bulletin board, art. 81 ET). It should be noted, in this regard, that the issue of the use of more modern means of communication between representatives and representatives (email; intranet for trade union use in the domain of the company, etc.) was raised judicially, with no action taken by lawmaker.

Judgment 281/2005 of the Spanish Constitutional Court, of 13 December 2005, recognised the right to use these communication tools provided that the normal activity of the company was not disturbed and that the use of such tools does not affect the intended use of the technology, concluding that the interest of the trade union should not prevail. The use of these tools should harmonise its management by the union and the achievement of the company's objective that led to its introduction in the company. According to the TC, it would be constitutionally lawful for the company to predetermine the conditions of their use, provided that it does not exclude them in absolute terms. Moreover, this ruling of the Constitutional Court enshrines the doctrine that the use of the company's technological equipment or resources for union purposes cannot cause higher cost or significant inconveniences for the employer.

The Lay 9/2021, of 9 of July, has provided a tiny step forward in the recognition of the use of new technologies of communication by workers' representatives. According to art. 19, the company must provide to the legal

---

42 H. Johnston and C. Land-Kazlauskas, *Organizing on-demand: Representation, voice, and collective bargaining in the gig economy*, n°. 94, ILO Conditions of Work and Employment Series, 2018, p. 1.

representation of the employees the means to perform their representative activity, including access to professional email of use in the company and the implementation of a virtual bulletin board, 'whenever it is compatible with the telework'. Many questions arise from this new obligation, as nothing clear is said about its limits and the consequences of its infraction. Once more, courts would have to delimitate this duty.

From a sociological perspective it is possible to find obstacles for the platform employees to collectively organise themselves, because, on the one hand, the precarious link between workers with their platforms (part-time and temporality of hiring) discourages union membership.[43] On the other hand, employees fear reprisals in case of affiliation. Finally, there is a clear rejection by workers of traditional forms of union organisation, especially the youngest among them,[44] whose jobs thus far have been marked by precariousness, which makes the penetration of the traditional union in this sector of activity even more difficult.[45] As a result of the meagre union membership and the low acceptance of the traditional union among the collective of the workers of the gig economy,[46] the implementation of the traditional union representative figures in the company is complicated. The difficulties for the implementation of union representation structures in the company do not derive, therefore, from the normative articulation of the levels of representation inside and outside the companies, given the broad powers of union self-organisation recognised in the legislation (arts. 2.2 and 4 of the *Ley Orgánica 11/1985 de Libertad Sindical*), but from the obstacles that the union faces in penetrating the company.

In a moment where trade unions suffer from a generalised discreditation (because of their own errors and as a consequence of neoliberalist attacks) and are not accustomed to these new technologies, platform workers have started to organise themselves by means of the technologies they use to work (WorkerTech), in some cases with help of minor trade unions.

---

43 A. Mejías García, *Elecciones sindicales. El preaviso electoral*, Tirant Lo Blanch, Valencia 2016, pp. 98–99.

44 H. J. Simón, 'Qué determina la afiliación a los sindicatos en España?' [2003] 41 *Revista del Ministerio de Trabajo y Asuntos Sociales* 80.

45 F. rocha Sánchez, 'La intervención de los sindicatos de clase en la economía de plataformas' [2018] 5 *Anuario IET de Trabajo y Relaciones Laborales* 87–88.

46 This conclusion is not contradictory with the positive assessment about traditional trade unions made by the workers of the platforms in the report; E. Voss and H. Riede *Digitalization and Workers' Participation: What Trade Unions, Company-Level Workers and Online Platform Workers in Europe Think*, (E. Voss and H. Riede, ETUC, September 2018, p. 50) and this is because, as stated therein, the surveyed platform workers were located through acts organised by unions.

This is the case of *RidersxDerechos*, a platform created within the *Intersindical Alternativa de Cataluña*, a union which attempts to be different from traditional unionism. This is how some strikes and protests have been organised, demanding better working conditions for platform workers, leading to a new way of unionism though *cyberunions*. As we shifted from factories to digital labour platforms, a new way of collective organisation has appeared.

Traditional Spanish trade unions have understood the risk of losing contact with platform workers and their claims. Therefore, they have not resigned themselves to representing the collective of workers in digital platforms. In this way, the traditional trade unions have learned from the 4.0 movements and, echoing the actions of platform workers, begin to explore digital tools to promote their union activity in order to achieve the affiliation of these non-standardised workers.[47] Consequently, they have taken certain actions in order to gain the recognition among them, creating apps for canalising their demands.

4. CONCLUSION

The traditional criteria for identifying subordinated work are still valid in order to qualify the nature of the contracts. The problem of qualification is that as courts give their decisions based on that criteria qualifying the relationship as an employment relationship, companies move toward new forms of organisation in order to make it more difficult to ascertain that the relationship is one of subordination. Hence, the nature of the relationship becomes less clear. One example of this is the decision in the UK of the Central Arbitration Committee about Deliveroo,[48] where, after a modification of the terms of the contract and the way the services were performed, the committee concluded that the rider is not a worker. It is likely that something similar will happen in the Spanish context.

Regardless of whether the criteria are still valid, what has become obviously out-dated is the employment legislation, which still operates in

47 For example, the actions of UGT regarding digital platforms of riders came from the many queries received through "Your union response", a tool developed in September 2017 through which the union approached and made itself available for digital platform workers (http://www.turespuestasindical.es).

48 Case Number: TUR1/985(2016) 14 November 2017. Confirmed by the England and Wales Court of Appeal (Civil Division) Decisions [2021] EWCA Civ 952. Case No: C1/2018/3104, 24 June 2021.

a productive context where employees relate to a single employer, both located and coexisting in the same place and where the workforce meets at the same time. The legislation hardly takes into account either the introduction of new technologies, the new form for providing services or the internationalisation of the productive system. It is recommended that a deep review of employment institutions be done. However, the moment does not have seem to be, up to now, particularly favourable to do such task, as neoliberalist tendencies have caused workers' organisations to be afraid of such a legal intervention. In the new political context, the Spanish government announced its intention to carry out a profound reform of *Estatuto de los Trabajadores*, in order to address these and other issues, but many obstacles must be overcome to do so.

On the other hand, the emergence of digital platforms has strengthened the trend toward the consolidation of a labour model without rights,[49] in an evolutionary process of relations between capital and labour that dehumanises the latter,[50] satisfying the desire of capital to avoid the obligations that may arise from the employment relationship. Precariousness emerges as a result. While new legislation protecting platform workers is discussed and, eventually, approved, platform workers have innovated and created new ways of unionism. Therefore, more dynamic instruments of organisation have been created, employing the tool used by platform workers – that is, digital technology. This is how an organisational movement of a digital nature (digital trade unionism), opposed to the traditional 'analogue' trade unions, has appeared. This is a more flexible way of organising, which allows national borders to be more easily crossed in the trade union organisation, providing a better response to the challenges posed by capital, and is clearly favoured by the internationalisation of the economy that long since transcended the borders of the nation-state, aiming to promote several global strikes.

The structures that have therefore emerged constitute representation bodies that denote the beginning of their path toward institutionalisation, constituting the origin of a new labour union movement, which, unlike the labour movement of the proletariat which emerged from the industrial revolution, would be characterised as being a labour movement of the precarious workers which results from the digital revolution – a movement which initially has sought for social support for its claims. Thus, after

---

49 G. Lyon Caen, 'The evolution of Labour Law' in AA.VV., *Labour Law in the post-industrial era*, Dartmouth Publishing Co Ltd., Aldershot 1994, p. 104.

50 A. Supiot, *Au-delà del'emploi,* Flammarion, Lonrai 2016, p. XVII.

the success of the denunciation campaigns promoted through platforms such as *change.org* or *avaaz.org* (platforms which could be described as generalists), other platforms and applications for the specific defence of fair platform working conditions have appeared. These include platforms such as *co-worker.org*, or *theworkerslab.com*, and applications such as *workitapp.org*, or new forms of organisation in cooperatives, such as the Spanish *Mensakas*,[51] which are channelling a new form of organisation of workers' mobilisation, laying the foundations of what could be considered a digital labour movement of international scope.

---

51 Created by the RidersXRights platform, this application is defined as the responsible food delivery app, raising the battle for rights in the field of competitivity by constituting a cooperative composed of former riders from various platforms (Deliveroo, UberEats, Glovo ...) which offer the same services as those.

PLATFORM WORK

The Dutch Case

Antoine Jacobs*

1. INTRODUCTION

Like in all Westernised countries, the digital economy in the Netherlands has been on the rise for several years. The Netherlands itself have become one of the centres of this world, as several digital companies have already established their global or European headquarters in the Netherlands, such as Google, Booking.com and Uber, among others. This has led to further platformisation on the labour market[1] where an increasing number of people are entering into labour relations for casual work that they have

* Emeritus Professor of Labour Law, Social Security Law and Social Policy at Tilburg University, atjmjacobs@hotmail.com.

1 M. Houwerzijl, 'Arbeid en Arbeidsrecht in een digitale platform samenleving. Een verkenning' [2017] 2 *TRA: Tijdschrift recht en arbeid* 3, 3–8.

found on the Internet. Given its nature, this kind of work may create legal questions for the parties in such contracts as well as for society as a whole. This chapter will provide a quick scan of the actual situation of platform work in the Netherlands.

For the sake of this chapter, 'platform work' is defined as 'all labour provided through, on or mediated by online platforms in a wide range of sectors where work can be of varied forms and is provided in exchange for payment'.[2] 'Platform economy' is defined as 'the economy, comprising, involving and resulting from these digital platforms'.[3] Currently, a number of tasks in the digital economy are recruited via Internet platforms. A platform ensures that buyers and providers of a mini-job who do not know each other physically can now be connected.

2. MAPPING THE MINI-JOB ECONOMY AND PLATFORM WORK IN THE NETHERLANDS

It is not easy to generate an accurate impression of the share of platform work in the Dutch labour market. There have been international studies concerning the size of crowd work, the 'mini-job economy' (in Dutch often called *Kluseconomie*),[4] the platform economy and platform work, among others. Research on the platformisation of work was conduction in 2016–2019.[5] According to that survey, it could be estimated that for some 270,000 inhabitants of the Netherlands, platform work is the primary source of income.

---

2 Z. Kilhorrer, W. P. De Groen, K. Lenaerts, I. Smits, H. Hauben, E. Giacumacatos, W. Waeyaert, J. P. Lhernould and S. Robin-Olivie, *Study to gather evidence on the working conditions of platform workers*, European Commission, Luxembourg 2020, p. 25; see also R. Florisson and I. Mandl, *Digital age: Platform work: Types and implications for work and employment – Literature review*, Eurofound, 2018, p. 2.

3 S. Graben, *Protecting workers in the Online Platform Economy: An overview of regulatory and policy developments in the EU*, OSHA, 2017, pp. 11–12; V. Prassl and M. Risak, 'Uber, TaskRabbit & Co. Platforms as employers? Rethinking the Labour Law of Crowdwork' in K. Ahlberg and N. Bruun, *The New Foundations of Labour Law*, Peter Lang, Frankfurt 2017, pp. 97–126.

4 *Klus* or *Klusje* is the Dutch word for a short, informal job. It may be compared with the German notion of mini-job.

5 U. Huws, N. H. Spencer, M. Coates and K. Holts, *The Platformisation of work in Europe: results from research in 13 countries*, Foundation for European Progressive Studies, Brussels 2019; A shared study by the University of Hertfordshire and Ipsos MORI, the Foundation for European Progressive Studies (FEPS), UNIEuropa, in which TNO participated for the Netherlands. See https://www.tno.nl/media/7841/2016-22_factsheet_netherlands_platform_economie.pdf.

Another research project, the COLLEEM survey,[6] published in 2018, estimated for the Netherlands the amount of those individuals who are 'predominantly' platform workers (i.e. those who earn 50% or more of their income via platforms and/or work via platforms for more than 20 hours a week) to be about 3% of the adult population, which would mean 400,000 individuals. However, these studies have been seriously contested for various reasons.[7] In any case, these surveys have covered too wide a collection of online platforms[8] to be useful for the focus of this chapter: digital labour platforms.

Three recent Dutch studies are more relevant. The first is a report from SEO in 2018.[9] The report estimated that in 2018, 0.34% of the Dutch labour market (i.e. 40,000 persons) are performing platform work. Of these individuals, 34% operate in the category of food delivery; 14% in the category of cleaning; 14% in the category transport of persons; 11% in the category of photography; and 27% in other categories such as bar personnel and care personnel, among other fields. However, a large part of these roughly 40,000 persons are not working full-time in the platform economy. Most workers are working fewer than 20 hours per week in this economy, although there are major differences in the number of hours worked by full-time taxi drivers, professionals or part-time meal delivery staff. This confirms that there is a large heterogeneity of platform work[10] which makes it impossible to give a description of 'the' platform worker.[11]

In 2020 the official statistical office of the Netherlands (CBS) published the results of its first study into what it called the mini-job economy in the Netherlands.[12] The CBS estimated that at the end of 2017 there were

---

6 A. Pesole, M. C. Urzi Brancati, E. Fernandez Macias, F. Biagi and I. Gonzalez Vazquez, *Platform Workers in Europe: Evidence from the COLLEEM Survey*, Publication Office of the European Union, Luxembourg 2018.

7 See for instance A. Piasna and J. Drahokoupil, *Digital labour in central and eastern Europe: evidence from the ETUI Internet and Platform Work Survey*, ETUI Working Paper, Brussels 2019, p. 12.

8 See for this variety, European Commission, *Online Platforms, Accompanying the Communication on Online Platforms and the Digital Single Market*, 2016.

9 B. ter Weel, S. van der Werff, H. Bennaars, R. Scholte, J. Fijnje, M. Westerveld and T. Mertens, *De opkomst en groei van de kluseconomie in Nederland*, SEO, Amsterdam 2018.

10 V. De Stefano, *The rise of the "just-in-time workforce": on-demand work, crowdwork and labour-protection in the "gig-economy"*, Conditions of Work and Employment Series No. 71. ILO, Geneva 2016.

11 R.F. Hoekstra, *Naar een normalisering van platformwerk*, Wiardi Beckman Stichting, The Hague 2019, p. 22.

12 S. van der Werff and B. ter Weel, *Werkenden in de kluseconomie in Nederland*, in the report *Dynamiek op de Nederlandse arbeidsmarkt*, CBS, The Hague 2020, pp. 64–76.

34,000 people working in this mini-job economy. The CBS report affirmed that most of the workers in this economy work fewer than 20 hours per week in these activities, although there are vast differences in the number of hours worked between professions. A significant part of the workers in the digital economy are young and highly educated, but especially in domestic services they are mostly educated to a lower level.

Building on the latter two reports, a report from January 2020 from a state commission about the functioning of the Dutch labour market regulations (Borstlap Committee)[13] estimated the share of platform work in the Dutch economy to be currently around 0.4% of the working population, which equals approximately 34,000 persons.[14] A recent publication of the official Social-Economic Council assesses the number of platform workers to be less than 1% of the labour market,[15] and a recent publication of the official Social and Cultural Planning Office held that platform work is the main type of occupation for between 0.4% and 2.8% of the working population.[16]

Interestingly, all these reports seem to confirm that the working conditions of crowdworkers and platform workers cannot be said to be substandard in general. This is very much related to the professions within which they are operating and whether they have other sources of income. The SEO study showed that there are large differences in income out of platform work between different workers: 25% works (including unpaid hours) for a maximum of €8 per hour, while in the upper quartile of the income distribution at least €19 per hour is earned.

3. VARIOUS TYPES OF WORK PLATFORMS

However, not all platform work has the same characteristics.[17] Some studies have recently been conducted on a number of work platforms in

---

13 Commissie Regulering van Werk, *In wat voor land willen wij werken? Naar een nieuw ontwerp voor de regulering van werk. Eindrapport van de Commissie Regulering van Werk (Report of the Borstlap-Commission)*, The Hague 2020.

14 R.F. Hoekstra, above n. 11, p. 17.

15 Sociaal Economische Raad, *Hoe werkt de platformeconomie*, 2020, p. 80 (referred to henceforth as 'SER-report').

16 J. Rözer, A. van der Torre and A. Roeters, *Platformisering en de kwaliteit van werk*, SCP, The Hague 2021.

17 R. Florisson and I. Mandl, above n. 2; Sociaal Economische Raad, above n. 15, pp. 7–10.

the Netherlands.[18] They perceived a great diversity and distinguished at least five types, with an increasing degree of involvement of the platform with the work of the platform worker. For instance,

Pawshake is a platform on which residents can search for available pet-sitters. It is up to the resident and the pet-sitter to determine the price, the form of pet-sitting and the pet-sitting periods. The platform does not in any way control or supervise the work.

Just Cargo is a platform on which companies can search for available persons who want to deliver packages to customers. The individuals must be available for at least five jobs per week and must complete an accepted job within a specified time period. But the platform leaves the determination of the price and the way in which the transport is performed entirely to the discretion of the contractor of the job. It exercises no supervision on the implementation of the work. No means of transport is made available by the platform.

Helping is a platform that offers a customer (usually private households) to request six potential domestic servants who are registered on the platform with references. The customer can choose from this selection and the platform leaves all arrangements to the customer and the preferred domestic servant, but it is helpful to the customer to find a replacement in case of illness or vacation.

Gig2U is a bus company platform that offers bus rides to available drivers. If they take such trips, they must also take them at the price set by the bus company and must use the bus of the bus company, but there are no other specific obligations.

Uber is a platform on which customers can order a taxi ride from available drivers who are registered on the platform. The driver who accepts this job must be able to take it immediately with his own car at the price determined by Uber. Frequently refusing to accept rides and bad references are rewarded by fewer – or even a total lack of – ride offers.

Another international study[19] considered digital labour platforms like LinkedIn, ZipRecruiter, Freelancer.com and Care.com as platforms which also act as an employment service.

This brief summary of existing platforms provides a good understanding of the variety of platforms and of the divergent ways in

---

18 P. Kruit and M. Ouwehand, *Platformarbeid: de ene platformwerk(nem)er is de andere niet* [2018] 58(7/8) *TRA: tijdschrift Recht en Arbeid.*

19 V. De Stefano and M. Wouters, *Should digital labour platforms be treated as private employment agencies?* ETUI Working Paper, Brussels 2019.

which platforms stay involved with the services they offer. There are many platforms on the Internet, which are quite passive. On those platforms, there are parties which are offering the jobs that are to be done; other parties are reacting to those offers, and ultimately, the result is that there are two parties who are entering into direct contact with each other to get the job done. This kind of platforms will be referred to here as simple digital labour platforms.

On the other hand, there are platforms that play a much more active role in organising the offers of jobs and the persons who are ready to do these jobs. New technology is one important driving force behind the emergence of these much more advanced digital platforms. They thrive thanks to the development of different matching algorithms and the wide use of smartphones by the broad public. These platforms are using interactive Internet systems to select the person that is going to perform the job, set the prices and other conditions of these jobs, charge the providers of the jobs, handle the payments of the performers of the jobs and potentially organising tax payments and insurance – thus fulfilling certain tasks which are traditionally done by employers. It is this last form of platforms that has given rise to a new business model in which significant value can be created and exchanged.[20] These platforms are herein referred to as complex digital labour platforms. They can be defined as 'economic agents providing virtual spaces for matching labour supply and demand via online technologies based on algorithmic management'.[21] Their services must be performed at a (specific) location and time by a (specific) person responsible for performing the task or service.[22] These complex digital labour platforms, which today are most researched,[23] are the platforms that match offers and demands of relatively standardised physical and, above all, labour-intensive work, as well as offering limited amounts of work and little income security.

---

20 For a description of the services of Uber, see: Case C-434/15, *Asociación Profesional Elite Taxi v. Uber Systems Spain SL*, ECLI:EU:C:2017:981.

21 J. Drahokoupil and B. Fabo, 'Outsourcing, offshoring and the deconstruction of employment: new and old challenges' in A. Serrano and M. Jepsen, *The deconstruction of employment as a political question*, Palgrace Macmillan, Basingstoke 2019, p. 33; J. Prassl, *Humans as a service. The promise and perils of work in the gig economy*, Oxford University Press, Oxford 2018.

22 U. Huws, N.H. Spencer, D.S. Syrdal and K. Holts, above n. 5.

23 S.P. Choudary, *The architecture of digital labour platforms: Policy recommendations on platform design for workers' wellbeing*, International Labour Organisation, Geneva 2018.

Various estimates based on surveys in many countries indicate only a very small fraction of the work force regularly performs work for complex digital labour platforms.[24] This chapter argues that the digital labour platforms do not employ much more than some ten thousands of people in the Netherlands and that they mostly perform platform work incidentally and during short periods during their lives. Not many lawyers and scholars cared about the minimal protection of the work and income of the more than 100.000 domestic workers in the Netherlands.[25] There have been in the Netherlands up to roughly 300,000 persons who were employed by so-called pay-rolling firms that exploited the exceptions in the common labour law, created to serve temporary work agencies. It took the Dutch legislator 10 years to ensure better protection for the pay-rolling workers.[26]

Presumably, the broad attention afforded to platform work is caused not so much by the actual numbers it concerns, as by a fear of a strong increase of this type of work in the future. There are as yet no official estimations about the future trajectory of platform work on the Dutch labour market. However, most researchers take it for granted that the mini-job economy in general and the role therein of the complex platforms will further expand, everywhere and in the Netherlands, in the near future.[27] The impact of the most recent economic downfall as result of the coronavirus crisis on the further development of the platform economy remains to be seen.[28] In the Netherlands, the initial indications are that this crisis has immediately led to an enormous increase in searchers for mini-jobs on the various labour platforms, but at the same time to a dramatic decline in the offer of mini-jobs via Helping (domestic personnel) and Uber (drivers).[29] However, it was quickly shown that the meal-delivery sector has been booming, and

---

24 R. Florrison and I. Mandl, above n. 2.

25 A.T.J.M. Jacobs, 'The Netherlands' in R. Blanpain, *International Encyclopedia of Labour Law and Industrial Relations*, Kluwer, Hague 2020, para. 59; V. De Stefano and M. Wouters, above n. 17, p. 7 wrote: '... domestic workers, whose employment via digital labour platforms is often neglected in the debate on platform-based work'.

26 A.T.J.M. Jacobs, above n. 23, para. 67. Payrolling was a specific business model of a number of companies that did not actively perform broker activities on the labour market but only offered the status of being a temporary work employer to employers which wanted to take on specific workers, but not as their own workers.

27 R.F. Hoekstra, above n. 11, pp. 21–24; SEO report above n. 9, pp. 36–39; see J. Rözer, A. van der Torre and A. Roeters, above n. 16, pp. 83–88 for a variety of estimations among Dutch experts.

28 J. Rözer, A. van der Torre and A. Roeters, above n. 16, pp. 88–89 and 94–95.

29 Reports in M. Arets, 'De impact van Corona op de vraag en aanbod van klusplatformen' [2020] *ZiPconomy*, https://www.zipconomy.nl/2020/04/de-impact-van-corona-op-de-vraag-en-aanbod-van-klusplatformen/.

in the long run it may be that the coronavirus crisis has given a boost to telework, and therefore, after the coronavirus-induced economic recession is over, platform work may indeed show a strong increase.

The Dutch economy is above all a services economy in a small but very densely populated country (17 million individuals in an area as large as Lombardia). That situation seems to be well suited for an increased use of services provided by labour platforms. For job seekers, the value of platforms is that the larger the platform is, the more job providers are on the platform – and vice versa. For those platforms to work effectively and efficiently, sufficient mass is needed. In cities or other places where a lot of people come together, it is relatively easy to arrange work by platforms, while in more rural areas it is more difficult for this work to be effective and efficient for various platforms. This minimum mass which is necessary to operate also leads to the fact that platforms have thus far been especially active and successful in the densely populated Randstad region of the Netherlands and some other large cities as well.

However, there is also another side of the coin: will a great deal of 'permanent work' conducted by employees evaporate in the future as a result of the rise of digital labour platforms in various economic sectors? There are as yet no estimations of that.

4. WHAT IS THE LEGAL POSITION OF PLATFORM WORK IN THE NETHERLANDS?

The SEO report has confirmed that workers in the mini-job economy are working under different conditions.[30] Some are working on a formal contract of employment, but many of them are independent working persons. Dutch law has notably two legal figures in the Civil Code at its disposal, under which the platform worker can be situated: the employment contract and the contract for services.[31] It is largely an either/or situation, as Verhulp has put it.[32] He is right in the sense that in the Netherlands there are not such intermediate worker categories as exist in Germany,

[30] SEO report, above n. 9, pp. 10–26.

[31] A.T.J.M. Jacobs, above n. 24, paras. 47–52.

[32] See the paper by E. Verhulp for a Conference of the European Commission on the notion of 'employee' in EU law and national laws, on The Personal Scope of Labour Law in Times of Atypical Employment and Digitalisation.

Italy, Spain and the UK.[33] However there are a number of legal avenues to engage personnel as 'employees-minus' or 'independents-plus'.[34]

Firstly, there is the difference between, on the one hand, open-ended employment contracts and, on the other hand, fix-term employment contracts[35] and zero-hours contracts,[36] which in the Netherlands (due to its strict dismissal control) leads to a much larger differentiation than in other countries. Secondly, there is the employment contract with temporary agency workers, which also gives those workers fewer employment rights, although this still is officially a contract of employment.[37] Thirdly, there are special employment rules for domestic workers. Those working under the tax rules of the Home Services Regulations have fewer employment rights although they are entitled to the minimum wage of circa €10 an hour.[38]

Fourthly, there is also the transport charter contract between the independent drivers and the job providers, but which under Dutch law may also be covered by the minimum wage legislation.[39] Lastly, there are a few specific categories of independent workers brought under the coverage of the social security acts for employees. Since the phenomenon of the platform work has appeared, the problem of categorising such work has also arisen.

Work found via the simple digital platforms does not create large problems. Those platforms can be considered as a further stage of development of the private placement services. They only bring together job providers and job seekers and withdraw subsequently. There is certainly not a contract of employment or a contract of service between the platform and the job seeker. Those platforms are only obliged to abide with the rules of 'job placement' as meant in ILO Convention 181, and implemented by the Dutch Act on intermediate services on the labour market, the WAADI Act.[40]

This opinion has recently been confirmed in a case concerning Helping,[41] a digital labour platform for cleaning personnel. The judge

---

33 F.G. Laagland and J. Kloostra, 'De Engelse tussencategorie als oplossing voor platformwerk: mythe of werkelijkheid?' [2019] 7 *Ondernemingsrecht* 41, 46–47.

34 A.T.J.M. Jacobs, above n. 23, para. 62.

35 A.T.J.M. Jacobs, above n. 23, para. 64/229.

36 A.T.J.M. Jacobs, above n. 23, para. 65.

37 SEO report, above n. 9, pp. 16–17; A.T.J.M. Jacobs, above n. 23, para. 66/232.

38 SEO report, above n.9, pp. 17–18/45–46; A.T.J.M. Jacobs, above n. 23, para. 59.

39 A.T.J.M. Jacobs, above n. 23, para. 139.

40 A.T.J.M. Jacobs, above n. 23, para. 254.

41 ECLI:NL:RBAMS:2019:4546; E. Verhulp, 'Platformwerkers verdienen meer!' [2018] 1 *Arbeidsrecht*.

ruled on 1 July 2019, in short, that there is no employment contract or temporary agency work contract between Helping and persons who carry out cleaning work via this online platform. That is why Helping cannot be obliged to apply the collective agreement for the cleaning industry. However, according to the judge, Helping performs the business of 'job placement'. That is why Helping, according to the judgment, is subject to the Dutch Act on intermediary services on the labour market, WAADI.

All EU countries have these kind of acts, which are implementing ILOILO Convention No. 181 and Directive 2008/104/EC, which are requiring states to allow private employment services provided that they operate in the framework of a sound general employment policy and a good regulatory environment.[42] Most of the time, national regulations on these services are quite rational, such as the prohibition (a) to charge workers fees or costs; (b) to offer their services during a collective labour conflict; and (c) to bind the working party to some sort of exclusivity. These requirements are indeed minimal but they are, at the same time, significant. Yet, it seems that they are neglected by several platforms. Moreover, this kind of regulation is the exact legal basis on which to intensify the labour market regulation of digital labour platforms, as we shall see in the following sections.

However, things are much more complicated with regard to complex digital labour platforms. As has been said above, this kind of platform uses matching algorithms so that the names of possible job seekers come up giving the platform the discretion to make the selection. The platform can limit or even fully determine the price for the provided job; they set the conditions for the execution of the job, charge the provider of the job with the payment; and hand (after a certain commission is deducted) the remaining payment over to the performer of the job, eventually taking charge of tax payments and insurance. Therefore, this kind of platform is very much fulfilling certain tasks that are traditionally done by employers.

It is no wonder that the conclusion can arise that the work relationships that they create are in fact employment contracts, in which they are the employer. Some of the platforms indeed have drawn that conclusion. In the Netherlands, meal-delivery service Thuisbezorgd.nl still has employment contacts with its workers which categorises them as temporary agency workers. In the past, this also occurred with certain meal-delivery services, such as Deliveroo, which from 1 January 2018, however, switched to engaging its workers only on a freelance basis.

---

42 V. De Stefano and M. Wouters, above n. 17, p. 3.

This platform, like most other complex digital labour platforms, takes the legal position that a platform worker is an independent person who is commissioned by the firm/person. The worker then performs assignments for this third party and is an entrepreneur. For that position they notably invoke the fact that job seekers are completely free to refuse a job offer.

In the Netherlands, there is a significant difference between an employee and a self-employed person. Genuinely self-employed persons are not covered by collective agreements, they are not entitled to the minimum wage, they are not paid for hours that have not been worked (no paid holidays and leave rights, no sick pay), they enjoy no dismissal protection, nor are they covered by the statutory unemployment and disability benefits schemes or by occupational pensions.[43] There is for them no employer to pay for their retraining and reintegration if they are ill or disabled. So due to the switch to the self-employment status, regulatory requirements governing employment may easily be circumvented, and responsibilities and market risks externalised. Therefore one can imagine that the notable switch to the self-employed status made by Deliveroo in 2018 has spurred this debate in the Netherlands. There have already been five Deliveroo court cases.

In the first judgment, on 23 July 2018,[44] the court ruled, in summary, that the contract for services that the rider had concluded with Deliveroo did not count as a contract of employment and that this rider was therefore not employed by Deliveroo. No appeal was lodged. On 15 January 2019, however, the Amsterdam District Court ruled in proceedings between FNV (the major Dutch trade union) and Deliveroo[45] that riders from Deliveroo are not self-employed, but can claim an employment contract. The court also ruled that Deliveroo is covered by the collective agreement for the Road Haulage Industry. Appeals were lodged. Furthermore, on 26 August 2019, the Amsterdam District Court ruled in proceedings brought by the Occupational Pension Fund for Road Haulage[46] that Deliveroo is obliged to apply the pension arrangements of this pension fund and must retroactively pay pension contributions for all its employees. An appeal was lodged.

43 A.T.J.M. Jacobs, above n. 23, para. 68.

44 ECLI:NL:RBAMS:2018:5183.

45 ECLI:NL:RBAMS:2019:198 and ECLI:NL:RBAMS:2019:210; A.T.J.M. Jacobs, above n. 23, para. 69.

46 ECLI:NL:RBAMS:2019:6292.

Very recently, the Amsterdam Court of Appeal in an appeal judgment of 26 February 2021,[47] on the above-mentioned judgment of the Amsterdam District Court of 15 January 2019, has established that the riders with Deliveroo do not have a choice between an employment contract and a contract for services. They have only signed contracts which in Deliveroo's view are contracts for services. To which persons Deliveroo offers these contracts is determined by an algorithm system, named 'Frank'. It offers such contracts notably on the criterion of who among the persons who have applied by logging in can most effectively execute the offered order.

The court has noticed that the persons concerned in theory but also in fact have the freedom to refuse orders offered by Frank, and that it has not been found that they are disadvantaged by such a refusal in future tender offers. The court also found that the riders have to provide their own means of transport and that they can have the delivery carried out by another person.

On the other hand, the court has also established that engaging meal deliverers is the core business of Deliveroo. Its contracts with its meal deliverers have many aspects that exhibit the characteristics of an employment contract. The freedom to organise the work according to the insight of the meal deliverer is in fact very limited. The GPS system allows Deliveroo to actually control work done by the delivery person. The remuneration is unilaterally determined by Deliveroo. It is also paid by Deliveroo and it pays for the deliverers' accident insurance. Most deliverers do not pay VAT because the tax authorities consider their work as 'hobby work' and not as running a business.

All these factors in favour of the classification of the contracts of the meal deliverers with Deliveroo, in the eyes of the Court of Appeal, outweigh the arguments in favour of classifying the agreements of Deliveroo with the meal deliverers as a contract of services. Therefore the Court of Appeal confirmed that the meal deliverers of Deliveroo are engaged on the basis of a contract of employment.

Appeal requested.

The Court avoided giving a general ruling on the nature of the employment relationships that persons conclude with platforms. It only made a statement about the nature of the contracts between Deliveroo NL and its meal deliverers. Moreover this Court gave only a judgment about the civil law character of the contract of the Deliveroo riders. It did not pronounce on the consequences for statutory labour law and social

[47] ECLI:NL:GHAMS:2021:392.

security law, tax law and collective agreements or occupational additional social security law on their contracts.

In the meantime, the Dutch trade union FNV has filed a complaint at the District Court of Amsterdam, 27 August 2020, based on its judgment of 15 January 2020, in which it requested on behalf of two meal deliverers that Deliveroo should offer these persons an open-ended employment contract as well as back-pay of salary over their average working week of respectively 22 and 28 hours during the last two years.

Additionally, the Dutch trade union FNV has filed a complaint at the District Court of Amsterdam, December 2020, in which it requested on behalf of several of its members that Uber would offer these taxi drivers an open-ended employment contract as well as pay them according to the collective agreement for taxi services. No judgment yet.

5. WHAT ARE THE CHALLENGES OF PLATFORM WORK FOR THE ORGANISATION OF THE LABOUR MARKET?

In all five aforementioned cases, the bulk of labour law applicable to subordinate work was at stake – not only the statutory labour law, but also the labour law in the collective agreements and the occupational social security law (pensions). These judgments will have consequences for statutory social security law and tax law, as well.

The arrival a few years ago of the complex digital labour platforms on the Dutch labour market has revived the classic debate about the nature of the contractual relationships in the grey zone between the contract of employment and the contract for services.[48] What should the classification of platform work be? Is this a contract of employment, is it a genuine contract for services or is it a contract for services in disguise – in reality, a contract of employment? Is the current assessment framework in Dutch labour law (the legal qualification of the employment agreement and employer) still suitable? It is clear that in the Netherlands platform work profoundly challenges the binary divide between employees and self-employed persons.

The labour lawyers who are now advocating for the qualification of platform workers as employees certainly have valid arguments as far as the

---

48 J.M. Van Slooten, 'Ter Visie – Platformarbeid: nog een reden tot rethinking van het arbeidsrecht' [2017] 6 *Tijdschrift voor Arbeid & Onderneming* 51, 52.

complex digital labour platforms are concerned. As we have seen, those platforms are using interactive internet systems to select the person that is going to perform the job, set the prices and other conditions of these jobs, charge the providers of the jobs, handle the payments of the performers of the jobs and may handle tax payments and insurance. Such platforms can set exclusivity requirements – for example, services cannot be placed on a competing platform – and it is difficult or even impossible to take customer reviews to another platform. All this can lead to the platform worker being independent on paper, but in practice strongly economically dependent on the platform company.

Taking economic dependency instead of subordination as the central criterion for the qualification of a contract instead of subordination has long been a proposal of some labour lawyers, far before the digital labour platforms were even invented. Why has this proposal not been followed? There has been a rich debate on this issue, but in brief, this suggestion would create new borderline questions and would expand the dominion of labour law quite far into the world of self-employment.[49] Therefore, until now in all countries the legislators and the courts have been reluctant to take economic dependency as the central criterion for the qualification of the contract of employment. What most courts were prepared to do, has been to take the aspect of economic dependency as one of a wide range of factors. Also legislators have not been prepared to take the radical step from subordination to economic dependency; some legislators have limited themselves to creating an intermediate category, like the British 'worker'; others, like the Dutch, have more incidentally created forms of 'employee-minus' and 'independents-plus'.

Certainly the rise of platform work has given new ammunition to this old debate, which in fact touches upon the very foundations of labour law. Courts are hesitant to qualify platform work in general terms as contracts of employment. What they are actually considering is that perhaps some kind of platforms may be qualified as employers, but others not.

If platform workers would be considered as workers under contracts of employment, this would certainly increase the price of labour. No wonder the platforms resist – as well as other actors. Economists and numerous politicians see platform work as an important issue for Dutch business and an asset in the future labour market. The Dutch like to see themselves at the helm of the advanced technological economies in the world. These forces

---

49 A.T.J.M. Jacobs, *Labour and the Law in Europe. A Satellite View on Labour and Social Security Law in Europe*, Wolf Legal Publishers, Nijmegen 2011, p. 28.

are not prepared to renounce of this position. They point at the freedom of enterprise which must prevail. And they have social arguments, as well. There are in Dutch society many people who prefer the independent status. They enjoy having the feeling of being their own boss and not being forced to associate with colleagues. The option to work in subordination should be chosen in liberty. Many people have to turn to platform work because they cannot find a preferred stable position with an open-ended contract of employment. Some platform users may counter that for them, the platforms can be a blessing. Due to the somewhat anonymous character of these platforms, they may find jobs that in the past were unreachable. These platforms often make work accessible for specific groups and thus increase labour participation and contribute to an inclusive labour market.[50] Although this may be true, when these platforms by way of their algorithms destroy precisely these advantages and combine it with minimal working conditions, then the blessings quickly fade away. Therefore, this entire debate leads many people to the conclusion that platform work should be better regulated.[51] But what kind of regulation?

In the Netherlands, the qualification of specific platforms as employers would certainly be a victory for the platform workers concerned, but not a very big one. These platforms will immediately switch to the 'employee-minus' models that Dutch law has to offer: fixed-term contracts; zero-hours contracts; and temporary agency contracts.

A recent very thorough scientific study[52] has revealed that even if platform workers are henceforward qualified as employees, their status in labour law is weak, assuming that in that case they will be offered very casual or short fixed-term contracts. They then still fall outside a great deal of labour law protections and social security benefits which are focused on long-term employment relationships. Who is going to guarantee them continued payment of wages in the event of illness, holidays, parental leave, and other issues? What must be the calculation of working hours and pay for the time platform workers spend looking for assignments or waiting between work? The dynamics of the platform work entails special risks of accidents at work and work-related health complaints. In the Netherlands,

---

50 J. Gautier, 'Hoofdstuk 6. Nieuwe technologieën en de match van vraag en aanbod' and K. Frenken and B. Straathof, 'Hoofdstuk 10. Online platforms op (en in plaats van) de arbeidsmarkt', both in B. ter Weel, *De match tussen mens en machin*, Preadviezen van de Koninklijke Vereniging voor de Staathuishoudkunde, Amsterdam 2015, p. 103 and p. 163.

51 J. H. Bennaars, 'Is platformwerk een bedreiging of een kans voor het arbeidsrecht? Het antwoord is ja' [2018] 28(6/7) *ArbeidsRecht* 8, 10–12.

52 R.F. Hoekstra, above n. 11, p. 17.

even 'employees' who work outside their boss's premises are not sure of their employers' liabilities and responsibilities. Furthermore, what will be the substance of protection against dismissal without valid grounds? The privacy rules for employees do not yet seem to be sufficiently geared toward particular problems concerning data portability, digital customer assessments and algorithmic discrimination. From a practical point of view, platform workers are extra difficult to bring together in collective action and in representative advisory bodies. Will they qualify for unemployment benefits schemes and for occupational pensions under the actual rules, and if so, who will pay the contributions? A complete overhaul of existing labour law and social security law will be needed to give such platform workers, even if they are qualified as employees, a sufficient level of social protection.

6. THE OPPOSITION PROPOSALS

The Dutch social democrats, which in recent years were in the opposition, have made their position clear in a draft for a Private Members Bill that they intend to bring in Parliament.[53] In short, the initiator made the following proposals:

(1) Reverse the burden of proof: a platform is by definition an employer, unless the platform company demonstrates that the platform only acts as a mediator/broker.
(2) Clarify the employment relationship: platform workers should be given the rights of employees if the relationship between the platform and the workers meets certain criteria, which can be included in the Wage Tax Act 1964 and the Social Insurance Financing Act. If these criteria are met, there is always an employment contract, with corresponding rights and obligations for the platform and the platform worker.
(3) Platform workers must be guaranteed a fair wage, a good pension and protection in the event of illness and disability.
(4) The legislation on health and safety and working hours should be applicable to self-employed persons. Where possible, this legislation is directly integrated into the algorithm that assigns work to platform workers.

53 Parliamentary Papers 35230, n. 1–2.

(5) Strengthen the negotiating position of platform workers: give self-employed persons, including platform workers, the opportunity to negotiate rates collectively by adjusting competition law.
(6) Data portability: the government should encourage the portability of the reputation data of platform workers and take action against platforms that prevent this.
(7) Participation: compulsory consultation and/or co-decision rights for platform workers in the event of a change in the operation of algorithms that assign work.
(8) Compliance: enforce laws and regulations that protect self-employed persons and employees.

It is submitted that the last proposal is easier said than done because of the international character of the complex digital labour platforms. Such platforms offer their services via a world wide web. They may easily escape any Dutch rule on those platforms by simply relocating the platform to another country where no such rules exist. In the Netherlands, problems with private and public international law have already been identified in doctrinal writing,[54] but there is no case law yet related to international platform workers. It is doubtful whether the undesirable developments of complex digital labour platforms can be stopped with merely national regulation.

7. THE WIDER CONTEXT OF THE FRAGMENTATION OF THE LABOUR MARKET

It is unlikely that the social democrats' proposals will swiftly lead to an act of parliament – not only because they come from the opposition, but also because many people in the Netherlands like to make small problems part of big problems for the sake of consistency in legislation. Therefore, the problems created by the platforms have been accommodated in the more fundamental problem of the fragmentation of the labour market.

This fragmentation is not only caused by the complex digital labour platforms, but also by many different forms of work that are now present on the labour market. Through various ways of splitting jobs into mini-jobs,

---

[54] M. Houwerzijl, 'European Cross Border Worker Mobility in the Light of Digitalisation of Labour. More Fragmentation underway?' in K. Ahlberg and N. Bruun, *The New Foundations of Labour Law*, Peter Lang, Frankfurt 2017, pp. 233–54.

many workers are prevented from building up substantial social protection. Whether it is in the 'employment-minus' or 'independent-plus' categories, or intermediate categories like the British 'worker' or in genuine or bogus independent work, the beds are not so well spread for the mini-job-workers as for the well protected, open-contract employees. And the beds of the former are cheaper than of the latter.

In the Netherlands, in recent years scholars and policymakers have qualified this phenomenon as the very uneven playing field between the status of employees (and then notably open-ended contract employees) and self-employed workers. This is not an exclusively Dutch problem, but for a variety of reasons this problem is more widespread in the Netherlands than elsewhere. This is demonstrated by the fact that the Netherlands are the frontrunners in Western Europe in fixed-term contracts and in self-employed workers.

As aforementioned, there are vast differences in the legal position of employees and self-employed individuals in the Netherlands.[55] Much of the costs incurred by having employees can be avoided by engaging workers as independent contractors. As Verhulp has formulated it:

> If the employer has the option of not having the work carried out by means of a subordinated relationship and engaging a self-employed person rather than an employee, he quickly lean in that latest direction of lower employment law obligations and risks.[56]

Moreover, for short-sighted individuals it sometimes may be more attractive to work as independent contractors than as employees. Their net income from the job may be higher than in the same job under a contract of employment. One of the factors here is certainly that in the Netherlands freelance workers do not pay income taxes over the first €7,500 of their income from free entrepreneurship.[57]

Modern labour and social security law in the Netherlands has charged the employers with an increasing load of social obligations. Employers must be responsible for an 'addressee' of employment law, social security law and other rules and regulations laid down in legislation. The employer is currently the point of contact in many areas for the protection and

---

55 A.T.J.M. Jacobs, above n. 24, para. 68.

56 E. Verhulp, above n. 29, p. 7.

57 The Rutte III government has begun to step-by-step scale down this facility.

equipment of working people, the prevention of illness and reintegration in the event of illness, among other areas. It is most often the employer who invests in the human capital of workers (for example, through training) and provides for the physical capital (for example, machines) with which the worker can increase his productivity. This is the Netherlands' brand of 'corporate social responsibility'.

However, when the employer disappears as a point of contact for all aspects of such a protection, the question arises as to how workers must obtain the desired protection. Therefore, the conclusion of many a scholar is[58] that in the regulation of work, bottlenecks will arise in the coming years due to the fact that certain activities can be organised more easily without an employer.

In the Netherlands, many people are still attached to the present system, which offers the working population a substantial degree of income and certainty to build their future. If, however, crowdwork in general is expanding, an increasing number of people doing (low-paid) commodity work no longer fall under the scope of employment and social security law protection. Also, the financing of the system of social security would be endangered – the Organisation for Economic Co-operation and Development and the European Commission have already warned the Netherlands of these effects.[59] All this concerns independent work, crowdwork and the mini-job economy in general,[60] and it applies to work found via complex digital labour platforms. If it expands incessantly, it will contribute to a reduction of the role of the socially responsible employer in society.[61]

Consequently, many economists, policymakers and employers in the Netherlands see platform work as part of the wider problem of the distorted playing field between employees and independent contractors. The debate therefore has a high fundamental value, because it applies not only to the field of the platform work, but also to the entire field of the crowdwork economy.

58 R.F. Hoekstra, above n. 11, pp. 35–57.

59 A.T.J.M. Jacobs, above n. 23, para. 68.

60 F. Dekker, 'Werken in de kluseconomie: een literatuurstudie' [2018] 45(2) *Beleid en Maatschappij* 189, 190–93; M.S. Houwerzijl, 'Juridische vraagstukken rond arbeid in de klusseneconomie' [2018] 45(2) *Beleid en Maatschappij* 208, 208–16.

61 G. Evers and F. Pot, *Platform werk ontwricht ons arbeidsbestel*, Economisch-Statistische berichten, 20.12.2018.

8. THE OPINIONS OF THE SOCIAL PARTNERS AND OTHER STAKEHOLDERS

Many employers are anxious to reap the fruits of the mini-job economy, but others are concerned that an excessive expansion of this mini-job economy may lead to a dismantling of the societal structures in the Netherlands. There are also employer concerns about the level playing field between existing companies and new players on the market, partly due to differences in employment conditions. The employers' association of temporary work agencies,[62] for instance, puts much emphasis on the necessity of a more equal playing field between employees and self-employed individuals and more clarity on the legal status of platform workers. It prefers self-regulation above new statutory law, but it also believes that the existing law on intermediary services (WAADI) should be applicable to platforms.

The main Dutch employers' confederation, VNO-NCW, has taken a cautious position.[63] It has stressed the importance of the gig sector for the Dutch economy. Platforms are contributing to high-tech new employment. Several platform companies have already chosen the Netherlands for their (European) headquarters, which also creates work for persons in other fields, such as marketing, communication, construction and other fields. Moreover, the platforms, because of their advanced methods, may better align supply and demand than the traditional intermediary services. Nevertheless, employers recognise that platforms are creating new questions about the systems of social security and labour regulation, and therefore the employers' associations see the desirability of new regulation. But they are vague about what this new regulation should be. The general employers' confederation requires an improvement of the investment climate and the societal support for platforms – a vision of the Netherlands and the EU on technology – and ultimately, improvement of the rules of the game and enforcement of competition law.

Considering all the threats of the mini-job economy to the entire system of the modern Dutch welfare society, the trade unions in the Netherlands are in favour of a containment of the expansion of the mini-job economy in general. They want to bring all sorts of bogus self-employment under the application of the law of the contracts of employment and under the collective agreement system and the social security schemes. The largest

---

62 Algemene Bond Uitzendondernemingen, *Wat is impact van platformwerk?*, ABU White Paper, 2019.

63 VNO-NCW, *Vision on the platform-economy*, 2019.

Dutch trade union, FNV,[64] would like to have the possibility to lay down rules for platform workers in the relevant collective agreements.

An initial problem here is European anti-trust law and competition regulation, which might stand in the way of collective bargaining, as introducing minimum employment terms and conditions for independent workers can be interpreted as 'price-fixing'; the EU competition rules do not allow general binding collective agreements for self-employed workers. Only if they can be qualified as 'false independent workers' then could collective agreements cover them (see CJEU in the FNV-KIEM case).[65] However, differentiating between genuine self-employment and bogus self-employment is not easy. Although the Dutch Competition Authority recently showed some leniency in this field,[66] this is a problem that remains to be solved. Independent workers also ought to have the right to collective bargaining.[67]

If this problem can be solved, then there comes the question: who is capable of representing the platform workers? The mainstream trade unions in the Netherlands do not consider the status of 'independent contractors' as incompatible with union membership. The main trade union (FNV) would like to see itself recognised as the primary representative union for these workers and to conclude agreements on behalf of platform workers. There exists already a riders' union, which is linked to FNV. However, smaller unions of independent persons may claim the right to collective bargaining for themselves.

More problematic is the situation concerning the employers. In other countries, platforms may refuse to recognise unions,[68] but in the Netherlands there are some signs that digital labour platforms were prepared to meet with workers' representatives on the working conditions on their platforms (for example, regarding a minimum tariff and the conclusion of private accident insurance). The Dutch Ministry of Social Affairs has already tried to bring the trade unions and the meal delivery platforms together and

64 FNV, *Riders verdienen beter*, FNV-Report, 2019.

65 Case C-413/13, *FNV Kunsten Informatie en Media v. Staat der Nederlanden*, ECLI:EU:C:2014:2411.

66 Autoriteit Consument & Markt, *Leidraad: Tariefafspraken voor zzp-ers*, July 2020.

67 See Case 123/2016 *Irish Congress of Trade Unions (ICTU) v. Ireland*, ECSR 12.09.2018; see also Resolution E.P. 15.07.2017 on a European agenda for the mini-job-economy (2017/2003/INI), para. 41; International Labour Organization, *Compilation of decisions of the Committee on Freedom of Association*, 6th Ed., Geneva 2018, para. 332 ff. notably 387 and 388.

68 N. Srnicek, *Platform Capitalism*, Polity Press, Cambridge 2017.

start a social dialogue.[69] Nevertheless, in the Netherlands there is certainly not such a thing as the Danish Hilfr.dk., a collective agreement for platform workers. There is no voluntary adherence to a code of conduct, like in Bologna or in Germany, nor are there signs of workers' involvement in digital labour platforms via works councils, as in Germany.[70]

Can platform workers exert pressure in this direction? In the Netherlands, workers, whether independent or otherwise, certainly have the right to organise. They have already staged collective actions a few times. But whether independent workers have the right to strike is uncertain, and even more uncertain is whether they have the right to take more aggressive forms of collective action. In 2015, a Dutch court prohibited a wild-cat action of independent postmen to block the gates of the official Dutch Post.[71] Moreover, even if the workers that use digital labour platforms have the rights to organise and to strike, can they freely exercise them, or must they be afraid that the digital labour platforms can punish them by their algorithmic systems? Out of desperation, they may have resort to even less legitimate action forms, like hacking the platform.[72]

The Dutch Parliament has already devoted a hearing to the legal position of platform workers and asked the Social-Economic Council to explore the possible options for the approach to the platform economy. The Social-Economic Council issued a study in the autumn of 2020.[73] The former Rutte III government decided to wait for the report of a special commission it had created to investigate all the problems of 'a future-proof operation of the labour market', the so-called Borstlap Commission.

9. THE BORSTLAP COMMISSION ON PLATFORM WORK

This commission of independent experts[74] was set up by the government to reflect on a 'future-proof' operation of the Dutch labour market.

69 Parliamentary Papers 35.074 T, p. 17.

70 K. Vandaele, *Will trade unions survive in the platform economy?*, ETUI Working Papers, Brussels 2018, pp. 22–23.

71 ECLI:NL:RBMNE:2015:5373.

72 J. van Slooten, *Collective action and crowd work*, Powerpoints University of Amsterdam, 2017.

73 Sociaal Econoische Raad, *Hoe werkt de plan-economie*, SER-Advies 20/09, The Hague 2020.

74 Report of the Borstlap Commission, above n. 13.

Consequently, the Commission considered it crucial that solutions for the problems caused by platform work are sought within this wider context of the discussion about a future-proof operation of the labour market. This debate should lead to a better balance between existing enterprises and new players on the market, by creating, *inter alia*, a more equal playing field between the various work relationships.

The Borstlap Commission showed concerns about some of the working people in the mini-job economy who may enter into a vulnerable position with uncertainty and sometimes low income. This may not be problematic when work in the mini-job economy is a side job, but it can be different when people have to live on those wages for a long time.

As to the digital labour platforms, this commission advised a more transparent position of the platform by a tailor-made regulation, which very much is based on a differentiation that exist between the various platforms.

The Borstlap Commission proposed that a digital labour platform should be considered as the 'employer' or a 'temporary agency employer' of the platform workers if:

1) the platform takes on the financial and administrative obligations associated with the agreement between platform and platform worker, or between platform worker and the user of the platform;
2) the platform itself also plays an independent and substantive role in the realisation and the execution of the agreement; and
3) the activities of the platform worker belong to the core business of the company that owns the platform.

If these conditions are fulfilled, the workers of the digital labour platforms will be automatically covered by the existing statutory labour law rules, by the collective agreements, by both statutory and occupational social security law and by the tax law for employees.

In case these conditions are not fulfilled, but the platform nevertheless plays the role of broker in concluding and financially executing the agreement between platform worker user and the commanding client, then the platform should in any case be responsible for organising the tax payments and premiums for the platform worker.[75]

[75] Borstlap report, above n. 13, p. 75.

10. RECENT DEVELOPMENTS

When it was released in mid-January 2020, the report of the Borstlap Commission provoked a number of comments, mostly favourable on the side of the governing coalition parties and the social partners, and largely negative on the side of the opposition parties. There were mixed critical responses from scholars. The former government (Rutte III) reacted to the Borstlap report. It launched the idea of a specific provision to be included in the Dutch law on the contract of employment:[76] 'He who is linked to assignments or clients via a digital platform and where this application exerts any influence on the way in which the work is obtained or performed, is presumed to perform this work on the basis of a contract of employment'.

The Rutte III Government left the progress on this idea to the new government which is due to come to power after the elections in March 2021. The former government had only been prepared to issue a prohibition for individuals under the age of 16 years to work as riders.[77] Apart from this, there are some European developments which may, in the near future, influence the Dutch legal situation of platform workers: firstly, there is the new EU regulation on promoting fairness and transparency for business users of online intermediation services,[78] which applies from 12 July 2020. This regulation may not affect employees but it certainly affects independent working persons, who qualify as 'business users'. When companies like Deliveroo and Uber claim to engage independents individuals, not employees, then these rules may be applicable to them.[79] Secondly, the new EU directive on the transparency of worker contracts requires implementation before 1 August 2022. The Dutch legislature cannot escape the question of platform work in the course of this framework, as platform workers fall within the scope of this directive if they are genuinely self-employed persons.[80]

Thirdly, the Council Recommendation of 8 November 2019, on access to social protection for workers and self-employed individuals,[81] clearly

76 Parliamentary Papers 29 544 B.

77 Regulation of 22 June 2020, Staatscourant (Official Gazette) 30 June 2020.

78 Council Regulation (EC) 1150/2019 of 20 June 2019 Regulation, (EU) 2019/1150 of the European Parliament and of the Council of 20.06.2019 on promoting fairness and transparency for business users of online intermediation services [2019] OJ L186/57.

79 V. De Stefano and M. Wouters, above n. 17, p. 7.

80 See recital no. 8 of Council Directive 2019/1152/EC of 20 June 2019 on Transparent and Predictable Working Conditions OJ L 186/105.

81 Council Recommendation 2019/C 387/01 of 8 November 2019 on access to social protection for workers and the self-employed, OJ C 387/1.

also refers to platform work and requires the member states to present before 15 May 2021 an action plan to improve their social security systems on the various aspects concerned. Lastly, it has been the intention of the European Commission to come up with proposals to improve the working conditions of platform workers.[82] Consultation with the European social partners about this intention has already begun.[83]

11. CONCLUSION

Since 2015, platform work has – in the Netherlands and elsewhere – provoked a lot of scholarly debate, although the size of this work is not yet considerable (in the Netherlands, it accounts for 0.4 per cent of the labour market, approx. 34,000 persons). It is difficult to predict the growth of platform work in the near future, especially now that the coronavirus crisis has upset many economic forecasts.

There is also a wide variety of platforms. Judging by the degree of involvement in the eventual relationship between the provider of the job and the performer of the job, there is a distinction between 'simple digital labour platforms' and 'complex digital labour platforms'. The former should be bound to the regulation of employment placement services (ILO Convention No. 181), and the latter require more far-reaching regulation. Many scholars see the solution of this problem in labelling the workers of such platforms as 'employees'. In line with the conclusion of the Borstlap Commission, this should only be done concerning complex digital labour platforms.

However, it is prudent to note that this is merely the beginning. The workers of such platforms need more fundamental adaptations in existing labour law and social security law. Proposals to that end have been tabled in the Dutch Parliament, which is a good step forward. However, the problem of the global dimension of platform work should not be ignored. Can merely national rules ever get a sufficient grip on complex digital labour platforms?

In the Netherlands there is much debate about these phenomena, and now the courts have issued initial judgments. Additionally, the government, parliament and the social partners have participated in the

82 COM (2020) 37 final.

83 COM (2021) 1127 final.

debate on platform work, but this had not yet led to agreements between the social partners, nor to statutory activities in this field. Obviously policymakers are slow to take steps as they – rightly – see platform work as part of the more complex phenomenon of the mini-job economy, which in the Netherlands has created an uneven playing field between the various relationships on the labour market.[84]

In conclusion, it is safe to say that the adaptation of the existing structures of labour law and social security law to the requirements of the new world of work is bound to become just as protracted an effort as the restoration of the Dome of Milano.

[84] In the near future, only certain incidental actions seem possible, spurred on by a number of EU legislative activities.

REGULATORY AND JURISPRUDENTIAL PERSPECTIVES ON PLATFORM WORK

The UK Case

Nicola Countouris*

1. INTRODUCTION. THE RELEVANCE OF PLATFORM WORK IN THE UK

In *'Sorry We Missed You'*, internationally acclaimed director Ken Loach vividly described the plight of millions of British workers trying to earn a living while being managed by a ruthless algorithm at the hands of unscrupulous employers operating in the so-called 'gig economy'. *'Sorry We Missed You'* was partly inspired by the even more tragic events that in January 2018 led to the death of Deutsche Post Delivery (DPD) courier Don Lane. Don had worked for DPD for nearly two decades when, in

* Director of the Research Department at the European Trade Union Institute (ETUI), Belgium; Professor of Labour Law and European Law, University College London (UCL), United Kingdom. This chapter is written in the author's personal capacity and the views expressed are the author's own.

December 2017, he collapsed at the end of a long and exacting round of pre-Christmas deliveries. It was not the first time the diabetes-suffering, self-employed franchisee had collapsed, including once into a coma while at the wheel of his DPD van.[1] DPD had a policy of applying a £150 charge to the company's couriers whenever the latter cancelled a round and were not able to arrange cover, and Don – according to his widow – had missed several hospital appointments because of that. In March 2017, nine months before Don's death, Frank Field MP, the Chair of the House of Commons Work and Pensions Committee, had written a letter to the CEO of DPD UK, Dwain McDonald, requesting explanations about his company's policy.[2] No action was taken before Don's death, and DPD only changed its contracts, granting self-employed drivers sick pay, in March 2018.

While not all those working in the gig economy are exactly in the same position as Don Lane, these forms of work have become synonymous with uber-precarious and unprotected working and living conditions. A 2019 report produced for the Trade Union Congress (TUC) and other trade union organisation, *Platform Work in the UK 2016-2019*, noted how, in the last three years, the 'number of people working for online platforms at least once a week has doubled from 4.7% of the adult population to 9.6%',[3] or approximately 4.6 million workers. A report published by the UK Department for Business, Energy and Industrial Strategy (BEIS) in 2018 had that figure at about 2.8 million.[4] Both reports, however, with slightly different nuances, suggest that gig work in the UK appears to have a number of fairly common features. For instance, it is strongly characterised by low levels of income and unpredictability of terms and conditions, especially working hours. Most gig workers are actually couriers, followed by other task workers employed through platforms such as Task-Rabbit, and workers in the urban transport sector. For the majority of those working through an app, gig work generates levels of hourly income that tend to fall significantly below the statutory minimum wage. While a majority of gig workers actually do so to supplement income derived from other forms of employment, approximately 10 per cent of them earn most of their income in the gig economy. Statistics also suggest that there is a large

---

1 R. Booth, 'DPD courier who was fined for day off to see doctor dies from diabetes', *The Guardian*, 5 Feb 2018.

2 Letter available at https://www.parliament.uk/documents/commons-committees/work-and-pensions/Correspondence/Frank-Field-to-Dwain-McDonald-DPD-7-03-2017.pdf.

3 University of Hertfordshire, *Platform Work in the UK 2016-2019* (2019), page 1, available at https://www.feps-europe.eu/attachments/publications/platform%20work%20in%20the%20uk%202016-2019%20v3-converted.pdf

4 BEIS, *The Characteristics of those in the Gig Economy – Final report* (Feb 2018), p. 5.

concentration of platform workers in larger cities such as London, and the majority of them tends to be relatively young.

The 2019 report produced by Hertfordshire University for TUC noted that:

> Nearly half (48.1%) of people doing platform work say they are in full-time employment, with 10.7% saying they are self-employed. Platform workers cannot be seen as a distinct and separate category on the labour market but can be found in all categories and form part of a diverse continuum of casual, precarious and on-call work.[5]

There is some virtue in looking at platform work as being distributed along a diverse range of contracts that, regardless of their employment status, are inherently characterised by high levels of casualization and precarity. The following sections elaborate further on the legal construction of platform work through a variety of different types of contractual arrangements or relations, as well as focusing on a number of particular challenges affecting the regulation of 'gig work'. But they also note that the inherently fragmented and discontinuous nature of some forms of platform work can adversely affect any legal claim to a contract of employment or even to a worker's contract, raising caution around the suggestion that only one in ten platform workers is self-employed.

2. THE LEGAL CONSTRUCTION OF PLATFORM WORK

At a basic level UK employment law distinguishes between three main employment statuses: the employee with a contract of employment or 'contract of service', as cursorily defined by s. 230 (1)-(2) ERA 1996; the 'self-employed' contractor employed under a 'contract for services', a concept which is predominantly a construction of common law courts and reasoning; and the intermediate category of 'worker' as defined by s.230(3)(b) ERA 1996 ('any other contract, whether express or implied ..., whereby the individual undertakes to do or perform personally any work or services for another party to the contract whose status is not by virtue of the contract that of a client or customer of any profession or business undertaking carried on by the individual'). This latter category

5 University of Hertfordshire, above no. 3, p. 1.

attracts some labour law protections (e.g. minimum wage under the Minimum Wage Act 1998, rules on working time and paid holidays under the Working Time Regulations 1998, statutory sick pay under the Social Security Contributions and Benefits Act 1992), but not all, and is notoriously excluded from unfair dismissal legislation.

The self-employed contractor category is not directly defined by any statute or regulation, and in practice it has emerged as a sort of 'residual category' for those persons that do not meet the legal tests used by courts and tribunals to define the concept of contract of employment or of 'worker' contract. Various contractual arrangements, from the more formal ones (e.g. franchisee, agent, personal service company) to the less formal ones (e.g. a variety of contractual arrangements loosely understood as amounting to contracts for services) can be relied upon in order to construe a work relationship as one of self-employment.

It is worth noting that in recent years the Supreme Court has clarified two important points in respect of the legal concept of self-employment. Firstly, in its decision in *Jivraj v Hashwani*,[6] it read the definition of 'employment' currently contained in s. 83(a) of the Equality Act 2010 ('employment under a contract of employment, a contract of apprenticeship or a contract personally to do work') as excluding from equality legislation at large all genuinely self-employed persons.[7] Secondly, in the case of *Bates van Winklehof*,[8] it established that 'workers' are in effect a kind of self-employed people, best understood as 'people who provide their services as part of a profession or business undertaking carried on by some-one else'[9] as distinct from 'those self-employed people who are in business on their own account and undertake work for their clients or customers'.[10] However, and in spite of these 'workers' being a sub-category or kind of self-employed persons, it is clear that they are not excluded from the scope of application of the Equality Act 2010.[11]

At a less superficial level it may be possible to identify at least two more relevant legal definitions of worker. Relevant in the sense that those working in the gig economy may be able to draw some rights from such legal definitions. The first one is the 'worker' definition contained in s. 296(1)(b) of Trade Union Labour Relations (Consolidation) Act 1992

---

6 *Jivraj v Hashwani* [2011] UKSC 40.

7 For a critique see M. Freedland and N. Kountouris, 'Employment Equality and Personal Work Relations – A Critique of *Jivraj v Hashwani*' (2012), *ILJ*, 56–66.

8 *Clyde & Co LLP & Anor v Bates van Winklehof* [2014] UKSC 32.

9 Ibid, para. 25.

10 Ibid, para. 31.

11 Ibid, Para. 46.

of 'an individual who works ... under any other contract whereby he undertakes to do or perform personally any work or services for another party to the contract who is not a professional client of his'. The second one is the definition of 'home worker' contained in s. 35(1) of the National Minimum Wage Act 1998, which does not insist on the relevant work being performed in a personal capacity (and thus ostensibly allowing for the occasional substitution of the worker by a substitute worker).

It is worth noting that, unlike labour law, tax law is much more binary, providing a fairly clear dichotomy between the employee and the self-employed contractor status, but also a strong presumption that several self-employed contractors (including those operating through personal service companies and, increasingly, franchise agreements) performing work 'personally', ought to be taxed (both in terms of their income tax and of their national insurance liabilities) on a par with standard employees working under a contract of employment.[12]

3. REGULATING APP-BASED WORK RELATIONS

This relatively broad and fragmented palette of definitions (and conceptualisations) of worker status has undoubtedly complicated the framing of platform work in a clear and consistent manner, including by courts. By and large, it can be suggested that a number of cases that have ended before employment tribunals (ET) have eventually resulted in a finding that various forms of platform work had to be framed as performed under 'worker' contracts. For instance, the widely commented ET decision in *Aslam v Uber*[13] concluded that the drivers had to be treated as 'workers' under the definition contained in s. 230(3)(b) ERA 1996, and were thus entitled to the National Minimum Wage as well as having a right to paid holidays. In 2021, this finding was finally upheld by the UK Supreme Court in its judgment *Uber BV v Aslam* [2021] UKSC 5. Several other ET decisions reached a similar conclusion in respect of a variety of other forms of platform work.[14]

---

12 See the Finance Act 2000 (Schedule 12), and successive amendments.

13 *Aslam v Uber BV* [2016] EW Misc B68 (ET) (28 October 2016); upheld by the Court of Appeal in *Uber BV v Aslam* [2018] EWCA Civ 2748, and by the Supreme Court in *Uber BV v Aslam*[2021] UKSC 5.

14 *Dewhurst v Citysprint uk ltd* (ET 2202512/2016, 5 Jan 2017); *Mr A Boxer v Excel Group Services Ltd* (ET 3200365/2016, 22 March 2017); Lange v Addison Lee Ltd (ET 2208029/2016, 25 September 2017).

Most tribunals, and courts, have reached these conclusions by recognising the importance of three key factors present in all these app-mediated work relations before them. The first factor is the presence of substantial levels of direction and control, albeit in the rather novel forms permitted by apps and algorithms. In that respect, the Supreme Court's suggestion is extremely insightful:

> Uber exercises control over the acceptance of the request by the driver in two ways. One is by controlling the information provided to the driver. [...] The second form of control is exercised by monitoring the driver's rate of acceptance (and cancellation) of trip requests.[15]

The second factor is the presence and substantial exercise of managerial powers, including disciplinary ones. This is quite evident from the 13 considerations that led the London Employment Tribunal to reclassify Mr Aslam and his colleagues as 'workers', as listed in paragraph 92 of the Uber ET decision, and as approved by the Employment Appeal Tribunal, the Court of Appeal and by the Supreme Court.[16] Paragraph 99 of the Supreme Court judgment rightly concludes that:

> the ratings are used by Uber purely as an internal tool for managing performance and as a basis for making termination decisions where customer feedback shows that drivers are not meeting the performance levels set by Uber.

The third factor is the glaring disconnect between the fiction of the contractual arrangements and the reality of what tribunals found almost invariably to be a contract for the performance of personal work, thus leading to the application of the 'sham contracts' *Autoclenz*[17] doctrine. As summarised by the Court of Appeal (with one judge, Underhill LJ, dissenting) in the *Uber* decision:

> We consider that the extended meaning of 'sham' endorsed in *Autoclenz* provides the common law with ample flexibility to address the convoluted, complex and artificial contractual arrangements, no doubt formulated by a battery of lawyers, unilaterally drawn up and dictated by Uber to tens

---

15 *Uber BV v Aslam* [2021] UKSC 5, paras. 96–97.

16 *Uber v Aslam* [2018] EWCA Civ 2748, para. 96. Uber BV v Aslam [2021] UKSC 5, para. 120.

17 *Autoclenz Ltd v Belcher* [2011] UKSC 41; A. Bogg, 'Sham Self-Employment in the Supreme Court' (2012) *ILJ*, 328; A.C.L. Davies, 'Sensible Thinking About Sham Transactions' (2009) *ILJ*, 318.

> of thousands of drivers and passengers, not one of whom is in a position to correct or otherwise resist the contractual language. As to the reality, not only do we see no reason to disagree with the factual conclusions of the ET as to the working relationship between Uber and the drivers, but we consider that the ET was plainly correct.[18]

It is worth noting that on this latter point, the Supreme Court judgment is slightly more nuanced, providing a reading of *Autoclenz* as effectively reversing the burden of proof for the employer to demonstrate that the written contractual documents do actually reflect the reality of the relationship. Now, to use the Supreme Court's words, 'there is no legal presumption that a contractual document contains the whole of the parties' agreement and no absolute rule that terms set out in a contractual document represent the parties' true agreement just because an individual has signed it.'[19]

Partly to address the suggestion by Uber that the drivers were free to work for multiple apps, including for competing companies, and were therefore genuine entrepreneurs, the Supreme Court stressed that this was a 'matter of fact and degree' and that:

> no evidence was adduced at the hearing in the employment tribunal ... that there was at that time any other app-based PHV transportation service operating in London or that drivers logged into the Uber app were as a matter of practical reality also able to hold themselves out as at the disposal of other PHV operators when waiting for a trip.[20]

This was an important conclusion to reach, as a different one could have excluded the drivers from workers' rights due to their providing services to a multitude of 'clients and customers' under s. 230(3)(b) ERA 1996.

In most cases appearing before employment tribunals, the claims made by the applicant workers revolved around an underpayment of statutory national minimum wage, or to breaches of the Working Time Regulations, including the right to paid annual leave, or to a mix of the two. While the finding that these app-based workers were indeed 'workers' under that statutory definition of s. 230(3)(b) ERA 1996 successfully entitled them to such rights, tribunals had to elaborate with a certain degree of

18 Court of Appeal, para. 105.
19 Supreme Court para. 85.
20 Supreme Court paras. 136–37.

sophistication on the question of when gig workers start accruing these rights in the course of their work.

In *Uber*, the Supreme Court fully endorsed the finding by the ET that 'all time spent by a driver working under a worker's contract with Uber London, including time spent "on duty" logged onto the Uber app in London available to accept a trip request, is "working time" within the meaning of the Working Time Directive and Regulations.'[21] It expressed some caution that this may not be the case if the drivers were also genuinely making themselves available on a competing platform,[22] but as noted above, it ultimately concluded that there was no factual evidence suggesting this practice. Ultimately, it is still accurate to suggest that one is a 'worker' and accrues worker's rights such as pay and paid holidays, from the moment they have switched on their app and are present within the geographical area of service to which their employer has designated them, although the simultaneous use of multiple apps may jeopardise this finding. This is arguably the consequence of a narrow understanding of the concept of 'personality' at work, and a rather counterintuitive one, as the law would not draw such an inference if a full-time (let alone a part-time) academic lawyer were also to offer legal services as a barrister or on a consultancy basis.

4. THERE'S A GAP IN YOUR APP! PROTECTIVE LOOPHOLES IN THE REGULATION OF THE GIG ECONOMY

By and large, the majority of decisions have thus far found app-based workers to be 'workers' in the technical sense of s.230(3)(b) ERA 1996, and have adopted a fairly generous concept of the temporal dimension of their work (from the moment the app is on). However it is also important to acknowledge at least two slightly less optimistic considerations that severely diminish the worker's protective implications of these decisions.

Firstly, it remains unclear why app-based workers who are found to be performing personal work – under the control of a main employer that also, de facto and de jure, exercises substantial amounts of managerial authority – ought to be classified as 'workers' entitled to some rights, as opposed to being seen as 'employees' entitled to all right contained in the

---

21 Para. 134.
22 Para. 135.

labour law statutes. In *Uber*, the Supreme Court identified not one, but five separate ways in which the platform exercised a substantial degree of control over the manner in which the drivers performed their work.[23] So why should they only be conferred a 'worker' status? At a superficial level, it could be suggested that this is a result primarily dictated by the specific litigation strategies designed by risk-adverse employment solicitors (and by the unions appointing them under their equally risk-adverse and chronically underfunded legal schemes). It is, in theory, easier to satisfy the benchmark for 'worker' status as opposed to that of 'employee'.[24] Thus far, the legal enquiry around 'worker' status has allowed workers and their counsel to sidestep the extremely frustrating 'mutuality of obligation' test that English courts insist imposing on the legal construction of contracts of employment. In essence, while in order to find that a person is an employee under a contract of employment, courts need to satisfy themselves that she and her employer are contractually bound by a sufficient degree of mutual obligations for future and continuous performance of the work-wage bargain – this *probatio diabolica* for all those on intermittent or casual contracts has yet to be imposed, or at least imposed with the same intensity, on 'worker' claims (though admittedly with some important inconsistencies).[25] But litigation strategies aside, it remains extremely disturbing that workers whom the courts and tribunals have found to be, in effect, subordinated and controlled by an employer are deprived from the full panoply of protective rights that labour law was designed to offer to all employees.

Secondly, and perhaps more worryingly, it is clear that some of the earlier successes registered by skilled workers' counsel are increasingly triggering a learning process by equally skilled employers' advisors and human resources professionals. For instance, it has become apparent that various operators in the delivery services sector have started amending the contracts they issue to their platform workers in order to introduce new clauses on substitution that could act as de facto exclusion clauses or 'defeat devices', by rejecting the 'personal' character of the work provided.

The most notorious of such cases underpins the litigation involving Deliveroo and the Independent Workers' Union of Great Britain (IWGB). In this case, the central question was whether Deliveroo riders could be

---

23 Supreme Court paras. 94–100.

24 For a critical appraisal of this position expressed in *Byrne Bros (Formwork) Ltd v Baird* [2002] ICR 667, see H. Dhorajiwala, 'Secretary of State for Justice v Windle: The Expanding Frontiers of Mutuality of Obligation?' (2017) ILJ, 268.

25 Ibid.

seen as 'workers' under the definition provided in s. 296(1)(b) TULRCA 1992. This, in combination with the provisions contained in Schedule A1 of the 1992 Act, would have allowed IWGB to trigger a statutory recognition procedure which, if successfully carried out, could have led to the forced recognition of the union by the company for the purposes of collectively agreeing a number of minimum terms and conditions of employment.

In November 2017, the Central Arbitration Committee, the adjudicative body tasked with discharging the statutory procedure under sch.1 of the Act, reached the conclusion that under the terms of a new contract issued by Deliveroo in May 2017 (just as various ETs across the UK were recognising more and more drivers and couriers as limb-b workers), Deliveroo riders were self-employed, and not workers. This was mainly because of a new substitution clause in the new contract, clause 8, providing that riders were free to 'engage others to provide the Services ... without the need to obtain Deliveroo's prior approval' (clause 8.1).[26] And although the High Court, where a judicial review against the CAC decision was lodged, agreed with the findings by CAC that 'most riders do not use substitutes', the fact that 'a few riders'[27] did so, with one providing evidence on behalf of Deliveroo to that effect, was sufficient to deny 'personality', and worker status, to all riders. It was clear that while, on occasion, a very small number of Deliveroo riders may have delegated to other riders, for a share of their fee, some delivery services assigned to them, the practice was far from widespread. This set of findings, in effect, also fatally affected the attempt by IWGB counsel to claim that the riders ought to be accorded the right to bargain collectively under Article 11 ECHR as, in the words of Supperstone J, that provision did not 'extend the right collectively to bargain beyond an employment relationship',[28] and the occasional and limited use of the substitution clause meant that there was none. This approach was confirmed by the June 2021 Court of Appeal judgment that affirmed that 'only workers in an employment relationship enjoy the particular protections arising from by the closing words of article 11 [ECHR]' and that 'riders are, genuinely, not under an obligation to provide their services personally and have a virtually unlimited right of substitution', this being 'a material factor in the decision whether they are in an employment relationship with Deliveroo',[29] effectively concluding that they did not.

---

26 *IWGB v RooFoods Ltd T/A Deliveroo*, Case Number: TUR1/985(2016).

27 *IWGB v CAC/Deliveroo*, [2018] EWHC 3342 (Admin), paras. 79–81.

28 Ibid, para. 36.

29 *IWGB v Deliveroo* [2021] EWCA Civ 952, paras 44, 77.

So while it is possible to argue that court cases have brought some hard-fought successes to a number of platform workers, it is also fair to say that unlike other countries, there has been a certain reluctance to litigate for the establishment of a full 'employment status', and perhaps more worryingly employers have started to make adjustments in order to escape the potential liabilities that they would accrue against their newly identified 'workers'. It is worth noting that the Watford Employment Tribunal sent a reference to the CJEU,[30] seeking a pronouncement on whether an 'individual [who] has the right to engage sub-contractors or "substitutes" to perform all or any part of the work or services required of him [is] to be regarded as a worker for the purposes of Directive 2003/88/EC'. In April 2020, the CJEU produced an order that, on the one hand, offered a very broad interpretation of the EU concept of 'worker', but on the other, concluded that a person would be prevented from being classified as a 'worker' where afforded the discretion 'to use subcontractors or substitutes to perform the service which he has undertaken to provide'.[31] This decision by the CJEU did not go amiss and partly underpinned the Court of Appeal's judgment in *Deliveroo*.[32] A better approach would establish the extent to which these kinds of clauses are genuinely and commonly used by a substantial share of the workforce, or whether their use is merely marginal or even just fictional.

5. PLATFORM WORK AND CONFLICTS OF LAW

English courts have so far resisted the attempts by platforms and their representatives to claim that the incorporation of part of their complex corporate value chain in a foreign jurisdiction would necessarily result in their being wholly or partly incompetent to adjudicate over the workers' claims. In the *Uber* case, for instance, the company's solicitors claimed that 'Uber' the company was in reality split into at least three separate legal corporate entities, not all of them incorporated under UK law. The first entity was Uber London Limited (ULL), a UK-registered company which, since May 2012, had held the Private Hire Vehicle (PHV) Operator Licence

---

30 Case C-692/19, *B v Yodel Delivery Network Ltd*, (2019/C 423/30).

31 Case C-692/19, para. 45. For a critical analysis see A. Aloisi, "Time Is Running Out' The Yodel Order and Its Implications for Platform Work in the EU' (2020), Italian Labour Law e-Journal, available at https://illej.unibo.it/article/view/11777.

32 *IWGB v Deliveroo* [2021] EWCA Civ 952, paras 64–74, 78, 82.

pursuant to the Private Hire Vehicles (London) Act 1998, as required by UK law. Its functions include making provision for the invitation and acceptance of PHV bookings and accepting such bookings. The second entity was Uber Britannia Limited, which holds or manages PHV Operator Licences issued by various local authorities outside London. The third entity was Uber BV (UBV), for all purposes a Dutch corporation and the parent company of the previous two companies. UBV holds the intellectual property rights in the app, and the app is of course responsible for a large part of the actual terms and conditions of employment/engagement of the drivers. Uber's solicitors maintained up until the Court of Appeal that 'the ERA and NMWA do not apply to any contract with UBV – Dutch law applies such that the claimants do not have any protection under UK employment legislation'.[33]

The issue was eventually dropped and was not brought before the Supreme Court. The ET and the subsequent appellate courts approached this question from the angle of deciding who was the entity performing the core employer functions. On paper there were two options. One was Uber UBV, and the other ULL. At paragraph 96 of the judgement, the CA agreed with the ET that ULL was the employer as the main 'point of contact between Uber and the drivers. It recruits, instructs, controls, disciplines and, where it sees fit, dismisses drivers. It determines disputes affecting their interests'. It therefore concluded that it was the employer and agreed with the view held by the ET that 'In view of the conclusion that ULL was the employer the conflict of laws issue became irrelevant, but for the avoidance of doubt the ET held that, on Rome I principles, English law would have been applicable in any event'.[34]

6. PLATFORM WORK AND COLLECTIVE BARGAINING

The *Deliveroo* decision, discussed above, highlights the complexities that trade unions can face when attempting to seek recognition for the purposes of collective bargaining with employers in the gig economy.

Exceptionally, some unions have succeeded in concluding agreements with a number of the key players in the courier sector. In February 2019, the union GMB announced the conclusion of a voluntary collective agreement

33 *Uber v Aslam* [2018] EWCA Civ 2748, para. 9.
34 Ibid, para. 32.

with delivery firm Hermes. The agreement grants to Hermes riders the choice of opting into a new peculiar employment status, namely that of 'self-employed plus'. Under the terms of the agreement, riders opting to become 'self-employed plus' receive a minimum hourly wage of £8.55 per hour (approximately 9% more than the national living wage rate at the time), and would be entitled to holiday pay on a pro rata basis up to 28 days per year. Undoubtedly this agreement constituted an important novelty in the British industrial relations landscape.

On the other hand, it is worth noting that a year prior to the agreement being concluded, a number of Hermes couriers, with the help of GMB, had successfully established before the Leeds ET that they should be regarded as workers and given the broader spectrum of employment rights to which limb-b workers are entitled.[35] This status, it will be recalled, also includes protection against discrimination, rights for whistleblowers and, under certain circumstances, a right to certain social security entitlements such as statutory sick pay. So in many ways, the GMB agreement was the product of concession bargaining, presumably with the view of avoiding either the risks or the expenses of a potential appeal by the employer.

It is worth noting that following the Supreme Court's decision in *Uber v Aslam*, GMB and Uber entered into a voluntary recognition agreement, with Uber agreeing to pay the statutory minimum 'living' wage to all its 70,000 UK drivers, calculated 'after accepting a trip request and after expenses' (and thus falling short of the broader definition of working time upheld by the Supreme Court).[36]

7. PLATFORM WORK AS A PARADIGM FOR THE FUTURE OF WORK IN THE UK: REFORM PROPOSALS

At the time of writing, it is clear that 'gig work' is no longer the niche phenomenon it used to be just half a decade ago. It is also clear that it has neither substituted the standard employment relationship nor the contract of employment as the core institution around which labour

35 *Leyland and others v Hermes*, Case Number: 1800575/2017, of 22 June 2018.

36 'Uber and GMB strike historic union deal for 70,000 UK drivers', 26 June 2021, available at https://www.gmb.org.uk/news/uber-and-gmb-strike-historic-union-deal-70000-uk-drivers

markets continue to operate. It is arguable that this may be neither an ambition nor a possibility in the immediate future. But the impact of the inherent insecurities of platform work is increasingly felt both by those in casual forms of work and those in more secure forms but who are at risk of substitution with less protected, platform-based working arrangements.

Platform work can adversely affect labour market institutions even without becoming the dominant paradigm for labour versus capital exchanges. It is worth considering that the emergence of lean-production, Toyotism and of what used to be called, in the 1980s and 1990s, the peripheral and numerically flexible labour force, did not completely displace pre-existing forms of vertically integrated forms of industrial and bureaucratic organisation, with their broadly secure and internalised labour markets. The emergence of the flexible workforce certainly ate into and eroded more secure forms of work, but essentially complemented the latter, without supplementing them. In doing so, it both created large pockets of atypical, and increasingly precarious, labour, employed though a range of agency, part-time and short-term or intermittent contracts, and generated a substantial amount of deregulatory pressures on more secure forms of work, both through the threat of substitution and through the emergence of the 'insider v outsider' false dilemma that essentially held to ransom employment protection policy for a good two decades.[37]

So in that sense, the threat by platform work to the future of work relations in the UK should not be understood as gig work becoming the new labour market paradigm, but as a new, and technologically enhanced, direct and indirect threat to the standard employment relationship. Uberism is in many ways 'Toyotism on steroids'. It will certainly hollow out some sectors (already populated by insecure forms of work) such as the urban transport and catering sectors, blurring completely the old distinction between core versus peripheral workforce and between functionally and numerically flexible workers. But most importantly, it will generate pressures on those sectors where jobs are still relatively secure, but where workers and unions are less able to resist implicit 'races to the bottom' and social dumping. Sectors such as medical care, primary and secondary and university education, construction and digital infrastructure and important areas

---

37 V. De Stefano, 'A Tale of Oversimplification and Deregulation: The Mainstream Approach to Labour Market Segmentation and Recent Responses to the Crisis in European Countries' (2014), ILJ 253.

of the public sectors or even civil service could be most exposed to this 'creeping uberisation' of work relations.[38]

It is worth noting that the two key reform proposals that have emerged in recent years as likely conceptual and political alternatives to the regulation of gig work, the proposals stemming from the so called Taylor Review,[39] essentially commissioned by the Conservative Prime Minster Theresa May, then in government, and the ones stemming from the Institute of Employment Rights' Manifesto,[40] essentially endorsed by the Labour Party in opposition, share the view that we may be witnessing, for all purposes, a creeping 'uberisation' of work relations. The Taylor Review's rose-tinted-glass approach to gig work saw this form of casual labour as part of a pattern of 'new business models based around matching sellers and buyers of goods and services meaning that people can make money in new ways ... [that are] forecast to grow'. It conceived of this type of labour as 'attractive to young people', with 'benefits to an individual choosing to work in this way include[ing] flexibility and control over how they work', merely acknowledging that 'this new way of working also raises questions about the suitability of the current employment law framework in addressing the needs of people actively choosing to work outside of the traditional employment model'.[41] Given this rather underwhelming critical assessment of the challenges presented by platform work, it is unsurprising that the crux of the solutions envisaged by the report in this domain was the adoption of a new employment status of 'dependent contractor' to replace the concept of limb-b worker (with some tweaks in terms of a looser requirement for personal work, and greater if vaguely phrased allowances for substitution clauses) and attracting a comparable set of rights to the one currently enjoyed by 'workers'.[42]

---

38 See N. Countouris, 'La gouvernance par les algorithmes et le récit alternatif du travail', in A. Supiot (ed.), *Le travail au XXIe siècle* (Les Editions de l'Atelier, 2019), 90.

39 M. Taylor et al, 'Good work: The Taylor review of modern working practices' (2017).

40 K.D. Ewing, J. Hendy and C. Jones (eds.), *A Manifesto for Labour Law: Towards a Comprehensive Revision of Workers' Rights* (IER, 2016), available at https://www.ier.org.uk/product/manifesto-labour-law-towards-comprehensive-revision-workers-rights/; cf. also, K.D. Ewing, J. Hendy and C. Jones (eds.), *Rolling Out the Manifesto for Labour Law* (IER, 2018), available at https://www.ier.org.uk/product/rolling-out-manifesto-labour-law.

41 M. Taylor et al, above no. 39, p. 28.

42 For an in-depth analysis of the Taylor Review, see K. Bales, A. Bogg and T. Novitz, '"Voice" and "Choice" in Modern Working Practices: Problems With the Taylor Review' (2018) *ILJ* 46–75.

The Institute of Employment Rights first approached the issue in its publication *A Manifesto for Labour Law: towards a comprehensive revision of workers' rights*[43]and then subsequently in the more detailed *Rolling out the Manifesto for Labour Law.*[44] Both documents were endorsed by the Labour Party in opposition and shared a novel approach to the regulation of non-standard work, including platform work, characterised by the principle of universalism, both in terms of universal coverage (across different forms of personal work) and in terms of protection (i.e. all labour rights to be enjoyed as a day-one right, and the abolition of qualifying periods). The central axis of this reform approach was a new definition of 'worker' that would have applied to every individual 'engaged by another to provide labour' and that is 'not genuinely operating a business in his or her own account'.[45] A second axis was a new definition of employer, centred around the idea of joint or dual-employership, whereby the employer is whoever 'substantially determines the terms on which the worker worked' and if:

> more than one party is so responsible (and regardless of whether one party is more responsible than the other, as long as both are 'substantially' responsible), the worker may address a claim against either or both putative employers.[46]

This would have covered both traditional employers and employers in the gig economy, whether operating by means of platforms such as Uber, or as mere intermediaries and crowdwork facilitators, such as Task-Rabbit and the like. A third essential element of this approach was the introduction of a strong, but rebuttable, legal presumption so that:

> Anyone providing their labour to another will be presumed to fall within the scope of [labour law], unless the end user or the service provider can demonstrate that the person providing the labour is performing a genuine entrepreneurial activity on their own account.[47]

The key objective of this approach would have been that of broadening the scope of application of labour law while trying to reduce the casualization dynamics inherent to all forms of casual labour, including those forms that are digitally mediated and facilitated.[48]

---

43 K.D. Ewing, J. Hendy and C. Jones (eds.) (2016), above no. 40.
44 K.D. Ewing, J. Hendy and C. Jones (eds.) (2018), above no. 40.
45 Ibid, p. 36
46 Ibid, p. 38.
47 Ibid, p. 37.
48 For a regulation of working hours see the suggestions at ibid, pp. 39–41.

At the time of writing, neither the Taylor Review nor the Manifesto project have received substantial implementation by means of legislation. By and large, they continue to represent the two primary approaches to the regulation of platform work – the first essentially aimed at offering palliative reforms, for all intents and purposes facilitating its spread, the second offering more structural reforms aimed at co-opting this form of work within a broadened and more secure labour rights framework. And with the UK no longer a member of the EU, it is clear that any EU reforms of the platform work phenomenon stemming from Brussels,[49] will only have a distant echo (though they may not necessarily be completely unheard) on this side of the Channel.

8. CONCLUSIONS

There is hardly any doubt that platform work is here to stay. The gig workforce can be understood in a continuum with other forms of casual labour which were already proliferating in the pre-digital world of work, but also as a digitally enhanced version of these pre-modern forms of precarious employment. The domestic policy debate leans towards recognising that platform work can have some short-term benefits for those who embrace it, whether willingly or not, but also conceding that ultimately it is storing longer-term problems both in terms of individual workers missing out on important rights and protections and in terms of broader societal costs. It does not represent a fair mutualisation of those risks that are inherent to every form of labour versus capital exchange, and it is clear that individual workers and societies at large end up absorbing most of these risks, whereas most the benefits accrue with businesses and, to a certain extent, consumers.

A clear manifestation of this unbalanced allocation of risks is emerging very visibly and poignantly in the context of the COVID-19 crisis. While the government was rushing to support employees with income-replacement schemes and businesses with interruption loan facilities, millions of

---

[49] European Commission, 'First phase consultation of social partners under Article 154 TFEU on possible action addressing the challenges related to working conditions in platform work', Brussels, 24.2.2021 C (2021) 1127 final; European Commission, 'Second-phase consultation of social partners under Article 154 TFEU on possible action addressing the challenges related to working conditions in platform work', Brussels, 15.6.2021 C(2021) 4230 final.

self-employed individuals on zero-hours contracts – working through personal-service companies, digital platforms or other intermediaries – were caught in a limbo of helplessness and faced poverty and destitution, in spite of the belated introduction of government schemes seemingly targeted at their needs.[50] Unions had to resort to litigation to ensure that gig-workers received at least some rights in the realm of EU health and safety law.[51] In the meantime, authoritative sources have reported[52] on large swathes of self-employed individuals, many of them gig workers, missing out on these schemes – just as, over the years, they missed out on a broad range of statutory and collective labour rights, while also failing to achieve the economic security and market autonomy typically enjoyed by successful businesses. A solution to the problem of platform work is now long overdue.

---

50 See N. Countouris, V. De Stefano, K. Ewing and M. Freedland, 'Covid-19 crisis makes clear a new concept of 'worker' is overdue', 9 April 2020, Social Europe Blog, available at https://www.socialeurope.eu/covid-19-crisis-makes-clear-a-new-concept-of-worker-is-overdue.

51 *R (Independent Workers' Union of Great Britain) v Secretary of State for Work and Pensions*[2020] EWHC 3050 (Admin).

52 The Fairwork Project, 'The Gig Economy and Covid-19: Looking Ahead' (September 2020); IF, 'Income protection for the self-employed and employees during the coronavirus crisis' 2 April 2020, available at https://www.ifs.org.uk/publications/14786.

PART II

EUROPEAN PERSPECTIVES

CROWDWORK AND WORK ON-DEMAND IN THE EUROPEAN LEGAL FRAMEWORK

Promises and Expectations

Luca Ratti*

1. INTRODUCTION

National legal systems are struggling to work out whether, and if so how, employment laws should apply to new forms of non-standard employment[1] including work in the so-called gig economy, performed through online platforms often located in countries different from where the person actually performs her tasks.[2] Many, but by no means all, of those working

* Associate Professor of European and Comparative Labour Law at University of Luxembourg, luca.ratti@uni.lu.

1 ILO, *Non-standard Employment Around the World*, Geneva 2016, pp. 7–10.

2 M. Cherry, 'A Global System of Work, A Global System of Regulation? Crowdwork and Conflicts of Law' [2019] 94 *Tulane Law Review* 1, 13.

in these jobs are migrant workers circulating within the EU or coming from third countries.[3]

A number of issues emerge in the EU regulatory space, such as the rise of non-standard work; the breaking down of work; micro-labour; the short duration of work; the use of algorithms to assign work, fix prices and to evaluate workers; uncertainty, insecurity, isolation and precarity; health and safety issues; and discrimination and fundamental rights.[4]

It seems that not all such issues have been addressed by the loose, stipulatory definition of 'collaborative economy' adopted by the EU Commission in the 2016 Communication 'A European agenda for the collaborative economy'. Referred to individuals providing their services, the document defines them as 'service providers who share assets, resources, time and/or skills – these can be private individuals offering services on an occasional basis ("peers") or service providers acting in their professional capacity ("professional services providers")'.[5]

In light of such a definition, the EU is now given the chance to better address a number of legal questions arising from the multi-level context typical of the union, taking into account the interests stemming from social partners and other civil society instances.[6]

A much clearer avenue has been taken by the EU Commission with the launch of two rounds of consultation on a possible action addressing the challenges related to working conditions of platform workers. In February 2021, the commission opened a consultation with social partners at the EU level according to Article 154(2) TFEU, already articulating its strategy to develop sustainable growth for platforms and tackle the most pressing issues for platform workers.[7] In June 2021, the commission

---

3 B. De Vries, 'The "Social Market Economy" in a (Heterogeneous) Social Europe: Does it Make a Difference?' [2019] *Utrecht Law Review* 47, 48.

4 V. Hatzopoulos, *The Collaborative Economy and EU Law*, Hart, Oxford 2018, p. 152.

5 EU Commission, Communication From The Commission To The European Parliament, The Council, The European Economic And Social Committee And The Committee Of The Regions, *A European agenda for the collaborative economy* (COM/2016/0356 final), Brussels 2016.

6 A documented criticism of the EU Communication on collaborative economy may be found in ETUC, 'The digital agenda of the European Commission: Preliminary ETUC assessment', https://www.etuc.org/documents/digital-agenda-european-commission-preliminary-etuc-assessment#.VwZsyoQzy-I. The ETUC has further elaborated on its claims in 'Towards fair digital work', https://www.etuc.org/sites/www.etuc.org/files/document/files/en-resol.digitalisation_adopted.pdf.

7 EU Commission, Consultation Document 'First phase consultation of social partners under Article 154 TFEU on possible action addressing the challenges related to working conditions in platform work' (C(2021) 1127 final).

published a second-phase consultation document, clarifying the possible direction of an EU intervention in the field of platform work.[8]

In this chapter, attention will be given to the margin of discretion for Member States to set their own regulatory standards and the degree of market access guaranteed (or required) by EU rules. Given the concurrent ability to legislate upon the EU and its Member States, this issue becomes increasingly important in the wake of the social disruptions brought about by the spread of platform work. Moreover, once it has been clarified that such a regulation of work in the gig economy can happen, it is crucial to determine what exactly is being regulated, whether that be the service which is provided (IT, consultancy, transport or others) or the individuals and platforms providing such service. Lastly, and more fundamentally, we may even question whether that of the legal status of individuals providing the service is really an EU problem or it simply replicates well established doctrines on the qualification of persons as workers in EU law. Some of these issues have been addressed by the case law of the Court of Justice of the EU (CJEU) and, more recently, by the same EU legislator. But the regulatory response still appears to be unsatisfactory and needs constant fine-tuning and updating, due to the mercurial nature of platform work as well as to its contractual background.

This chapter will address some issues which have emerged from the debate on platform work, taking as a point of reference the EU legal framework. Section 2 will consider how the scope of EU law fits into the legal challenges brought by platform work. Section 3 will map the relevant case law of the CJEU and assess its effectiveness on future cases. Section 4 will then examine the EU legislator's initiatives that can serve as starting point to regulate platform work. Section 5 will conclude, elaborating on opened issues that still necessitate a legal response, particularly in light of the 2021 initiative from the commission to thoroughly regulate platform work.

2. THE ROLE OF EU LAW BETWEEN *SEIN* AND *SOLLEN*

The underlying question surrounding this section can be summarised as follows: is there any room for EU law in the entire debate on the regulation

8 EU Commission, Consultation Document 'Second-phase consultation of social partners under Article 154 TFEU on possible action addressing the challenges related to working conditions in platform work' (C(2021) 4230 final).

of platform work? At first glance, it may seem that the inherently transnational nature of such form(s) of work – particularly crowdwork – serves as a good argument for the intervention of the EU as a supranational actor in the fixation of common rules. As suggested by an OECD study, the global nature of modern firms renders it easier to '(re)allocate resources, scale up and down, and enter and exit markets, including internationally', taking advantage of the differences between labour markets in terms of business environment and employment protection.[9]

It may therefore be questioned whether the EU is best placed – compared to its Member States – to intervene in the field and, if so, which forms such intervention may be compliant with general principles of EU law. Whenever such a question arises, Article 5 TEU comes into play, as the EU is entitled to intervene in so far as its action meets the double test of proportionality and subsidiarity. Particularly, the latter deserves some attention here.

Article 5(3) states that:

> in areas which do not fall within its exclusive competence, the Union shall act only if and in so far as the objectives of the proposed action cannot be sufficiently achieved by the Member States, either at central level or at regional and local level, but can rather, by reason of the scale or effects of the proposed action, be better achieved at Union level.[10]

Its explanatory protocol[11] further emphasises that any

> draft European legislative act (...) should contain some assessment of the proposal's financial impact and, in the case of a European framework law, of its implications for the rules to be put in place by Member States, including, where necessary, the regional legislation. The reasons for concluding that a Union objective can be better achieved at Union level shall be substantiated by qualitative and, wherever possible, quantitative indicators.

Because platform work is a field of intervention with no predetermined boundaries, the legislation that some European Member States have passed so far cannot be considered either comprehensive or exhaustive of all forms of intervention. This appears to be an argument in favour of a more general

9 OECD, *Going Digital: Shaping Policies, Improving Lives*, OECD Publishing, Paris 2019.
10 TEU, Article 5(3).
11 Protocol On The Application Of The Principles Of Subsidiarity And Proportionality, Official Journal of the European Union [2004], C-310/207.

intervention of EU law in the field,[12] in particular since the dis-harmonised way in which national parliaments and governments have been legislating in recent years is directly proportional to their inability to really tackle the most pressing needs of digital workers. This may play in favour of a purely top-down approach to govern the complex set of legal issues arising from a regulatory intervention, which in some fields of law in particular appears over-fragmented.[13] The same EU legal framework on the provision of services (Directive 2006/123 and Article 56 TFEU) seems not entirely well equipped to accommodate the regulatory needs of platforms, which operate under the umbrella of Article 16, Charter of Fundamental Rights of the European Union (CFREU) on the freedom to conduct business.[14]

A 2019 study from the European Trade Unions Institute (ETUI) shows that more and more Member States are intervening, directly or indirectly, to regulate some aspects of platform work, either by stretching existing categories (oftentimes intermediate between subordination and self-employment) and extending to them the typical labour law protections, or by selecting specific areas of intervention (tax, social security, work accidents insurance).[15] This may lead to a situation in which the EU legislator, acknowledging the patchwork resulting from such diverse domestic legislation, considers it necessary to legislate with the aim to improve the functioning of the internal market (Articles 114 and 115 TFEU) or to harmonise social policies on the basis of Article 153 TFEU.

The legal test based on Article 153 is that of competence, a pivotal question for EU law. The list of 'fields' in which the union is entitled to intervene 'with a view to achieving the objectives of Article 151'[16] includes an encompassing number of aspects that could be taken into account while legislating on platform workers, in particular related to improved living and working conditions and with proper social protection. A number of important topics deserve attention from an EU perspective.

---

12 M. Finck, 'The Sharing Economy and the EU' in N. Davidson, M. Finck and J. Infranca, *The Cambridge Handbook of The Law of the Sharing Economy*, CUP, Cambridge 2018, p. 264.

13 K. Pantazatou, 'The Taxation of the Sharing Economy' in W. Haslehner, G. Kofler, A. Pantazatou and A. Rust, *Tax and the Digital Economy: Challenges and Proposals for Reform*, WKI, Alphen upon Rhine 2019, p. 215.

14 P. Hacker, 'UberPop, UberBlack, and the Regulation of Digital Platforms after the Asociaciòn Profesional Elite Taxi Judgment of the CJEU' [2018] 14 *European Review of Contract Law* 80, 94.

15 I. Daugareilh, C. Degryse and P. Pochet, *The platform economy and social law: Key issues in comparative perspective*, 10, ETUI Working Paper, Brussels 2019.

16 Article 153(1), TFEU.

In the first place, the improvement of platform workers' health and safety becomes crucial, as the typically precarious working conditions of individuals working via app (drivers, riders, etc.) may lead to an increase in work accidents with serious consequences but no liability rules in place.[17]

Furthermore, remuneration – as a central issue of all contracts involving the provision of personal service – calls into question the ability of EU law to establish minimum conditions applicable to all workers, or at least specific categories.[18] The experienced field in this regard is that of posted workers, where EU law has sensibly evolved since the first Rush Portuguesa case,[19] via Directive 96/71 and the relevant (and unfortunate) case law Viking/Laval/Rüffert, until the more recent Directive 2014/67 (the 'enforcement directive') and the recast Directive 2018/957, fixing more generous minimum conditions for posted workers.[20]

A third item that could well fit into the list enshrined in Article 153 TFEU is the protection against unfair termination of the contract. While being crucial for the entire field of labour law, this proved to be uneasy to exercise, and despite its constitutional umbrella (Article 30CFREU) remains dead letter in EU law.

Another pressing issue not listed in the competences of the EU legislator in the social policy title, but rather in title II (Provisions having general application), is the protection of the individual's privacy and personal data (Article 16 TFEU). In the world of platform work, this includes proper privacy tools, as well as limitations on algorithmic monitoring and surveillance.

The collective aspects of platform work also need some consideration under EU law. Here, the main point concerns the fact that whenever the law does not qualify platform workers as employees, the *Albany* doctrine[21]

---

17 S. Garben, *Protecting Workers in the Online Platform Economy: An overview of regulatory and policy developments in the EU*, EU-OSHA, Luxembourg 2017, p. 24; M. Tran and R.K. Sokas, 'The Gig Economy and Contingent Work: An Occupational Health Assessment' [2017] 59 *Journal of Occupational and Environmental Medicine* 63–66. The risk seems to be confirmed by the US bureau of labour statistics data: see https://www.bls.gov/opub/btn/volume-8/fatal-occupational-injuries-to-independent-workers.htm.

18 J. Berg, *Income security in the on-demand economy: Findings and policy lessons from a survey of crowdworkers*, ILO, Geneva 2016, p. 23.

19 Case C-113/89, *Rush Portuguesa Ld^{a} v. Office national d'immigration*, ECLI:EU:C:1990:142.

20 R. Zahn, 'Revision of the Posted Workers Directive: A Europeanisation Perspective' [2017] *Cambridge Yearbook of European Legal Studies* 187.

21 Case C-67/96, *Albany International BV v. Stichting Bedrijfspensioenfonds Textielindustrie*, ECLI:EU:C:1999:430; Case C-180/98, *Pavel Pavlov and Others v. Stichting Pensioenfonds Medische Specialisten.*, ECLI:EU:C:2000:428.

does not in principle apply. While at a political level, the EU Commission showed open support to the exclusion of gig-economy workers agreements from the ambit of EU anti-trust rules,[22] according to the current state of EU law any agreement concluded between platforms and a plurality of workers is likely to fall under the scope of Article 101 TFEU, and can therefore be attacked as a restraint of competition.[23]

For what concerns the social protection of platform workers, Article 153(1)(c)–(k) leave the door open for an EU initiative. The limits thereof are quite clearly stated by the same norm, where it provides that:

> the provisions adopted pursuant to this Article: shall not affect the right of Member States to define the fundamental principles of their social security systems and must not significantly affect the financial equilibrium thereof (Article 153(4) TFEU).

The reach of any intervention of EU law is, on the contrary, far less clear from a competence perspective, particularly because of the substantive differences between social protection referred to standard employees and that extensible to non-standard employment or even self-employment.[24]

Last but not least, quite like (or even more than) standard employees, platform workers need not to be discriminated against. The issue has been already explored with regards to 'algorithmic discrimination'[25] and may lead to a serious intervention of EU law, since its non-discrimination legal

22 https://www.ft.com/content/0cafd442-f673-11e9-9ef3-eca8fc8f2d65.

23 Further remarks in I. Lianos, N. Countouris, and V. De Stefano, 'Re-thinking the competition law/labour law interaction: Promoting a fairer labour market' [2019] 10 *European Labour Law Journal* 291; D. Schieck and A. Gideon, 'Outsmarting the gig-economy through collective bargaining – EU competition law as a barrier?' [2018] 32 *International Review of Law, Computers & Technology* 275; A. Aloisi and E. Gramano, 'Workers Without Workplaces and Unions Without Unity: Non-Standard Forms of Employment, Platform Work and Collective Bargaining' in V. Pulignano and F. Hendrickx, *Employment Relations in the 21st Century: Challenges for Theory and Research in a Changing World of Work*, Kluwer Law International, Alphen upon Rhine 2019, p. 107.

24 P. Schoukens, 'Digitalisation and social security in the EU: The case of platform work: from work protection to income protection?' [2020] 22 *European Journal of Social Security* 434; M. Matsaganis, E. Özdemir, T. Ward and A. Zavakou, *Non-standard employment and access to social security benefits*, n. 8 Research note, Brussels 2015.

25 N. Countouris and L. Ratti, 'The Sharing Economy and EU Anti-discrimination Law' in N. Davidson, M. Finck and J. Infranca, *The Cambridge Handbook of The Law of the Sharing Economy*, Cambridge University Press, Cambridge 2018, pp. 494–95; M. Kullmann, 'Platform Work, Algorithmic Decision-Making, and EU Gender Equality Law' [2018] 34 *International Journal of Comparative Labour Law and Industrial Relations* 1–21.

framework constitutes one of its most developed fields of intervention, capable of making it a general principle of EU law with horizontal direct effect.[26]

It seems therefore that, at least on paper, the EU is empowered by its treaties to intervene through secondary law (typically minimum harmonisation directives or even regulations), or at least recommendations or decisions. But even beyond the items listed in Article 153 TFEU, it seems that a regulatory intervention should not forget essential aspects for platform workers, such as reputational mechanisms,[27] working time and shifts[28] and third-party liabilities.[29] All such items raise, however, a more fundamental question in the distribution of competences between the union and its Member States. Domestic labour laws have been historically designed to protect the rights of working people through the combination of a technical tool – the contract of employment – and a number of protective rules (on health and safety, work accidents, working time, etc.).[30] Trying to figure out the exact aims and reach of a supposed intervention of EU law in the protection of platform workers calls into question the very starting point of any labour law enquiry: should EU law redefine what a worker is, in order to include platform workers as well as other non-standard forms of employment, or should it leave untouched its long-established definitions and reserve specific measures to platform workers?

When the legal basis of an EU legislative act is questioned, even more stringent issues arise, such as the scale of the union's intervention, its effectiveness, its financial impact (particularly on small and medium-sized enterprises when it comes to labour law rules)[31] and its ability to stimulate the creation of new employment (or at least not to depress labour demand).

---

26 Case C-144/04, *Werner Mangold v. Rüdiger Helm*, ECLI:EU:C:2005:709.

27 A. Aloisi, V. De Stefano and S. Silberman, 'A Manifesto to Reform the Gig Economy', http://www.pagina99.it/2017/05/29/a-manifesto-to-reform-the-gigeconomy/.

28 V. De Stefano, 'The rise of the "just-in-time workforce": On-demand work, crowdwork and labour protection in the "gig-economy"' [2016] 37 *Comparative Labor Law & Policy Journal* 471, 477–78.

29 G. Valenduc and P. Vendramin, *Work in the digital economy: sorting the old from the new*, ETUI Working Paper No. 3, Brussels 2016, p. 46.

30 B. Veneziani, 'The Employment Relationship' in B. Hepple and B. Veneziani, *The Transformation of Labour Law in Europe*, Hart, Oxford 2009, p. 99.

31 According to Article 153(2)(b), the European Parliament and the Council 'may adopt, in the fields referred to in paragraph 1(a) to (i), by means of directives, minimum requirements for gradual implementation, having regard to the conditions and technical rules obtaining in each of the Member States. Such directives shall avoid imposing administrative, financial and legal constraints in a way which would hold back the creation and development of small and medium-sized undertakings'.

3. A CONTEXTUALISATION OF LEGAL TESTS IN THE CASE LAW OF THE CJEU

Before the CJEU ruled in the well-known cases *Uber Spain* and *Uber France*, much expectation was addressed to the Luxembourg court, as a consequence of a piecemeal panorama in the case law of national courts, particularly referred to the legal position of drivers and riders vis-à-vis their platform. For their importance in the overall discourse on the legal qualification of work performed on demand via app, the two cases on Uber require some attentive analysis.

A first case was brought before the CJEU in August 2015 by the *Juzgado Mercantil* No 3 de Barcelona (Spain), asking whether the activity pursued by Uber – consisting 'of acting as an intermediary between the owner of a vehicle and a person who needs to make a journey within a city' – must be considered to be 'merely a transport service or must it be considered to be an electronic intermediary service or an information society service, as defined by Article 1(2) of Directive 98/34/EC'.[32] The question revolved around the legal nature of the service, dealing only indirectly with the legal status of the persons involved thereby. Such status was not crucial for the claimant – a taxi drivers' association based in Barcelona – inasmuch as the focus was entirely concentrated on the (allegedly) unfair competition perpetrated by Uber against established taxi companies that operated under a licence.

The opinion delivered in May 2017 by AG Szpunar mainly focused on the nature of the service provided and on their consequences in terms of unfair competition. However, he did not consider the characterisation of the service with regards to the individuals actually driving the vehicles for Uber. In that respect, AG Szpunar noted that while the control exercised by the platform on its drivers

> is not exercised in the context of a traditional employer-employee relationship, one should not be fooled by appearances. Indirect control such as that exercised by Uber, based on financial incentives and decentralised passenger-led ratings, with a scale effect, makes it possible to manage in a way that is just as – if not more – effective than management based on formal orders given by an employer to his employees and direct control over the carrying out of such orders.[33]

---

32 Request for a preliminary ruling from the *Juzgado Mercantil* No 3 de Barcelona (Spain) lodged on 7.08.2015 – C-434/15, *Asociación Profesional Élite Taxi v Uber Systems Spain, SL*, ECLI:EU:C:2017:981.

33 Opinion of Advocate General Szpunar delivered on 11.05.2017, C-434/15, *Asociación Profesional Elite Taxi v. Uber Systems Spain, SL*, ECLI:EU:C:2017:364, para. 52.

Certainly, this may not lead immediately to the conclusion that Uber's drivers 'must necessarily be regarded as its employees', as the controversy 'is wholly unrelated to the legal questions before the court in this case'.[34] However, Uber cannot be considered as a mere

> intermediary between drivers willing to offer transport services occasionally and passengers in search of such services. On the contrary, Uber is a genuine organiser and operator of urban transport services in the cities where it has a presence. While it is true, as Uber states in its observations in the case, that its concept is innovative, that innovation nonetheless pertains to the field of urban transport.[35]

This led AG Szpunar to conclude that:

> a service that connects, by means of mobile telephone software, potential passengers with drivers offering individual urban transport on demand, where the provider of the service exerts control over the key conditions governing the supply of transport made within that context, in particular the price, does not constitute an information society service within the meaning of those provisions.[36]

The case gathered a conspicuous number of intervenients, both from the institutions (the EFTA Surveillance Authority and the EU Commission) and from the Member States (Finland, Greece, Ireland, the Netherlands, Poland and Spain), and presented the court 'with a highly politicised issue that has received a great deal of media attention',[37] attention from which the AG did not escape, clearly drawing a distinction between those platforms merely intermediating services, such as Airbnb or Booking.com, and the ones that materially employ humans in the service provided.[38]

The Grand Chamber of the Court of Justice substantially followed the arguments raised by its AG, considering the intermediation services provided by Uber 'as forming an integral part of an overall service whose main component is a transport service'. As a consequence, such service 'must be classified not as "an information society service" within the meaning of

---

34 Ibid., para. 54.
35 Ibid., para. 61.
36 Ibid., para. 94.
37 Ibid., para. 1.
38 L. Woods, 'Uber: a taxi service or an app? Analysis of an ECJ Advocate-General's view' [2017] *EU Law Analysis* http://eulawanalysis.blogspot.com/2017/05/uber-taxi-service-or-app-analysis-of.html.

Article 1(2) of Directive 98/34, to which Article 2(a) of Directive 2000/31 refers, but as "a service in the field of transport" within the meaning of Article 2(2)(d) of Directive 2006/123' and 'of Article 58(1) TFEU'.[39] In fact, as already decided in *Grupo Itevelesa*, 'the concept of "services in the field of transport" includes not only transport services in themselves but also any service inherently linked to any physical act of moving persons or goods from one place to another by means of transport'.[40]

Albeit in *obiter dicta*, the court followed its AG also in the legal characterisation of the relationship between the platform and its 'service providers', by observing that:

> Uber exercises decisive influence over the conditions under which that service is provided by those drivers. On the latter point, it appears, inter alia, that Uber determines at least the maximum fare by means of the eponymous application, that the company receives that amount from the client before paying part of it to the non-professional driver of the vehicle, and that it exercises a certain control over the quality of the vehicles, the drivers and their conduct, which can, in some circumstances, result in their exclusion.[41]

The three elements of a) the decisive influence over the service conditions, b) the maximum fare and c) the control over the drivers' conduct must be highlighted, particularly because the court refers to them as hypothetical grounds for the 'exclusion' of drivers from the platform, that is, the termination of their contract. Although these are criteria used to distinguish a transportation service from mere intermediation, the platform's influence and control turn out to be at the same time unambiguous indicators of the type of contractual relationship existing between the platform and its drivers.

The issue was less decisive in the similar case *Uber France*.[42] The case was brought before the CJEU in June 2016 on the basis of a provision in the French transport code, which considered a criminal offence the activity of exercising a transport service without a licence.[43] AG Szpunar

---

39 Case C-434/15, *Asociación Profesional Elite Taxi v. Uber Systems Spain SL*, ECLI:EU:C:2017:981, paras. 40 and 48.

40 Case C-168/14, *Grupo Itevelesa SL and a. v. Oca Inspección Técnica de Vehículos SA and Generalidad de Cataluña.*, ECLI: EU:C:2015:685, para. 45.

41 Case C-434/15, *Asociación Profesional Elite Taxi v. Uber Systems Spain SL*, ECLI:EU:C:2017:981, para. 39.

42 Case C-320/16, *Uber France*, ECLI:EU:C:2018:221.

43 Request for a preliminary ruling from the *Tribunal de grande instance* de Lille (Regional Court, Lille) (France) lodged on 6.06.2016 – *Criminal proceedings against Uber France SAS*, C-320/16.

also delivered his opinion on this case, concluding that the provision included in the transport code falls outside the scope of application of Directive 98/34,[44] since this provision:

> does not prohibit and does not penalise an activity which is in the nature of an information society service in a general fashion, but only in so far as the activity amounts to an act of complicity in the exercise of another activity, one that is illegal and, moreover, one that falls outside the scope of Directive 98/34, as amended.[45]

The CJEU – in its Grand Chamber composition – further developed the AG's arguments, recalling that in the *Elite Taxi* case it was found that the control exercised by Uber over its drivers was a decisive factor to infer that:

> the intermediation service at issue in that case had to be regarded as forming an integral part of an overall service the main component of which was a transport service and, accordingly, had to be classified, not as an 'information society service' within the meaning of Article 1(2) of Directive 98/34, but as a 'service in the field of transport' within the meaning of Article 2(2)(d) of Directive 2006/123.[46]

Consequently, the court concluded that 'intermediation service did not come under Directive 2006/123, since services in the field of transport are among those expressly excluded from the scope of that directive pursuant to Article 2(2)(d) thereof'.[47] Probably because this second case goes more directly to the point of considering Uber's services as transport services, it fails to further expand on the factual description of the drivers' contractual relationship with the platform, thus leaving the legal qualification issue unresolved. Although it quoted *Elite Taxi* when describing the way Uber drivers actually work, the court did not even recall its case law on the qualification of a worker according to EU law.

In this respect, the *FNV Kunsten* case should be mentioned, as it deals directly with the 'false self-employed'. The case was referred by a

---

44 Council Directive 98/34/EC of 22 June 1998 laying down a procedure for the provision of information in the field of technical standards and regulations and of rules on Information Society services, as amended by Directive 98/48/EC of the European Parliament and of the Council of 20 July 1998.

45 Opinion of Advocate General Szpunar delivered on 4 July 2017, C-320/16, *Uber France*, ECLI:EU:C:2017:511, para. 34.

46 CJEU, C-320/16, *Uber France*, ECLI:EU:C:2018:221, para. 22.

47 Ibid., para. 23.

Dutch court[48] and concerned the ability of an association representing self-employed workers (substitute musicians of an orchestra) to conclude collective agreements that did not infringe competition law rules on cartels. As AG Wahl put it, the underlying question was to understand whether the *Albany* exception 'covers provisions of collective agreements which regulate aspects of the professional relationship between self-employed persons and their customers or clients, and, if so, under what conditions'.[49] While the AG radically excluded such agreements from the exception – on the argument that self-employed individuals were to be considered undertakings for the purpose of Article 101 TFEU[50] – the court more broadly considered that this finding

> cannot, however, prevent such a provision of a collective labour agreement from being regarded also as the result of dialogue between management and labour if the service providers, in the name and on behalf of whom the trade union negotiated, are in fact 'false self-employed', that is to say, service providers in a situation comparable to that of employees.[51]

The court recalled that 'the classification of a "self-employed person" under national law does not prevent that person being classified as an employee within the meaning of EU law if his independence is merely notional, thereby disguising an employment relationship'.[52] From this it should be inferred that whenever the individuals concerned performed their job exactly in the same manner as the musicians they substituted, there should be no distinction in terms of legal treatment. Alternatively, if they 'enjoy more independence and flexibility than employees who perform the same activity, as regards the determination of the working hours, the place and manner of performing the tasks assigned, in other

---

48 Request for a preliminary ruling from the *Gerechtshof The Hague* (Netherlands) lodged on 22 July 2013 – C-413/13, *FNV Kunsten Informatie en Media v. Staat der Nederlanden*, ECLI:EU:C:2014:2215.

49 Opinion of Advocate General Wahl delivered on 11 September 2014, C-413/13, *FNV Kunsten Informatie en Media v. Staat der Nederlanden*, ECLI:EU:C:2014:2215, para. 2.

50 Case C-180/98, *Pavel Pavlov and Others v. Stichting Pensioenfonds Medische Specialisten*, ECLI:EU:C:2000:428, paras. 73–77. This, in turn, justifies the fact that 'social policy considerations which justified the *Albany* exception for workers cannot be considered valid with regard to the self-employed': Opinion of Advocate General Wahl delivered on 11 September 2014, C-413/13, *FNV Kunsten*, para. 38.

51 Case C-413/13, *FNV Kunsten Informatie en Media v. Staat der Nederlanden*, ECLI:EU:C:2014:2411, para. 31.

52 Ibid., para. 35.

words, the rehearsals and concerts',[53] they must be considered as truly self-employed. Although the CJEU left it entirely to the referring court to ascertain, on the basis of a factual assessment, the real nature of the legal status of such allegedly self-employed workers, the case confirms the court's inclination to deprive a service provider of its status of independent entity 'if he does not determine independently his own conduct on the market, but is entirely dependent on his principal'.[54]

Critics of this line of reasoning have stressed the inopportune resurgence of a clear-cut binary divide between workers and self-employed individuals,[55] which seems to contradict the recent evolution of a number of European legal systems, where the creation of grey and intermediate zones through legislation or case law pointed in the opposite direction.[56] Also, such a binary way of thinking may lead to a substantive lack of protection for an increasing number of legal relationships that do not technically fall under the traditional scope of labour law, but nevertheless present similar needs of protection.[57] As a consequence, particularly after the Lisbon Treaty and the enactment of the CFREU, the concepts of 'undertaking' and 'restriction of competition' referred to by Article 101(1) TFEU should be reformulated, in order to build a continuum of personal relationships that, based on pre-defined criteria, include false self-employed as well as dependent self-employed workers.[58]

The factual assessment of *FNV Kunsten* resulted in a clear qualification of substitute musicians as falsely self-employed by the Gerechtshof 's-Gravenhage. The Dutch court found that those substitutes had 'the same duties as employees; they play from the same sheet music as the employees; they have to follow the same strict schedule for rehearsals and concerts; and they have to perform their duties in person and thus they cannot replace themselves'.[59]

53 Ibid., para. 37.

54 Ibid., para. 33.

55 M. Freedland and N. Kountouris, 'Some Reflections on the "Personal Scope" of Collective Labour Law' [2017] 46 *Industrial Law Journal* 52, 66–67.

56 For an overview cf. B. Waas and G.H. van Voss, *Restatement of Labour Law in Europe, Volume I, The Concept of Employee*, vol. 1, Hart, Oxford 2017, p. xxvii.

57 I. Lianos, N. Countouris and V. De Stefano, 'Re-thinking the competition law/labour law interaction: Promoting a fairer labour market' [2019] 10(3) *European Labour Law Journal* 291.

58 Ibid., p. 308.

59 E. Grosheide and B. Ter Haar, 'Employee-like worker: Competitive entrepreneur or submissive employee? Reflections on ECJ, C-413/13, FNV Kunsten Informatie' in S. Bellomo, N. Gundt, M. Łaga and J.M. Miranda Boto, *Labour Law and Social Rights in Europe: The Jurisprudence of International Courts. Selected Judgements*, Gdańsk University Press, 2018, p. 31.

In a broader reflection of how *FNV Kunsten* has contributed to clarification of the legal position of platform workers, it must be recalled the argument for which:

> the status of 'worker' within the meaning of EU law is not affected by the fact that a person has been hired as a self-employed person under national law, for tax, administrative or organisational reasons, as long as that person acts under the direction of his employer as regards, in particular, his freedom to choose the time, place and content of his work (see judgment in *Allonby*, C-256/01, EU:C:2004:18, paragraph 72), does not share in the employer's commercial risks (judgment in *Agegate*, C-3/87, EU:C:1989:650, paragraph 36), and, for the duration of that relationship, forms an integral part of that employer's undertaking, so forming an economic unit with that undertaking (see judgment in *Becu and Others*, C-22/98, EU:C:1999:419, paragraph 26).[60]

This argument raises the question of whether platform workers may qualify as 'false self-employed' within the meaning of the criteria elaborated by the CJEU and further implemented by the domestic court. If the criteria are those of a) freedom to choose the time, place and content of his work, b) sharing of the employer's commercial risk and c) forming an integral part of the employer's undertaking, it may not be difficult to have a number of drivers and riders, as well as of crowdworkers, included in the falsely self-employed category.

Additional guidance to the analysis came from the CJEU in the preliminary ruling *B v. Yodel Delivery Network*.[61] The case concerned a courier engaged on the basis of a self-employment contract to deliver parcels in two different areas. The relevant terms in the contract, other than explicitly excluding any employment status, required the courier to have adequate insurance cover. They provided that the person is not obliged to render services personally and s/he is expressly permitted to engage subcontractors; they required the individual not to perform her services exclusively for the courier company; and they excluded any obligation by the latter to provide work to the courier, coupled with the freedom of the courier not to accept deliveries.[62] On the basis of this factual assessment, the referring court asked the CJEU to answer whether Directive 2003/88/EC

---

60 Case C-413/13, *FNV Kunsten Informatie en Media v. Staat der Nederlanden*, ECLI:EU:C:2014:2411 para. 36.

61 Reference for a preliminary ruling from the Watford Employment Tribunal (United Kingdom) made on 19 September 2019 – C-692/19, *B v Yodel Delivery Network Ltd*, ECLI:EU:C:2020:288.

62 Ibid., paras. 7–34.

concerning certain aspects of the organisation of working time precludes provisions of national law which require an individual to undertake to do or perform all of the work or services required of him, 'personally' in order to fall within the scope of the directive. In particular, the CJEU was tasked to clarify if the right to engage substitutes may lead to exclude a worker status for the purposes of Directive 2003/88, in all circumstances or at least 'in respect of any period of time when exercising such right of substitution (so that he is to be regarded as a worker in relation to periods of time actually spent performing work or services)'.[63] The CJEU decided the *Yodel* case with an order on 22 April 2020. Based on its previous jurisprudence, the CJEU recalled that a 'worker' in EU law is 'a person who performs services for and under the direction of another person for a certain period of time in return for which he receives remuneration'.[64]

While this concept left it open to the court to elaborate additional criteria for the application of the working time directive, the binary divide methodology reiterated in *FNV Kunsten* only allowed for a small re-interpretation of the concept of 'worker', leaving genuine self-employed individuals who are economically dependent on one client outside the scope of any protection under EU labour law rules.[65] This is exactly what happened in the case. According to the court's order, some features of the work relationship, namely the 'choice of the type of work and tasks to be executed, the manner in which that work or those tasks are to be performed, the time and place of work, the freedom in the recruitment of his own staff,' may reflect a self-employment status, which is for the referring court to ascertain. In doing so, the British judge should take into account some guiding principles, focused on the choice of the service provider: to use subcontractors or substitutes to perform the service; to accept or not accept the various tasks offered by his putative employer, or unilaterally set the maximum number of those tasks; to provide his services to any third party, including direct competitors of the putative employer; and to fix his own hours of 'work' within certain parameters and to tailor his time to suit his personal convenience rather than solely the interests of the putative employer, provided that, first, the independence of that person does not appear to be fictitious and, second, it is not possible

63 Ibid.

64 Case C-316/13 *Fenoll*, ECLI: EU: C2015:200, para. 27.

65 N. Kountouris, 'The Concept of "Worker" in European Labour Law: Fragmentation, Autonomy and Scope' [2018] 47(2) *Industrial Law Journal* 192, 214.

to establish the existence of a relationship of subordination between that person and his putative employer.[66]

Concentrating its interpretation on those factual elements, in *Yodel* the CJEU seems to underestimate the strategic behaviour of most platforms vis-à-vis their workers, which perpetuates the typical gig economy business model wherein an indefinite plethora of individuals are – on paper – free to determine their schedule and even nominate substitutes, but de facto result in performing work similar to subordinate workers.[67] The many issues which the CJEU was not able or entitled to resolve in the *Yodel* decision are still undetermined and deserve increased attention from the national and/or European legislator. In the following section, certain pieces of EU law will be considered.

4. ROLE AND AMBITION OF EU LEGISLATIVE INITIATIVES

The way in which the EU legislator approached the societal disruptions deriving from the advent of the platform economy is wide in its reach and multi-layered in its sources, but still appears to be disorganised and sectoral. The first explicit move undertaken by the EU Commission to intervene in the field dates back to 2015, when the *Digital Single Market Strategy* came out.[68] Based on the premise that the state of the market was fragmented and incomplete, the commission pushed for the creation of 'the right conditions for a level playing field' that may allow business to operate more transparently in the market. In doing so, the commission pleaded for an overall assessment to cover: (a) transparency in search results; (b) platforms' usage of data; (c) relations between platforms and suppliers; (d) inter-platform movement; and (e) illegal content. The aims of the *Digital Single Market Strategy* were limited per definition, and did not include the legal status of platform workers, nor any social measure that platforms may adopt in order to at least make their use more transparent.

In 2016 the EU Commission published two distinct documents, conceived to orient EU legislative bodies in the direction of future

66 Ibid., para. 45.

67 R. Buendia, 'The Court of Justice of the European Union's Order on B v Yodel Delivery Network', [2020] *Comparative Labor Law & Policy Journal* – Dispatch No. 24 – United Kingdom.

68 EU Commission, *A Digital Single Market Strategy for Europe*, Brussels, 6.5.2015 COM(2015) 192 final.

intervention. The first was the aforementioned *Communication on the European agenda for collaborative economy.*[69] While focusing on employment law-related concerns, the commission came up with a general recommendation to Member States, focused on a double, conflicting aim: on the one hand, people should be supported to make full use of their potential, stimulated in their participation in the labour market and contribute to boost competitiveness; and on the other hand, fair working conditions and adequate and sustainable social protection must be ensured. To this end, Member States have been urged to:

> assess the adequacy of their national employment rules considering the different needs of workers and self-employed people in the digital world as well as the innovative nature of collaborative business models; [and] provide guidance on the applicability of their national employment rules in light of labour patterns in the collaborative economy.[70]

A second document – the Communication *Online Platforms and the Digital Single Market Opportunities and Challenges for Europe* – addressed more specifically the role of online platforms.[71] The drivers to shape a new regulatory landscape were, firstly, the de-regulation of existing telecommunication services 'as part of its 2016 proposal for revising telecommunication rules';[72] secondly, the need to ensure content-wise social responsibility from platforms (i.e. protecting minors, banning hate speech and incitement to hatred, ensuring copyrights, etc.); and thirdly, the protection of consumers and business, in the form of a revision of the Unfair Commercial Practices Directive[73] and of a proposal for a regulation on fairness and transparency for business users of platforms.[74]

---

69 EU Commission, *Communication on the European agenda for collaborative economy*, June 2016 (COM(2016) 356 final).

70 Ibid., at 13.

71 EU Commission, *Communication Online Platforms and the Digital Single Market Opportunities and Challenges for Europe*, Brussels, COM(2016) 288/2.

72 A. Savin, 'Regulating internet platforms in the EU – The emergence of the "Level playing field"' [2018] 34 *Computer Law & Security Review* 1219, where also references to the recast rules deriving from the Directive 2018/1972 establishing the European Electronic Communications Code, adopted in December 2018.

73 For this purpose, the commission produced a specific document: see Guidance on the Implementation/Application of Directive 2005/29/EC on Unfair Commercial Practices, COM(2016) 320 final.

74 Proposal for a Regulation of the European Parliament and of the Council on promoting fairness and transparency for business users of online intermediation services, COM(2018) 238 final.

In May 2017, based on a report by its Committee on the Internal Market and Consumer Protection, the European Parliament adopted a resolution that called for an intervention by the EU Commission directed to fix the legal uncertainty concerning work performed via digital platforms.[75] But still, a more robust intervention was needed, since political uncertainty and strategic resistance by some Member States hindered a fully-fledged centralised intervention by the EU.

Meanwhile, on the 'social side' of Europe, the commission had proclaimed in November 2017 the European Pillar of Social Rights. Its solemn proclamation may be seen as a clear indication of the EU Commission's political will to enhance social rights and further streamline the social acquis. This patchwork of institutional initiatives toward the introduction of a more coherent set of rules for platforms, consumers and workers led to a number of tangible results, whose value and efficacy must be here considered.

4.1. REGULATION 2019/1150: ANYTHING OTHER THAN TRANSPARENCY RULES?

The increasing awareness among the EU legislative institutions further stimulated the commission to insist on the enactment of some legal instruments before the end of its mandate (November 2019). In this context, the adoption of Regulation 2019/1150 on fairness and transparency for business users of platforms[76] constituted a crucial step to ensure not only a more transparent service to European consumers, but also a better 'working' environment for platform workers. The regulation was adopted in June 2019 and applies as from 12 July 2020. Social issues are not explicitly addressed by Regulation 2019/1150, which is instead focused on the role of 'business user',[77] 'online intermediation services',[78]

---

75 European Parliament, 'European agenda for the collaborative economy', 2017/2003(INI).

76 Regulation 2019/1150 of the European Parliament and of the Council of 20 June 2019, on promoting fairness and transparency for business users of online intermediation services.

77 Defined as 'any private individual acting in a commercial or professional capacity who, or any legal person which, through online intermediation services offers goods or services to consumers for purposes relating to its trade, business, craft or profession' (Article 2(1), Reg. 2019/1150).

78 Defined as 'services which meet all of the following requirements: (a) they constitute information society services within the meaning of point (b) of Article 1(1) of

'provider of online intermediation services'[79] and on the protection of consumers.[80] Additionally, work performed via platforms is not mentioned in the indicative list of online intermediation services covered by the regulation.[81] This has correspondence in the legal basis chosen for the adoption of the regulation, undoubtedly identifiable in Article 114 and Article 26 TFEU.[82] However, labour law issues as such are not excluded from the scope of application of the regulation, which therefore allows, under specific circumstances and to a certain extent, its provisions to find application, particularly when the service provision by an individual may qualify as, or resemble to, the performance of work.

The global nature of platforms has been thoroughly addressed by the Regulation, which provides that its norms

> should apply to providers of those services regardless of whether they are established in a Member State or outside the Union, provided that two cumulative conditions are met. Firstly, the business users or corporate website users should be established in the Union. Secondly, the business users or corporate website users should, through the provision of those services, offer their goods or services to consumers located in the Union at least for part of the transaction.[83]

The regulation provides some general standards that platforms may guarantee, concerning transparency and fairness of their terms and conditions,[84] the conditions for the restriction in the use of platforms or

---

Directive (EU) 2015/1535 of the European Parliament and of the Council (12); (b) they allow business users to offer goods or services to consumers, with a view to facilitating the initiating of direct transactions between those business users and consumers, irrespective of where those transactions are ultimately concluded; (c) they are provided to business users on the basis of contractual relationships between the provider of those services and business users which offer goods or services to consumers' (Article 2(2), Reg. 2019/1150).

79 Defined as 'any natural or legal person which provides, or which offers to provide, online intermediation services to business users' (Article 2(3), Reg. 2019/1150).

80 Defined, on the basis of an established case law of the CJEU, as 'any natural person who is acting for purposes which are outside this person's trade, business, craft or profession' (Article 2(4), Reg. 2019/1150).

81 Recital (11), Reg. 2019/1150.

82 Article 1(1), Reg. 2019/1150 provides that 'the purpose of this Regulation is to contribute to the proper functioning of the internal market by laying down rules to ensure that business users of online intermediation services and corporate website users in relation to online search engines are granted appropriate transparency, fairness and effective redress possibilities'.

83 Recital (9), Reg. 2019/1150.

84 Article 3, Reg. 2019/1150.

the suspension and termination of the relevant services thereof,[85] and the reputation that business users may get from consumers or clients.[86]

What is crucial in order to enucleate the legal position of platform workers is the definition of 'business user'. While referring to the two elements of a) acting in a commercial or professional capacity and b) offering goods or services related to its trade, business, craft or profession, such a definition seems to include what workers on-demand via app and crowdworkers are typically asked to do when performing their contracts with the platforms. Therefore, the definition of 'business user' may encompass the provision of services by any individual operating through an online platform and fulfilling the tasks assigned thereby.

Applying to work on-demand platforms and to crowdwork platforms the provisions on fairness, suspension and termination and ratings may ultimately be beneficial to the individuals involved. Changes in contractual terms, for instance, may be subject to notification and give business users the chance to unilaterally terminate the contract before the expiry of any notice period. Moreover, any restriction or suspension of the provision of online services to a given business user may be documented in writings and justified 'with a statement of reasons for that decision on a durable medium'.[87] Also, the ranking of the services provided by a business user may be subject to explicit and transparent parameters in order to let business users adequately understand them. Whenever the use of such parameters can influence ranking against 'remuneration paid by business users or corporate website users to the respective provider, that provider shall also set out a description of those possibilities and of the effects of such remuneration on ranking'.[88]

Albeit covering a number of important aspects of the contractual relationships between platforms and their 'business users', the regulation is highly unsatisfactory and seems mono-dimensionally focused on transparency and information, as if full awareness of contractual terms could resolve the multitude of legal issues raised by platforms' operations. The reasons for this reticence from the EU legislator may be linked to the degree of spontaneous distributive effects of the internal market, which resulted in a limited progress of positive integration in this field.[89]

---

85 Article 4, Reg. 2019/1150.

86 Article 5, Reg. 2019/1150.

87 Article 4(1), Reg. 2019/1150.

88 Article 5(3), Reg. 2019/1150.

89 D. Adamski, 'Lost on the Digital Platform: Europe's Legal Travails with the Digital Single Market' [2018] 55 *Common Market Law Review* 719, 720.

All in all, the regulation appears to be merely a first step toward the protection of the public interest of fair and socially responsible performance of work tasks through platforms. The complexity of platforms' reality suggests ample room for improvement. What the regulation failed to address was to 'take into consideration different platform types and sizes and their respective business models' in order to obtain a coherent picture of their market and their behaviour.[90] Furthermore, its market access nature prevented the regulation from including mandatory substantive rules aimed at limiting platforms' prerogatives concerning, *inter alia*, control, monitoring, remuneration, individual and collective redress.

4.2. THE EUROPEAN PILLAR OF SOCIAL RIGHTS AS A STEPPINGSTONE

The proclamation of the European Pillar of Social Rights (EPSR) significantly contributed to reorienting the EU Commission's action towards social objectives. In fact, not only does the Pillar rely on existing *aquis*, but also further explores regulatory territories to date unaffected by EU law. Its main objectives build on existing general principles of EU social policy, such as the aim of 'full employment and social progress' as well as that of 'a high level of protection and improvement of the quality of the environment' (Recital 1),[91] and further elaborate on a miscellaneous set of standalone rights and principles.[92]

Principle no. 5 of the EPSR, focused on 'secure and adaptable employment', combines two significant commitments: on the one hand, 'innovative forms of work that ensure quality working conditions shall be fostered' (letter c); and on the other hand, 'employment relationships that lead to precarious working conditions shall be prevented (including by prohibiting abuse of atypical contracts)' (letter d). Principle no. 12 on 'social protection' ambitiously aims to acknowledge the right to adequate

[90] A. Savin, 'Electronic Services with a Non-electronic Component and Their Regulation in EU Law' [2019] 23 *Journal of Internet Law* 26.

[91] S. Garben, 'The European Pillar of Social Rights: Effectively Addressing Displacement?' [2018] *European Constitutional Law Review* 210.

[92] In reality, the terminology and significance of the 'principles' enshrined in the EPSR is all but clear and risks undermining the normative content of some of its propositions: F. Hendrickx, 'European Labour Law and the millennium shift: from post to Pillar' in F. Hendrickx and V. De Stefano, *Game Changers in Labour Law: Shaping the Future of Work*, KLI, Alphen upon Rhine 2018, p. 49.

social protection to all workers and, under comparable conditions, the self-employed, 'regardless of the type and duration of their employment relationship'. Principle no. 4 on 'active support to employment' similarly extends to 'everyone' 'the right to timely and tailor-made assistance to improve employment or self-employment prospects'.

One could even go beyond the letter of some of those principles, wondering for instance whether other guarantees might be extended to all kind of workers, even self-employed individuals. This may be the case of the provision on 'Minimum income' contained in Principle no. 14, for which

> everyone lacking sufficient resources has the right to adequate minimum income benefits ensuring a life in dignity at all stages of life, and effective access to enabling goods and services. For those who can work, minimum income benefits should be combined with incentives to (re)integrate into the labour market.

These principles as well as other more general propositions contained in the EPSR constitute, if not a proper legal basis, at least the political driver to understand future developments of EU law in the social sphere. As accurately recorded by the EU Commission, each EPSR principle refers to a number of past, present or future initiatives to which the institutions of the EU are committed.

The Commission Staff Working Document monitoring the implementation of the EPSR[93] presents a relevant number of initiatives as if the pillar itself generated all of them, or at least its momentum favoured their adoption or implementation.[94] While this appears controversial, and most initiatives are in fact 'repackaging exercises',[95] the usefulness of the EPSR in assembling diverse regulatory initiatives under the same policy umbrella – labelled as the *Social fairness package*[96] – must be positively

---

93 Commission Staff Working Document accompanying *Communication From the Commission to the European Parliament, the Council and the European Economic and Social Committee*, monitoring the implementation of the European Pillar of Social Rights, COM(2018) 130 final.

94 A clear example is the adoption – pursuant to long and consuming negotiations – of the recast Directive on the Posting of Workers 2018/957.

95 S. Garben, 'The European Pillar of Social Rights: An Assessment of its Meaning and Significance' [2019] 21 *Cambridge Yearbook of European Legal Studies* 101, 106–7.

96 More at: https://www.europarl.europa.eu/legislative-train/theme-deeper-and-fairer-internal-market-with-a-strengthened-industrial-base-labour/package-social-fairness-package.

welcomed and may even have interpretative repercussions in the CJEU case law.

In terms of policy-making, the proclamation of the EPSR has undoubtedly enriched the European semester process,[97] particularly in areas so far immune to EU labour law. Major examples in this respect come from the EPSR Principles on fair and adequate minimum wages and on access to social housing, which may give rise to coercive – albeit non-sanctionable – country-specific recommendations to tackle domestic deficiencies in the levels of protection.[98]

4.3. SOCIAL PROTECTION: FOR ALL?

The first recognised descendant of the EPSR is the 2019 Recommendation on Social protection for all forms of employment.[99] The act originates from the 2016 'Access to Social Security Initiative',[100] aimed at widening as much as possible Member States' action in the field of social protection.[101] The starting point of this action was that standard employment contracts, which constituted the normative and economic basis to build social protections systems in Europe, have progressively lost their predominance. This risks leaving an increasing number of individuals outside statutory protections, by reason of their non-standard working patterns.[102] The aim was, in particular, to include under a broader umbrella of social protection non-standard employment, self-employment and new forms of employment such as employee-sharing; job-sharing; interim management; casual work; ICT-based mobile work; voucher-based work; portfolio work;

---

97 S. Bekker, 'The European Semester Process: Adaptability and Latitude in Support of the European Social Model' in F. Vandenbroucke, C. Barnard and G. De Baere, *A European Social Union After the Crisis*, CUP, Cambridge 2018, p. 238.

98 S. Garben, 'The Constitutional (Im)balance between "the Market" and "the Social" in the European Union' [2016] *European Constitutional Law Review* 23, 46–48.

99 Council Recommendation (2019/C 387/01) of 8 November 2019 on access to social protection for workers and the self-employed.

100 COM [2016] 710 final.

101 According to the Stakeholder Consultation document circulated in 2017, 'social protection' encompasses all social benefits in cash and kind, with typical ones being benefits in case of: unemployment, sickness, accidents at work and occupational diseases, invalidity, old-age, pre-retirement, death (i.e. survivors' pensions and death grants), maternity/paternity, parental and family obligations and the need for health care or long-term care.

102 EU Commission, *Access to social protection for all forms of employment. Assessing the options for a possible EU initiative*, 2018, pp. 11–13.

crowd employment; and collaborative employment.[103] A number of social transfers were precluded to non-standard forms of work, such as those covering unemployment, sickness, health care, maternity and parental benefits, work-related sickness, work accidents and others.[104] Moreover, non-standard workers are massively affected by the risk of in-work poverty and social exclusion.[105]

The primitive proposal from the commission was to intervene with a directive, based on Articles 153(1)(c), Articles 151 and 352 TFEU, focusing on the following principles: a) ensuring similar social protection rights for similar work; b) tying social protection rights to individuals and making them transferable; c) making social protection rights and related information transparent; and d) simplifying administrative requirements.[106] Considering the serious limitations on the EU's actions deriving from subsidiarity and proportionality enshrined in Article 5 TEU, as well as the concern that social protection should be a self-standing right to which all citizens should be entitled against the state,[107] in November 2019 the commission opted for a looser intervention in the field, in the form of a recommendation addressed to all Member States, significantly reducing the importance and impact of the measure.[108] The recommendation is based on Article 3 TEU, on Articles 9 and 151 TFEU and on the relevant Principle enshrined in the EPSR – namely, Principle 12, for which 'regardless of the type and duration of their employment relationship, workers, and, under comparable conditions, the self-employed have the right to adequate social protection'.[109] The recommendation covers a wide range of benefits, including: (a) unemployment benefits; (b) sickness and healthcare benefits; (c) maternity and equivalent paternity benefits; (d) invalidity benefits; (e) old-age benefits and survivors' benefits; and (f) benefits in respect of accidents at work and occupational diseases.

---

103 Explicit reference to I. Mandl, M. Curtarelli, S. Riso, O. Vargas Llave, Oscar and E. Gerogiannis, *New forms of employment*, Eurofound, 2015.

104 European Social Policy Network, *Access to social protection for people working on non-standard contracts and as self-employed in Europe. A study of national policies*, European Commission, Brussels 2017, p. 33.

105 EU Commission, above n. 101, p. 17.

106 COM [2017] 2610 final.

107 ETUC Position: Proposal for a Council Recommendation on Access to Social protection for Workers and the Self-Employed, 12 April 2018: https://www.etuc.org/sites/default/files/document/files/etuc_position_proposal_for_a_council_recommendation_on_access_to_social_protection_for_workers_and_the_self_employed.pdf.

108 S. Garben, above n. 93, pp. 117–18.

109 Council Recommendation (2019/C 387/01) of 8 November 2019 on access to social protection for workers and the self-employed, Recitals (1) to (4).

It leaves instead outside its scope both social assistance measures and minimum income schemes (Article 4). When building their own social protection systems, Member States are required to implement the principles of formal coverage, effective coverage, adequacy and transparency (Article 5), all of which are listed in Article 7 and detailed along the document.

The implementation of such principles by the recommendation, however, is weakened by the lack of precise definitions of what a 'worker' and a 'self-employed' individual are. Compared to its previous versions, the document has abandoned the definition of 'worker' as including a person working 'under the direction' of another one in return of remuneration. Because the 'direction' is problematic for a number of non-standard relationships,[110] particularly in the platform economy, this anomy risks augmenting uncertainties and leads to inefficacy of the action. This is further amplified by the lack of enforceability mechanisms, even at governance level.[111]

Moreover, the operational definition of 'type of employment relationship' contained in Article 7(a) – 'one of the various types of relationship between a worker and an employer that can differ with regard to the duration of employment, the number of working hours or other terms of the employment relationship' – is highly unsatisfactory and neglects quasi-subordinate employees as well as casual, intermittent and probably on-demand platform workers. Moreover, the same formal coverage principle, recognised to 'ensure access to adequate social protection for all workers and self-employed persons' (Article 8) is undermined by the need to take into account 'national circumstances' and also by its voluntary application to the self-employed (Article 8(b)).[112]

As concluded by Aranguiz and Bednarowitz,

> access to social protection should be facilitated and granted to all individuals engaged in genuine employment irrespective of whether a person is a worker or a self-employed person, whether or not engaged in standard or non-standard work. At EU level, there are available mechanisms which could pave the way

---

110 A. Aranguiz and B. Bednarowitz, 'Adapt or perish: Recent developments on social protection in the EU under a gig deal of pressure' [2018] 9 *European Labour Law Journal* 342.

111 S. Sabato and B. Vanhercke, 'Towards a European pillar of Social Rights: From preliminary outline to a Commission Recommendation' in B. Vanhercke, S. Sabato and B. Bouget, *Social policy in the European union: State of Play 2017*, Etui/Ose, Brussels 2017, p. 89.

112 The same applies to unemployment benefits, also made voluntary for self-employed workers (Article 9).

towards recognition of the social standards that ought to apply to all. The social standards have to be safeguarded once and for all by highlighting that social protection is not for granted, it is not certainly a bonus to be enjoyed only by an exclusive group of workers. Quite the contrary, it must remain as a normal corollary feature of employment, typical or atypical; otherwise the vulnerable workforce engaged in non-standard work, be it gig or other, will continue to be trapped in the vicious circle of flexibility and precarity.[113]

4.4. THE 2019/1152 DIRECTIVE ON TRANSPARENT AND PREDICTABLE WORKING CONDITIONS: ANOTHER BROKEN PROMISE?

The second, long-awaited product of the EPSR is the Directive on Transparent and Predictable Working Conditions (TPWC Directive, 2019/1152),[114] whose significance, if compared to other legislative initiatives, derives from its legal efficacy.[115]

In its original form, drafted by the EU Commission, the proposal contained a number of provisions aiming to improve the position of a wide array of working people. In the impact assessment, the commission indicated some two to three million workers as the target group, including platform workers.[116] While the first draft referred to all workers irrespective of the type of contractual relationship,[117] the council heavily criticised the move to introduce a pan-European definition of worker and, based also on concerns on the respect of subsidiarity, significantly diluted the ambition of the document.[118]

---

113 A. Aranguiz and B. Bednarowitz, above n. 109, p. 345.

114 Directive (EU) 2019/1152 of the European Parliament and of the Council of 20 June 2019 on transparent and predictable working conditions in the European Union.

115 B. Bednarowicz, 'Workers' rights in the gig economy: is the new EU Directive on transparent and predictable working conditions in the EU really a boost?' [2019] *EU law analysis blog* http://eulawanalysis.blogspot.com/2019/04/workers-rights-in-gig-economy-is-new-eu.html.

116 Commission Staff Working Document Impact Assessment Accompanying the document Proposal for a Directive the European Parliament and of the Council of 20 June 2019 on transparent and predictable working conditions in the European Union, SWD (2017) 478 final.

117 EU Commission's proposal (Article 1(2)): This Directive lays down minimum rights that apply to every worker in the Union.

118 Council of the European Union, Proposal for a Directive of the European Parliament and of the Council on transparent and predictable working conditions in the European Union – General approach, Inter-institutional File: 2017/0355 (COD), 14 June 2018, 10054/18, pp. 4–5.

It was then for the European Parliament to mediate, by proposing to add that the material rights provided by the directive should apply to

> a natural person who, for a certain period, performs services for and under the direction of another person in return for remuneration in the case of dependency or subordination between the former and the latter. Persons who do not fulfil such criteria do not fall within the scope of this directive. Member States shall ensure that all the persons to which this Directive applies can make effective use of those minimum rights within the framework of national law or practice, including collective agreements.[119]

Similarly, while the original draft left Member States free to exclude from the personal scope of the directive those 'workers who have an employment relationship equal to or less than 8 hours in total in a reference period of one month. Time worked with all employers forming or belonging to the same enterprise, group or entity shall count towards that 8 hours period',[120] the Parliament proposed to delete this prerogative on the assumption that all workers must enjoy the same rights irrespective of the hours worked.

The final version of the directive is more limited in its scope and reverts to the more traditional language of 'worker'.[121] The directive, in fact, 'lays down minimum rights that apply to every worker in the union, who has an employment contract or employment relationship as defined by the law, collective agreements or practice in force in each Member State with consideration to the case law of the Court of Justice of the European Union' (Article 1(2)). Immediately after, the directive scales down, providing a potential exclusion referred to

> workers who have an employment relationship in which their predetermined and actual working time is equal to or less than an average of three hours per week in a reference period of four consecutive weeks. Time worked with all employers forming or belonging to the same enterprise, group or entity shall count towards that three-hour average (Article 1(3)).

This seems, however, in contradiction with Recital (12), which provides that:

> workers who have no guaranteed working time, including those on zero-hour and some on-demand contracts, are in a particularly vulnerable situation.

119 http://www.europarl.europa.eu/doceo/document/A-8-2018-0355_EN.html?redirect.

120 EU Commission's proposal (Article 1(3)).

121 B. De Vries, above n. 3, p. 58.

> Therefore, the provisions of this Directive should apply to them regardless of the number of hours they actually work.

Recital (21) clearly acknowledges the specific situation of on-demand workers, by assuming that whenever it is

> not possible to indicate a fixed work schedule because of the nature of the employment, such as in the case of an on-demand contract, employers should inform workers how their working time is to be established, including the time slots in which they may be called to work and the minimum notice period that they are to receive before the start of a work assignment.

These recitals are embodied by Article 11 (Complementary measures for on-demand contracts), which provides that

> Where Member States allow for the use of on-demand or similar employment contracts, they shall take one or more of the following measures to prevent abusive practices: (a) limitations to the use and duration of on-demand or similar employment contracts; (b) a rebuttable presumption of the existence of an employment contract with a minimum amount of paid hours based on the average hours worked during a given period; (c) other equivalent measures that ensure effective prevention of abusive practices.

As it is common in the social policy field, Directive 2019/1152 is subject to the non-regression principle, impeding Member States to reduce the 'general level of protection already afforded to workers',[122] and it is of minimum harmonisation – not affecting Member States' discretion 'to apply or to introduce laws, regulations or administrative provisions which are more favourable to workers or to encourage or permit the application of collective agreements which are more favourable to workers.'[123]

Let alone that information rights appear clearly unfit to significantly enhance the contractual positions of workers vis-à-vis their employer, the

---

122 Article 20(1), Directive 2019/1152.

123 Article 20(2), Directive 2019/1152. This is also clear from Recital 47, for which the Directive 'lays down minimum requirements, thus leaving untouched Member States' prerogative to introduce and maintain more favourable provisions. Rights acquired under the existing legal framework should continue to apply, unless more favourable provisions are introduced by this Directive. The implementation of this Directive cannot be used to reduce existing rights set out in existing Union or national law in this field, nor can it constitute valid grounds for reducing the general level of protection afforded to workers in the field covered by this Directive. In particular, it should not serve as grounds for the introduction of zero-hour contracts or similar types of employment contracts'.

directive's Achilles heel remains its ambiguous and 'hybrid' definition of worker.[124] Its references to both national laws, collective agreements and practice, and to the consideration of the CJEU case law risk undermining its applicability beyond the scope of traditional labour laws. The same 'influence', if ever, of the CJEU jurisprudence in the field is limited to the ambit of EU directives and regulations, because of its purposive nature and limited aspirations.

Albeit significant, the improvements in the elaboration of such definitions are to be strictly referred to the facts of each case decided by the CJEU, as is demonstrated by the fact that the *Lawrie-Blum* test was never nominally abandoned by the court.[125] It was, instead, the factual adaptation of such a test that allowed the CJEU to include an increasingly wide spectrum of personal work relationships, much beyond the field of workers' free movement governed by Article 45 TFEU.[126]

The most important interpretative tool to avoid a restrictive approach in the reading of Article 1(2), Directive 2019/1152 remains the argument of *effet utile* – often overlapped with teleological interpretation[127] – which may give the CJEU the opportunity to enlarge the directive's personal scope. The recitals of the directive, which are normally utilised to run such purposive interpretation, show that the need to guarantee all workers 'an adequate degree of transparency and predictability as regards their working conditions' (Recital (6)) is particularly evident for the new forms of work, and may lead to a situation in which almost only platform workers are kept in a state of 'uncertainty with regard to the applicable rights and the social protection' (Recital (4)).

It remains, instead, a mere optimistic (and circular) assertion that Article 1(2) may help 'domestic workers, on-demand workers, intermittent workers, voucher-based workers, platform workers, trainees and apprentices' fall within the scope of the directive (Recital (8)), the condition for this

---

124 B. Bednarowicz, 'Delivering on the European Pillar of Social Rights: The New Directive on Transparent and Predictable Working Conditions in the European Union' [2019] 48 *Industrial Law Journal* 604, 613.

125 S. Giubboni, 'Being a Worker in EU Law' [2018] 9 *European Labour Law Journal* 223.

126 M. Risak and T. Dullinger, *The Concept of "Worker" in EU Law: Status Quo and Potential for Change*, ETUI, Brussels 2018, p. 23.

127 R. Rebhahn, 'Effet Utile – Towards a General Principle of Law?' in L. Tichy, M. Potacs and T. Dumbrovsky, *Effet Utile*, Charles University, Prague 2014, p. 147; J. Cruz Villaça, 'Le principe de l'effet utile du droit de l'Union dans la jurisprudence de la Cour' in *The Court of Justice and the Construction of Europe: Analyses and Perspectives on Sixty Years of Case Law*, Springer, Cham 2013, p. 279; S. Mayr, 'Putting a Leash on the Court of Justice? Preconceptions in National Methodology v Effet Utile as a Meta-Rule' [2011] 4(2) *European Journal of Legal Studies* 3.

being that they fulfil the criteria established by the CJEU for determining the status of a worker.

On a positive note, the definition of worker contained in Article 1(2) seems at least capable of providing sufficient room to include those who work under disguised contractual forms, whose independency is merely notional (Recital (8)).[128] Refining the tests already used in *FNV Kunsten* may prove to be beneficial in a number of occasions, particularly in the light of national jurisprudence in the field.[129]

5. TOWARD A COHERENT EU STRATEGY ON PLATFORM WORK

The overall picture of the interactions between policy initiatives, regulatory intervention, and the case law of the CJEU is multifaceted. The current EU Commission, on the basis of what its predecessor already planned, is willing to deliver in the shortest period possible a comprehensive response to the needs of platform workers, and showed its willingness by putting the initiative amongst the 100 days priorities by EU Commissioner on Jobs and Social Rights.

Such initiative became reality in February 2021. The commission consulted social partners on their disposition to initiate social dialogue according to Article 154(2) and 154(3) TFEU.[130]

The commission's consultation document is particularly interesting in addressing the main concerns on platform work, leaving to social partners the task to further identify other issues. According to the commission, a number of challenges deserve attention from the social partners, namely the clarification of the employment status of platform workers and their working conditions; their access to social protection; their ability to get collective representation and bargaining; the cross-border dimension of platform work; its algorithmic management; and training and professional opportunities for platform workers.

The commission's consultation document, on the one hand, is broad enough to accommodate any initiative from the social partners, particularly when it comes to issues such as collective representation and

---

128 B. Bednarowicz, above n. 114, p. 621.

129 See, for further references, Chapters 2 to 8 in this volume.

130 EU Commission, Consultation Document "First phase consultation of social partners under Article 154 TFEU on possible action addressing the challenges related to working conditions in platform work" (C(2021) 1127 final).

collective bargaining, or even algorithmic management, some of which have been already the object of local or national agreements between social partners. On the other hand, the document is not detailed enough to let us appreciate the consistency of the EU's action, nor its technical aspects.

For instance, while it seems advisable that the EU intervenes in order to discourage the misclassification of platform workers, the document fails to clarify whether a (rebuttable or absolute) presumption on employment status will be introduced, nor if different approaches (such as that of introducing a third category between subordinate employment and self-employment) will be undertaken. On platform workers' classification, the room for manoeuvre for social partners and collective bargaining is relatively limited, being an issue typically reserved to national legislators, and implying delicate constitutional balances.

A substantial step forward is made by the overall purpose to enhancing working conditions of platform workers, an overarching rationale further articulated into specific measures that could be quite easily introduced at EU level. The main measures can be summarised as follows.

a) First of all, the consultation document mentions transparency and predictability of working conditions. The aspect of predictability is of particular importance, for the widespread use of zero-hours or on-demand contracts not engaging the platform and neither the client to grant a given amount of work occasions.
b) Secondly, the document mentions surveillance and performance appraisal, two items already on the forefront of platform workers' claims at the domestic level.
c) In the third place, the consultation document focuses on earnings and working time: while on earnings it seems the role of EU law is limited (at least in terms of reversing current practices of considering platform work as cognitive piecework),[131] on working time the perspective seems to be much more promising, the established case law of the CJEU serving as a good basis to further enhance working time-related entitlements.
d) Fourthly, the consultation document calls into question health and safety at work, and recalls the already existing ability of national labour inspectorates to help guaranteeing the respect of health and safety both for on-demand workers and for crowdworkers.

---

131 A. Felstiner, 'Working the Crowd: Employment and Labor Law in the Crowdsourcing Industry' [2011] 32 *Berkeley Journal of Employment and Labor Law* 143.

e) Fifthly, the consultation document addresses the need to ensure access to social protection, which is both a domestic issue for the systems of social security – rarely involved as a consequence of the low level of income and the formal self-employment classification of platform workers – and a transnational problem of the law applicable in transnational operations. The aforementioned recommendation on social security for all forms of employment may find further relevance if social partners decide to pick up this issue and require Member States to enlarge the scope of application of social security, possibly based on the temporary measures already undertaken during the 2020–2021 pandemic for the benefit of self-employed workers.
f) Finally, the document addresses the debated topic of collective representation and collective bargaining of platform workers. While at domestic level, the document mentions a number of autonomous initiatives by consolidated and newly born trade unions, which have concluded collective agreements particularly in the field of delivery services, at EU level the commission leaves unresolved the pivotal issue of the compatibility with EU competition law of any form of collective bargaining for the self-employed. As expressly clarified in the document, the consultation 'does not address the issue of potential impacts of EU competition law, notably prohibitions under Article 101(1) TFEU, on platform work'.[132]

Not all the crucial features in the regulation of platform work addressed by the consultation document may be picked up by social partners, in case they would welcome the invitation to negotiate on the topic. Some of them seem, in fact, hardly manageable in the context of the European social dialogue process. Failing a willingness to negotiate, it will be for the EU Commission to further substantiate its proposal and address the complex articulation of protection needs from a regulatory standpoint.

In June 2021, the EU Commission launched a second phase consultation with social partners, pursuant to Article 154(3) TFEU.[133] While the document is still quite general, an important step forward can be seen in

132 EU Commission, Consultation Document 'First phase consultation of social partners under Article 154 TFEU on possible action addressing the challenges related to working conditions in platform work' (C(2021) 1127 final), 20.

133 EU Commission, Consultation Document 'Second-phase consultation of social partners under Article 154 TFEU on possible action addressing the challenges related to working conditions in platform work' (C(2021) 4230 final).

its 'proposed objectives'. The document makes an explicit reference to the purpose of 'supporting the sustainable growth of digital labour platforms in the EU', while ensuring decent working conditions to people working through platforms.[134]

The document further elaborates on a number of challenges, stressing in particular the need to ensure that: a) people working through platforms have – or can obtain – the correct legal employment status in light of their relationship with the platform and gain access to associated labour and social protection rights; b) fairness, transparency and accountability in algorithmic management; and c) clarity on applicable rules for all people working through platforms operating across borders.[135]

As correctly pointed out in the two consultation documents, the EU legislator already intervened in the field of platform business from an internal market perspective. This, however, left a number of issues unresolved, particularly concerning platforms' liabilities and the recognition and enforcement of individual rights upon business users. On the social side, the picture is also still incomplete, as the efforts put on social protections seem not to have reached the expected results in terms of effectiveness and coverage.

EU law scholars so far disagree not only on the way to tackle platform workers' weakness, but also whether a tailored intervention would be more desirable than simply adapting existing legal tests or frameworks. For instance, and because of the variety of subordination tests employed by domestic courts, there is no clarity on the qualification issue. The second phase consultation document pays specific attention to the status of platform workers, envisaging different possible avenues of intervention, such as a rebuttable presumption, a mere shift in the burden of proof, or an administrative or certification procedure.[136] On the qualification issue, some scholars argue that employment law duties should be levied where doing so will discourage domination of workers by companies or by market forces: holding platforms to employment duties is therefore justified on these grounds.[137] Others proposed to consider platform workers as

---

134 Ibid., p. 19.
135 Ibid., p. 20.
136 Ibid., p. 21–22.
137 B. Rogers, 'Employment Rights in the Platform Economy: Getting Back to Basics' [2016] *10 Harvard Law & Policy Review* 479, 480.

agency workers,[138] or as intermediated by mere employment agencies,[139] or even as virtually posted workers, with the aim of resolving the question of the applicable law.[140] In the context of a broader analysis, it has also been argued to conceive platform work globally, thus using as a blueprint the existing legislation of maritime law, more adaptable to the virtually infinite horizons of platform work.[141]

It is a matter of fact that in the European regulatory space some pieces of legislation may be used notwithstanding the qualification of platform workers as employees, self-employed, third-categories or even falsely self-employed. This is particularly the case of anti-discrimination law. Most of its self-standing rights, in fact, operate irrespective of individual's legal status. Both the recast (2006) and the 2000 directives seem to leave enough space for the inclusion of any kind of relationship between an individual providing her service for a platform and the platform itself. This may help tackling algorithmic discrimination, as well as discriminatory assessments (ratings) or other conditions that platform workers live discriminatorily compared to standard workers.[142]

Conversely, the issue of collective representation and collective bargaining on platform workers still remains unsettled, for it appears that the CJEU is very much prudent to extend the *Albany* immunities beyond bogus self-employment[143] and so must be the same Commission while granting bargaining rights to platform workers.[144]

---

138 L. Ratti, 'Online Platforms and Crowdwork in Europe: A Two-Step Approach to Expanding Agency Work Provisions?' [2017] 38 *Comparative Labor Law & Policy Journal* 477, 500–7. The idea was to build on a stretched interpretation of Directive 2008/104, in line with what the CJEU did in the Betriebsrat case (Case C-216/15, *Betriebsrat der Ruhrlandklinik gGmbH v Ruhrlandklinik gGmbH* ECLI:EU:C:2016:883).

139 V. De Stefano and M. Wouters, *Should digital labour platforms be treated as private employment agencies?* ETUI brief #07, Brussels 2019.

140 CSL (Chambre des salariés, Luxembourg), Conference Nouveau monde du travail, nouveau droit du travail, Luxembourg, 7.11.2019.

141 M. Cherry, 'Beyond Misclassification: The Digital Transformation of Work' [2016] 37 *Comparative Labor Law & Policy Journal* 544, 596.

142 N. Countouris and L. Ratti, 'The Sharing Economy and EU Anti-Discrimination Law' in N. Davidson, M. Finck and J. Infranca, *The Cambridge Handbook of The Law of the Sharing Economy*, CUP, Cambridge 2018, p. 486.

143 I. Lianos, N. Countouris and V. De Stefano, above n. 56, p. 291.

144 EU Commission, Consultation Document 'First phase consultation of social partners under Article 154 TFEU on possible action addressing the challenges related to working conditions in platform work' (C(2021) 1127 final), 20.

The recent activism by the EU Commission is a remarkable effort to attribute substantive rights to platform workers. Based on the rights and principles recognised by the EPSR, the commission's intention to intervene in the field must be seen as an important step toward the establishment of a level playing field, not only for the workers involved, but also for the platforms. It remains to be seen how far social partners at the EU level are willing to be part of the regulatory machinery and, in the negative, which legal tools ('hard' or 'soft') the Commission will employ.

COLLECTIVE WORKERS' RIGHTS FOR WORKERS IN THE GIG ECONOMY

Filip DORSSEMONT*

1. INTRODUCTION

Numerous studies have attempted to analyse the phenomenon of digitalisation from a labour law perspective.[1] The question of whether workers who provide their services through a digital platform (or application) are bound by an employment contract and perform their work in a subordinate relationship continues to both captivate and divide the epistemic community of labour lawyers. The employment contract is often seen to be gateway to the application of labour law. The question that seems to have occupied the majority of authors is whether the relationship between the platform and the worker can be construed as an employment relationship, that is, as a relationship based upon *legal* subordination.

* Full Professor of Labour Law at Catholic University of Louvain (UCLouvain), Visiting Professor at Free University Brussels (VUB), filip.dorssemont@uclouvain.be.

1 See *inter alia*: M.A. CHERRY, 'Beyond misclassification: the digital transformation of work' [2016] 37 *Comparative Labor Law & Policy Journal* 577–602; V. DE STEFANO, 'The rise of the "just-in-time workforce": on-demand work, crowd work and labour protection in the "gig-economy"' [2016] 37 *Comparative Labor Law & Policy Journal* 471–504; J. PRASSL and M. RISAK, 'Uber, Taskrabbit, & Co: Platforms as Employers? Rethinking the Legal Analysis of Crowdwork' [2016] 37 *Comparative Labor Law & Policy Journal* 619–51.

It is therefore the individual relationship that is highlighted. This concern is probably explained by the aforementioned *idée fixe* that a worker can only gain access to the application of labour law through the employment contract. However, collective labour relations and their fragmentary legal institutionalisation actually predate the invention of the employment contract.

The relationship between platform workers taken collectively and the platform, conditioned by their ability to organise, to defend and promote their interests, is often overlooked. It is more or less a no-brainer to state that the law of industrial relations in many countries is modelled on an industrialised society. But are its legal categories so fossilised and impermeable that they risk to obscure a new mode of work organisation, or are they sufficiently lively or auto-poetic to allow platform workers to resist?[2]

This question cannot be developed exhaustively, or even systematically, in the context of this chapter. It will focus on the human rights that constitute the foundations of collective labour relations law enshrined in high-profile legal instruments (constitutions, international and European charters). The issue will also be addressed and illustrated on the basis of provisions of Belgian and French labour law. It is therefore right to speak of fundamental rights. These human rights are the freedom of association, the right to collective bargaining, the right to collective action and the right to information and consultation. The recognition of the freedom of association and the right to collective bargaining constitute the opening bars of the International Labour Organization (ILO) Declaration on Fundamental Principles and Rights at Work (1998). The right to strike has not been mentioned.

Both rights underpin the right of workers to defend and promote their rights and interests, including the more substantive fundamental principles and rights listed in this declaration. In short, the object of research is not to be confused with the more classical topic of the qualification of the employment relationship of platform workers. Above all, the fact that some of these workers cannot be qualified as workers bound by an employment contract is not sufficient to deprive them of trade union freedom. The notion of 'worker' is not monolithic and can be understood in a different way with regard to the enjoyment of the fundamental rights underlying

2 'Auto-poetic' in the sense of G. Teubner: G. Teubner, *Law as an autopoietic system*, Blackwell, Oxford 1993.

the right of collective relations, such as freedom of association, the right to collective bargaining and the right to information and consultation.

This chapter will not address the more specific issue of the practical obstacles, inherent to the precariousness of the employment relationship, which prevent an effective exercise of these fundamental rights, which presupposes a more stable insertion in a working community.[3] Nor will it deal with the question of the limits of these fundamental rights, particularly those arising from EU competition law.

2. FREEDOM OF ASSOCIATION

A potential convergence of constitutional practices is a relevant element in the interpretation of certain European instruments, such as the European Convention on Human Rights. Hence, it is worthwhile to take a birds-eye view of some constitutional interpretations of the recognition of the freedom of associations. Two questions should guide such a study. Firstly, do constitutions enshrine a specific right to organise, that is, to establish trade unions? Secondly, does this right also cover workers in general, irrespective of the status of the employment relationship? An initial survey of the French legal order highlights the usefulness of such a project. The preparatory work on the Preamble to the 1946 Constitution shows that the person who can defend his rights and interests through trade union action and join the trade union of his choice is a worker *sensu lato*. This notion includes both private and public sector workers, as well as craftsmen, agricultural workers tradesmen and members of the professions who would also be entitled to these rights.[4] Italian doctrine, having been confronted with a constitutional provision on freedom of association where employers are ignored, is leaning towards a recognition of freedom of association in favour of self-employed workers, *a fortiori* those who are in a state of economic dependence on certain entrepreneurs (i.e. the case of *parasubordinati*).[5] This approach seems to be beneficial for platform workers.

---

3 V. De Stefano, 'Non-standard works and Limits on Freedom of Association: a Human Rights-Based Approach' [2017] 46 *Industrial Law Journal* 185–207.

4 See on this subject: V. Ogier-Bernaud, *Les droits constitutionnels des travailleurs*, Economica, Paris 2003.

5 See: M. V. Ballestrero, *Diritto sindicale*, G. Giappichelli, Turin 2004, pp. 104–07; G. Ghezzi and U. Romagnoli, *Il diritto sindacale*, Zanichelli, Bologna 2001, pp. 45–47; G. Giugni, *Diritto sindacale*, Cacucci, Bari 2000, pp. 67–69; L. Lazzeroni,

In the absence of substantial 'vernacular' references, it is necessary to refer first to European and international instruments to identify the holder of trade union freedom.

Article 11 of the European Convention on Human Rights (ECHR) complements the generic recognition of freedom of association with the recognition that *everyone is entitled to form and join trade unions for the defence of his or her interests.* Given the specificity of the trade union in relation to the association, it is difficult to accept that anyone can found or join a trade union and that the means of collective defence of *any* interest fall within the scope of this recognition. They should logically be reserved for workers. A judgment of the Grand Chamber of the ECHR seems to us to identify the 'worker' in question. In the *Sindicatul Pastoral Cel Bun v. Romania* judgment,[6] the court had to consider whether members of the clergy of the Romanian Orthodox Church could invoke freedom of association vis à vis their bishopric. Romania contested this applicability by denying that the popes (i.e. priests) were bound by an employment contract. This exercise presupposed an interpretation of the concept of a worker who could invoke freedom of association. The Grand Chamber seems to insist only on the quid pro quo of subordination, work and remuneration. Neither the origin of this relationship (a civil law contract or a vow of a sacral nature), nor the source of financing (the church or the state) are relevant. In another earlier judgment on freedom of association (negative), *Sigurdur Sigurjonsson v. Iceland,* the court held that the distinction between self-employed and subordinate workers is not relevant in determining whether or not Article 11 ECHR is applicable to the case at hand.[7] The court held that Article 11 ECHR enshrines both the generic freedom of association and the specific trade union freedom. This position is valid insofar as it concerns the assessment of issues relating to freedom of association or trade union rights at the individual level. However, this distinction seems relevant when assessing the question of essential or important means for the defence of the interests of a member of a trade union. This obligation to provide essential means has only been recognised in favour of trade unions.

The European Social Charter (ESC) recognises freedom of association for workers and employers without specifying these notions. The use of the

'Libertà sindacale e contrattazione collettiva: una norma impegnativa', in L. Gaeta, *Prima di tutto il lavoro. La costruzione di un diritto all'Assemblea Costituente*, Ediesse, Rome 2014, pp. 229–54.

6 *Sindicatul Pastoral Cel Bun v. Romania*, no. 2330/09, 9 July 2013, ECHR.

7 *Sigurdur Sigurjonsson v. Iceland*, no. 16130/90, 30 June 1993, ECHR.

English word (*workers*) pleads in favour of a broad interpretation of the word 'worker'. The same is true for the opening up of trade union freedom to retired workers and the unemployed.[8] M. Nikkola, a former member of the committee, also considers that so-called 'self-employed' workers would fall within the scope of Article 5 of the ESC[9]

Convention No. 87, adopted within the ILO, takes a stronger stance. Its Article 2 states that: 'Workers and employers, without distinction whatsoever, shall have the right to establish and, subject only to the rules of the organisation concerned, to join organisations of their own choosing without previous authorisation.'[10]

The phrase 'without distinction of any kind' seems to argue for the broadest possible understanding of the word 'worker'. This is what the latest version of the Compilation of Decisions of the Committee on Freedom of Association, renamed Compilation (2018), states:

> By virtue of the principles of freedom of association, all workers – with the sole exception of members of the armed forces and the police – should have the right to establish and join organisations of their own choosing. The criterion for determining the persons covered by that right, therefore, is not based on the existence of an employment relationship, which is often non–existent, for example in the case of agricultural workers, self-employed workers in general or those who practise liberal professions, who should nevertheless enjoy the right to organise.[11]

It should also be noted that this maxim of jurisprudence, which was listed in the previous case law of 2006, has been confirmed by the Committee on Freedom of Association.[12]

---

8 See in this regard: A. Jacobs, 'Article 5. The right to organize', in N. Bruun, K. Loercher, I. Schoemann and S. Clauwaert, *The European Social Charter and the employment relation,* Hart, Oxford 2017, p. 235. The author refers to a 2010 Statement of Interpretation of the European Committee of Social Rights.

9 M. Mikkola, *Social Human Rights of Europe,* Karelactio Legisactio, Porvo 2010, p. 242.

10 J.Hodges-Aeberhard, 'The right to organise in Article 2 of the convention No 87. What is meant by workers without distinction "whatsoever"?' [1989] 128 *International Labour Review* 177–94.

11 International Labour Office, *Freedom of Association, Compilation of decisions of the Committee on Freedom of Association,* ILO nr. 387, Geneva 2018.

12 See, in this respect, the cases listed in S. Borelli and J.M. Serrano García, 'Il necessario riconoscimento dei diritti sindacali ai lavoratori dell'economia digitale', in C. Alessi, M. Barbera and L. Guaglianone, *Impresa, lavoro e non lavoro nell'economia digitale,* Cacucci, Bari 2019, pp. 537–56 and cases nr. 2686 (Dominican Republic); 2868 (Panama); nr. 2888 (Poland).

The reference to agricultural workers is not purely coincidental. Convention No. 141 (ILO) defines its scope of application very broadly. Article 2 states that:

> For the purposes of this Convention, the term *rural workers* means any person engaged in agriculture, handicrafts or a related occupation in a rural area, whether as a wage earner or, subject to the provisions of paragraph 2 of this Article, as a self-employed person such as a tenant, sharecropper or small owner–occupier.

Convention No. 141 tries to delimit its scope according to the concept of employer. It thus reverses the classic semantic approach of defining the concept of employer according to the worker. In the spirit of the convention, there is a watertight division between the worker and the employer. The convention applies to 'all categories of rural workers, whether they are wage earners or self-employed' (Article 3). Article 2 (2) states:

> This Convention applies only to those tenants, sharecroppers or small owner–occupiers who derive their main income from agriculture, who work the land themselves, with the help only of their family or with the help of occasional outside labour and who do not
>
> (a) permanently employ workers; or
> (b) employ a substantial number of seasonal workers; or
> (c) have any land cultivated by sharecroppers or tenants.

Instead of examining the question of whether a worker is in a state of subordination to an employer, a revolution of a Copernican nature is needed. The question that should be asked is whether a worker can be qualified as an employer. If not, he or she could invoke freedom of association. In other words, although employers are disqualified in a second stage, self-employment does not exclude falling within the scope. In short, the first real question is whether a farmer is an employer who employs workers. If he is not, he falls within the scope of Convention No. 141. It is interesting to note that the convention does not settle the question of whether an agricultural worker managing an undertaking has economic 'autonomy'. The right of farmers to form or join a 'trade union' is to be assessed on an autonomous basis.

It is sufficient in my view that farmers have the right to set up a professional organisations endowed with the essential prerogatives for the collective defence of the interests of its members. In fact, this idea was put forward in a judgment of the European Court of Human Rights, stating that the mere fact that domestic law prevents farmers from joining a trade union within the meaning of domestic law is irrelevant, provided that the constitution of such a professional organisation is indeed possible according to another statute.[13]

The ILO's openness to the freedom of association of all workers, regardless of whether they have concluded a contract of employment, is consistent with the history of French and Belgian labour law. In France[14] and Belgium,[15] laws providing a legal status for trade unions and professional unions were put in place before the invention of the employment contract. The legal invention of the trade union thus preceded the recognition of an atypical contract based on a relationship of subordination between the signatory parties. Moreover, the Waldeck Rousseau Law as well as the Law on Professional Unions have opened this status to self-employed persons exercising a liberal profession.[16,17]

In keeping with this long French liberal tradition, a recent amendment to the French Labour Code recognised the right of self-employed workers using one or more electronic networking platforms to 'set up a trade union organisation, to join it and to assert their collective interests through it' in order to carry out their professional activity.[18]

3. RIGHT TO COLLECTIVE BARGAINING

The recognition of the freedom of association for workers is not limited to the right to pay dues. It implies that the state recognises so-called essential means for workers to defend and promote their interests in

13 *Manole and the Direct Farmers of Romania v. Romania*, no. 46551/06, 16 June 2015, ECHR.

14 See, in this respect, the Waldeck Rousseau Law (1884) which predates the law.

15 In Belgium, the invention of the 'employment contract' dates back to the Law of 10 March 1900 on the employment contract (H. Velge, *Elements of Belgian Industrial Law*, Librairie Dewit, Brussels 1927, pp. 39–129).

16 See Article 2 of the Waldeck Rousseau Law (March 21, 1884) and Article 2 of the Law on Professional Unions. In both acts, the scope of application is defined in terms of persons practising the same profession or trade.

17 For a comparative study of these two laws from a historical perspective, see: 'The Belgian law on Professional Unions (1898) as an *avatar of* the Waldeck Rousseau law (1884)?' [2006] *Annales de la Faculté de droit de Strasbourg* 169–91.

18 Art. L. 7342-6.

relation to antagonists. The European Court of Human Rights has identified a limited number of these so-called essential means. In the *Demir and Baykara*[19] judgment, the court, overruling its earlier case law, recognised that the right to collective bargaining is indeed an essential means. Its case law on collective bargaining concerns only workers bound by a contract of employment. The court has not yet had the opportunity to rule on whether self-employed workers can also invoke a right to collective bargaining.

However, the ILO Committee on Freedom of Association (FAC) has had occasion to consider the right to collective bargaining invoked by self-employed workers. In a collective complaint (No. 2888), the FAC thus condemned Poland by considering:

> 1084. The Committee recalls that the term 'organization' used in Convention No. 87 means any organization of workers or of employers for furthering and defending the interests of workers or of employers (Article 10), such organizations should therefore have the possibility of engaging in collective negotiations in the interest of its members. The Committee notes, however, the Government's indication that the model of labour relations in the country does not permit self-employed or independent professionals to enter into negotiations. The Committee recalls in this regard that, by virtue of the principles of freedom of association, all workers – with the sole exception of members of the armed forces and the police – should have the right to establish and join organizations of their own choosing. The criterion for determining the persons covered by that right, therefore, is not based on the existence of an employment relationship, which is often non-existent, for example in the case of agricultural workers, self-employed workers in general or those who practise liberal professions, who should nevertheless enjoy the right to organize [see Digest of decisions and principles of the Freedom of Association Committee, fifth (revised) edition, 2006, para. 254]. The Committee therefore, like the Committee of Experts, requests the Government to take the necessary measures, including where necessary, the amendment of the legislation in order to ensure that all workers, without distinction whatsoever, including self-employed workers and those employed on the basis of civil law contracts, enjoy the right to establish and join organizations of their own choosing within the meaning of Convention No. 87. Further, recalling that Convention No. 98 protects all workers and their representatives against acts of anti-union discrimination and that the only possible exceptions from its scope of application are the police, armed forces and public servants engaged in the administration of the State, the Committee requests the Government to ensure

19 *Demir and Baykara v. Turkey*, no. 34503/97, 12 November 2008, ECHR.

that all workers and their representatives enjoy adequate protection against acts of anti-union discrimination regardless of whether they fall into the definition of employees under the Labour Code or not.

The committee thus decided not to dissociate the recognition of freedom of association from the right to collective bargaining. In principle, this approach implies that recognition of a worker's right to form and join a trade union implies recognition of the essential means for the defence of members' interests. These include the right to collective bargaining of the union in question.[20]

The question of whether self-employed workers have the right to collective bargaining is unfortunate, given that only organisations can invoke this right, as opposed to workers. Sometimes, specific statutory instruments regulating collective bargaining require an *aggiornamento*. In Belgium, it must this be noted that the *Loi sur les conventions collectives et les commissions paritaires* is not applicable to self-employed workers. It defines workers as 'persons who, by virtue of a contract of employment or otherwise than by virtue of a contract of employment, provide work under the authority of another person'.[21]

The recognition of the right to collective bargaining for the benefit of organisations representing platform workers does not imply an obligation on the part of the platform to enter into any negotiations, even if the representative organisation so requests. Such recognition imposes an obligation on the head of state to promote and encourage bargaining, as well as an obligation to respect the outcome of bargaining. It can only be observed that the *Loi sur les conventions collectives et les commissions paritaires* is not sufficiently auto-poetic to serve as a framework for formalising the results of such negotiation.

The exclusion of self-employed workers from collective bargaining by Irish competition law has been the subject of a collective complaint to the European Committee of Social Rights.[22] This is not the first time that the

---

20 For a more in-depth study on the position of the ILO with regard to the right to collective bargaining of the independent workers, see: X. Beaudonnet, 'Le droit de négociation collective des travailleurs considérés come indépendants au regard des norms de l'organisation international du travail' in D. Dumont, A. Lamine and J.B. Maison, *Le droit de négociation collective des travailleurs indépendants*, Larcier, Brussels 2020, pp. 55–86.

21 Article 2 §1 1) *Loi sur les conventions collectives et les commissions paritaires.*

22 Collective Complaint nr 123/2016. See: S. Borelli and J.M. Serrano García, above n. 12, pp. 537–56.

Council of Europe has been confronted with the vicissitudes of competition law and its impact on the freedom to bargain. In the case *Swedish transport workers Union v Sweden*, the European Court of Human Rights did not want to censure a decision of the Swedish authority declaring a clause in a collective agreement null and void on the basis of free competition law. This judgment predates the landmark *Demir and Baykara* judgment, and therefore could not take into account the recognition of the right to collective bargaining.[23]

In it decision in the Irish case, the committee affirms, as do the ILO supervisory bodies, that self-employed workers should enjoy the right to bargain collectively through organisations representing them, including in respect of remuneration for the services they provide, subject only to such restrictions as are prescribed by law, pursue a legitimate aim and are necessary in a democratic society (Article G of the Charter). It considers that the general prohibition of collective bargaining in favour of the self-employed was excessive. On the other hand, the committee considers that this non-compliance has been resolved following a legislative amendment (Competition [amendment] Act 2017), which recognises the right to collective bargaining for a specific category of workers such as actors recruited as dubbing actors, musicians recruited as session musicians and others. The committee considers that the prohibition of collective bargaining for self-employed persons, as well as for journalists recruited as freelance journalists and two more generic categories (bogus self-employed workers and economically dependent self-employed workers specified in an order issued by the Minister), was excessive. The discretionary vagueness surrounding the Minister's intervention led to a joint dissenting opinion of Mr Stangos and Ms Kresal.

4. RIGHT TO COLLECTIVE ACTION

The historiography of collective action and its legal construction by state law reveals that the combinations of journeymen (boycotts) and their legal regime preceded both the emergence of the strike and its late legal recognition, and the very invention of the employment contract. In an auto-poetic way, the criminal incriminations prohibiting the coalition of workers (the Le Chapelier Law 1791) and the concept of the freedom

23 *Swedish Transport Workers' Union v. Sweden*, no. 53507/99, 18 July 2006, ECHR.

to work have been mobilised to the detriment of people who would be qualified retrospectively as workers in a state of subordination.

Why not overturn this auto-poetic dynamic by dissociating the right to strike from the status of worker in a state of subordination? Such an approach presupposes extending the scope *ratione personae* of the right to strike as well as its scope *ratione materiae* in favour of a broader conception of collective action, which could include the boycott of platforms that do not respect the dignity of their 'collaborators'.

In France, a recent amendment to the French Labour Code has effectively recognised the right of self-employed workers using one or more electronic networking platforms in the exercise of their professional activity to take part in 'concerted refusals to provide their services ... with a view to defending their professional claims'.[24] The recognition of this right is implicit, and can be inferred from the statement that these movements:

> may not, except in cases of abuse, engage their contractual responsibility, or constitute grounds for breaking off their relations with the platforms, or justify measures penalising them in the exercise of their activity[25]

The use of the phrase '*concerted* refusal movement' suggests that it is a collective movement. Although the refusal to provide services may occur before or after the conclusion of a commercial contract, the explicit prohibition of sanctions in the contractual sphere suggests that this means of collective action has been conceptualised according to the image of the strike. It is mobilised *ex post*. In other words, the French Labour Code suggests that the platform worker who 'refuses' to respond to a call is already in a contractual relationship with the platform. If one had considered that this link is created only after having responded to an appeal, the refusal to respond to it could never engage contractual liability. In such a reading, the means of collective action does not resemble a strike, but a boycott, or as it was once called, a combination or coalition.

This reform of the Labour Code was foreshadowed by the case law of the Italian Constitutional Court as well as the Italian Court of Cassation allowing certain self-employed workers to resort to strike action.[26] This option remains reserved for so-called self-employed workers who are in a

24 Art. L. 7342-5 Code du travail.

25 Art. L. 7342-5 Code du travail.

26 See: M. V. Ballestrero, above n. 5, pp. 298–99; G. Ghezzi and U. Romagnoli, above n. 5, pp. 200–01; G. Giugni, above n. 5, pp. 232–33.

state of dependency and who do not themselves employ workers. Rather than reserving the right to strike or coalition to workers who are in a state of legal subordination, it would be more coherent to reserve it to economic actors who are not employers, nor entrepreneurs with autonomy in the management of their economic risks. Although the right to collective action is recognised for both workers and employers, the disqualification of an economic actor as a *subordinate* worker does not necessarily imply in Italian law a requalification as an employer.

A legislative reform as planned in France is lacking in Belgium. The question therefore arises as to whether the classical or historical basis for the right to strike under Belgian Law, the *Loi sur les Prestations d'intérêt public en temps de paix*, is sufficiently lenient to legitimise a recourse by self-employed persons to the refusal to provide their services. In this respect, it should be noted that the formula of 'collective and voluntary cessation of work'[27] does not refer to the person who performs the work, nor to the nature of this work (subordinate or self-employed). On the other hand, it is difficult to disregard the contextual reference in that law to the Belgian act on collective agreements and joint committees which would imply that the work in question must be performed by persons falling under the latter legislative act. Inevitably, this presupposes that the worker performs his or her work *under the authority of* the platform.

In a more contemporary approach to the basis of the right to strike and collective action, it is better to turn to international instruments.

Supervisory bodies are often silent on the precise question of whether self-employed workers can strike. On the other hand, the ILO has made it clear that freedom of association should be extended to some self-employed workers. It is clear that strikes are seen as an inseparable corollary of freedom of association, or as the most powerful means of defending workers' interests promoted by trade unions.[28] If freedom of association and the self-employed go hand in hand, like freedom of association and the right to strike, there should logically be an 'associative' relationship between self-employed workers and the right to strike.

In the *Hrvatski* case *liječnički sindikat v. Croatia*, the European Court of Human Rights found a violation of the right of a doctors' and dentists' trade

---

27 Article 1 of the Law of 19 August 1948.

28 Inseparable corollary: International Labour Office, *Freedom of Association, Compilation of decisions of the Committee on Freedom of Association*, ILO nr. 754 Geneva 2018. and 'most powerful means': *Hrvatski liječnički sindikat v. Croatia*, no. 36701/09, 27 November 2014, ECHR.

union to strike.[29] There is nothing in this case to suggest that the union was organising only doctors or dentists with an employment contract. The government of Croatia did not dispute at all that the union in question could invoke freedom of association and the right to strike. However, it would be presumptuous to consider that this judgment definitively and explicitly settles the question of the ownership of the right to strike in favour of self-employed workers.

5. RIGHT TO INFORMATION AND CONSULTATION

In the area of employee involvement, the question arises as to whether platform workers have the right to be informed and consulted through their representatives. Article 23 of the Belgian Constitution recognises a right to information and consultation for 'everyone', without specifying its purpose. The Law on the organisation of the economy, establishing works councils, defines the concept of employee by reference to the employment contract – without, however, excluding the King's power to assimilate certain categories of persons who, without being bound by an employment contract or an apprenticeship contract, provide work under the authority of another person.[30] Such a royal decree assimilating digital workers to platform workers does not exist and would seem problematic. Either some of these workers work under the authority of the platform, and then the existence of an employment contract seems obvious, or they do not work under its authority, and the King will not be able to assimilate them.

Apart from the threshold of workers required, another obstacle must be highlighted. The establishment of a works council presupposes that employees can be attached to the company, defined as a technical operating unit on the basis of economic and social criteria. The preponderance of social criteria seems to indicate that its workers carry out their tasks within a working community. It is not so obvious that workers who have a 'virtual' link with a platform can be counted as full members of such a community. Against this overly historicising interpretation of the enterprise, it should be noted that the act on the organisation of the economy also views the notion of enterprise from a more 'corporatist' angle, that is, as an enterprise run by a *legal person*.[31]

29 *Hrvatski liječnički sindikat v. Croatia*, no. 36701/09, 27 November 2014, ECHR.
30 Article 14 para. 1 2° Law on the Organisation of the Economy.
31 Article 14 para. 2 Law on the Organisation of the Economy.

The digitalisation of work organisation will inevitably raise the question of the applicability of Collective Labour Agreement No. 39. This convention, concluded in *tempore non supecto* (1983), establishes an obligation to inform and consult on the social consequences of the introduction of new technologies. Such an obligation exists as soon as 'the employer has decided on an investment in a new technology and when this investment has significant collective consequences with regard to employment, work organisation or working conditions'.[32] It must be implemented 'no later than three months before the start of the implementation of the new technology'.[33] The information to be disclosed in writing to the works council – or, where there is no such body, to the trade union delegation – should specify 'the nature of the new technology, the factors justifying its introduction and the nature of the social consequences it entails'.[34] The decision creates an obligation 'to consult with employee representatives on the social consequences of the introduction of the new technology'.[35] The word 'concertation' is interesting in that it suggests a more dynamic and interactive exchange of views than mere consultation.

However, the applicability and usefulness of this provision will depend on the conditions attached to these obligations. For an obligation to exist, the investment decision must have significant collective consequences, that is:

> affecting 50 per cent and 10 or more *workers in* a given occupational category or all occupational categories where there is a change in employment, work organisation or working conditions resulting from the introduction of the new technology, where all such occupational categories comprise fewer than 100 workers[36]

This raises the question of whether digital workers who have not concluded an employment contract with the employer concerned can be considered as belonging to 'a specific occupational category'. It should be noted that there is no explicit requirement in the collective agreement that this should be an occupational category of employees with an employment contract with the employer in question.

---

32 Article 2 §1 Convention Collective nr 39.
33 Article 2 §1 Convention Collective nr 39.
34 Article 3 §1 Convention Collective nr 39.
35 Article 2 §1 Convention Collective nr 39.
36 Article 2 §2 Convention Collective nr 39.

If the threshold of 100 employees has actually been reached on the basis of those who are undoubtedly under an employment contract – for example, those who carry out administrative tasks for the platform – or a lower threshold for the institution of an employee delegation; then the institution of a works council or an employee delegation seems conceivable. The prerogatives of the works council and the trade union delegation are not limited to information and consultation on social, economic and financial matters relating to employees in the strict sense. The works council has the power to monitor legality.[37] In the case of trade union delegation, this legality control is limited to the so-called social legislation. Nothing leads to a restrictive interpretation of the concept of social legislation. This competence is not in any way reduced to the fate of workers in the strict sense, but it is exercised by all persons concerned by the exercise of freedom of enterprise, provided that they are affected by the application of any general provisions of relevance to the enterprise. In addition to this specific task, it is worth mentioning the task assigned to the works council 'to examine all measures likely to promote the development of a spirit of collaboration between the head of the company and its staff'.[38] As this latter notion has not been defined by law, nothing seems to be opposed to a broader definition of the notion of personnel than workers unquestionably under a contract of employment, *a fortiori* in a sector of an economy which claims to be collaborative.

An overview of the European doctrine on the issue of digital workers gives the impression that platforms such as Deliveroo and Uber are organised at the European level. Sooner or later the question will arise as to whether these structures could not be qualified as groups of undertakings with a community dimension within the meaning of Directive 2009/38, which presupposes that a threshold of 1000 employees has been reached at group level and that at least one undertaking which is a member of the group employs at least 150 employees in one Member State, and at least one other undertaking which is a member of the group employs at least 150 employees in another Member State.

The purpose of the information as defined by the subsidiary requirements could be a catalyst for requesting information that also concerns 'digital employees'. In this respect, reference should be made to formulas included in the description of the purpose, such as 'the probable development of the activities, production and sales of the community–scale undertaking or group of undertakings' as well as 'the introduction of new

37 Article 15 (f) Law on the Organisation of the Economy.
38 Article (i) Law on the Organisation of the Economy.

working methods'.[39] This directive does not resolve the problem of the 'community' definition of the digital worker, since the concept of worker is not defined in the directive and is not relegated to the contracting parties to the agreement. Only the concept of employee representatives has been defined by reference to the law of the Member States. This lack of legislation therefore casts doubt on the national or European, or even autonomous, nature of the concept of employee. It would be foolhardy to imagine that the court would opt for an autonomous scope. Such an approach – justified by the 'fundamental' nature of the right to information and consultation – could generate a discrepancy with the explicitly national approach to the concept of employee in other directives on information and consultation of employees.[40] An approach to the concept of the 'worker' through national law would, moreover, imply taking account of digital employees according to a variable geometry, depending on the state of jurisprudence in the country concerned.

6. CONCLUSION

The 'platform' worker continues to be a challenge for labour law specialists. This chapter has tried to demonstrate that an analysis of the holding of fundamental rights allows us to build a bridge that allows these workers to have a say in the industrial relations system. This question cannot be approached in isolation from the international, European and national legal order recognising the underlying fundamental rights. The answer to this question will not be identical for all legal orders concerned. It depends on the permeability of each legal order to deal with workers who are still atypical.

The impermeability of certain national legal systems must not prevent these workers from fully enjoying the fundamental rights recognised in international and European legal orders. Such a perverse use of these national instruments is an obstacle to international cooperation. It is not difficult to identify both the fundamental right and the most permeable

39 Point 1 a) Subsidiary Requirements Directive 2009/38.

40 See Article 2 Directive 2002/14/EC of the European Parliament and of the Council of 11 March 2002 establishing a general framework for informing and consulting employees in the European Community; and Article 2 of Council Directive 2001/23/EC of 12 March 2001 on the approximation of the laws of the Member States relating to the safeguarding of employees' rights in the event of transfers of undertakings, businesses or parts of undertakings or businesses.

legal order for integrating platform workers. Freedom of association *sensu stricto*, the right to form and join a trade union and *a fortiori* the generic freedom of association, cannot be denied them. However, such a right to pay a membership fee to a structure is deprived of its useful effect if these workers are not given the essential means to defend their interests through collective action to conclude collective labour agreements. Comparing the different legal orders, it is clear that the ILO, through its supervisory bodies, has developed by far the most open position in collective bargaining. Collective Complaint No. 123/2016 has provided a unique opportunity for the European Committee of Social Rights to rally to the position adopted by the ILO supervisory bodies.

PLATFORM WORK IN EUROPE

A Comparative Analysis

Maria Teresa Carinci and Filip Dorssemont*

1. THE EXTENT OF 'PLATFORM WORK'

Before examining the legal issues that platform work poses, it is necessary to first ask (as do all the national reports on the matter in this book) what the current extent of the phenomenon is and, thus, concretely, how many 'platform workers' there are.

---

* Full Professor at University of Milan and Full Professor at Catholic University of Louvain (UCLouvain), Visiting Professor at Free University Brussels (VUB). This chapter is the result of the authors' shared reflections, though Filip Dorssemont wrote sections 1 and 3, while Maria Teresa Carinci wrote section 2.

All national reports highlight the lack of official statistics on the quantitative impact and growth of the introduction of 'platform work' on the active population concerned.

One of the main reasons for the lack of official data lies, in all probability, in the fact that – as is well known – most of the workers used by the platforms have a self-employment relationship with a platform and often even a totally informal relationship. This makes data collection extremely difficult. Only unofficial estimates can thus be used.

Unofficial data specific to each country shows that the estimates for each country are very divergent from one survey to another.

Data on the percentage of the active population involved in the gig economy is most common. It is complemented by data that distinguishes between workers who are mainly dependent upon the income derived from platform work and those who gain complementary income from platform work.

The overall tendency is that the proportion of gig workers is growing rapidly, although it usually never exceeds 5 per cent, with the exception of a Trade Union Confederation report that indicates a tantalising 9.6 per cent of the adult population in UK and also 10.4 per cent of the active population in Germany, according to a COLLEEM survey carried out in 2018.[1]

All in all, the dominant feature is that of a male and less-than-middle-aged worker.

If the numbers are, therefore, growing rapidly, it is urgent to ask what these workers' status is and what applicable individual and collective protections they have.

2. CONTRACTUAL RELATIONS AND APPLICABLE PROTECTIONS

2.1. SUBJECT MATTER OF THE RESEARCH: 'WORK VIA PLATFORM'

A juridical debate must begin with definitions. We must, therefore, first ask ourselves what is meant by the term 'platform work'. This term is in

1 N. Countouris, 'Platform Work: Regulatory And Jurisprudential Perspectives. The UK Case' *in this volume*, section 1 and R. Krause, '"App-Based" Work: The German Case' *in this volume*, section 2.

everyday usage and, at first glance, is actually very broad and generic in meaning because it encompasses all those employment contracts entered into *using* an online (digital) platform or an application on a smartphone (or some other such device) by virtue of which people undertake to carry out their tasks either completely online (crowdwork, cloudwork) or in the physical world (gig work; on-demand work). Clearly, such employment contracts can vary widely from each other depending on the *role* the platform actually plays:[2] the platform may act as a mere intermediary, limiting itself to bringing the parties to the employment contract into contact with each other, that is, the subordinate or self-employed person and the employer or principal (intermediary platforms). On the contrary, the platform can act as a staff leaser, that is, arrange for a worker to go to a user, who manages and coordinates that person's activities for their personal benefit (staffing platforms). Lastly, the platform can act as an employer or principal in the event the employer or principal makes the employee work directly for it, subordinate or self-employed work, thus making the employee part of the user's organisation, in order to provide a service to third parties ('work via platform').[3] It is clear that only the judge in a specific employment dispute can decide what role the platform plays. In theory, however, one can debate whether the rules of national judicial systems are already suitable to incorporate these new forms of work.

Given the particular interest this subject has in labour law, the reports gathered in this book all focus on the last form of employment contract mentioned above, namely, so-called 'work via platform' – specifically, that employment agreement by which people, connected to the platform via an app on their smartphones, conduct their activities entirely in the physical world ('work on-demand via app'). Indeed, this was the first form of 'work via platform' to disseminate in various countries and for which case law was called on to decide, given that the cases examined mostly concerned food delivery platform riders and taxi-hailing platform drivers (only in the German judicial system is there a ruling on the issue of crowdworking offered only via web).[4]

The basic question that is asked is whether the kinds of contractual relationships that exist in the various judicial systems are suitable to also

---

2 R. Krause, above n. 1, section 3.1.

3 See the different kinds of platforms presented by F. Kéfer, 'Platform Work: The Belgian Case' *in this volume*, section 4 and A.T.J.M. Jacobs, 'Platform Work: The Dutch Case' *in this volume*, section 3.

4 R. Krause, above n. 1, section 3.2.

include 'work via platform' within their scope and to provide the necessary employee protection, or if ad hoc legislation is necessary.

To this end, the national reports cited in this book cover very different situations.

In all the legal systems examined, except in France (where laws were passed before case law stepped in, given that the first French law on the matter was passed in 2016),[5] the judges were the first to have to face the problem of the legal framework of 'work via platform'. It was they who had to decide what status to give these workers by making reference to the kinds of contractual relationship already present in the various systems. In some countries there were two traditional kinds of contractual relationships: the subordinate employment contract; and the self-employment contract. These are distinct from each other depending on whether the employer has directive power and, in some legal systems, the addition by law of some specific[6] or supplementary[7] criteria established by law. In other areas, there are three traditional kinds of contractual relationships: the subordinate employment contract; the self-employment contract; and a subspecies of 'weak' self-employment contract, provided for in various forms and governed by law (the 'employee-like person' in Germany; the 'hetero-organised worker' in Italy; the 'TRADE' in Spain; the 'worker' in the UK).

Subsequently, other national legislators passed specific laws governing 'workers via platform' in general (in Belgium)[8] or other specific categories of platform worker involved in 'workers via platform' (the riders working for food delivery platforms in Italy[9] and France).[10]

2.2. THE CLASSIFICATION OF 'WORK VIA PLATFORM' BY JUDGES: TENDENTIAL ACKNOWLEDGEMENT OF THE SUBORDINATE NATURE OF THE EMPLOYMENT RELATIONSHIP

Starting from the position taken by the judges, one notices that there was an initial tendency in case law not to classify 'workers via platform' as

5 B. Gomes and T. Sachs, 'Making Work Platforms Accountable Or Safe? The Battle Between the Legislator And Judges. The French Case' *in this volume*, section 2.

6 R. Krause, above n. 1, section 3.2.

7 F. Kéfer, above n. 3, section 4.

8 F. Kéfer, above n. 3, section 4.4.

9 Law Decree 101, 3 September 2019, converted into law N. 128/2019.

10 By way of art. 44 Mobility Act Law, 24 December 2019.

subordinate workers but, instead, as *tout court* self-employed workers or 'weak' self-employed workers.[11] This is essentially because some typical elements of the contract binding the worker to the platform seem to indicate – at first glance – an absence of those stringent features that distinguish subordinate work. These features include: the continuity of constraint, which constitutes a prerequisite for the employer to exercise power (a platform worker, on the other hand, is free – apparently – to accept or refuse single assignments);[12] the platform's directive or disciplinary power (concealed by the 'automated' operation of the algorithm); and an exclusive personalised service (which is called into question by clauses that make it possible for workers to be replaced by others).[13]

Only later – after very thorough investigations – did the judges, in almost all the judicial systems, reveal that the freedom of the worker to choose whether, when and how to work was, in actual fact, only apparent.[14]

UK case law is an exception to this interpretative trend as it continued to classify people working for a platform as 'workers', but this was essentially because the workers' solicitors opted for a 'prudent' defence strategy.[15]

It thus emerged that since it was the algorithm that arranged the allocation of assignments, the worker is not at all free to choose whether to work and how to work, but is, instead, forced to accept as many assignments as possible and to perform them to the letter of the 'automated' instructions sent by the algorithm to the worker's smartphone in real time

---

11 Turin Court of Appeal, 4 February 2019, and Italian Court of Cassation, 24 February 2020, N. 1663, both of which classified Uber Eats riders as 'hetero-organised workers'; Tribunal of Milan, 28 March 2021, which classified shoppers via platform as 'hetero-organised' workers; M.T. Carinci, 'Case Law Approaches and Regulatory Choices on Platform Work: The Italian Case' *in this volume*, section 2; Tribunal Superior de Justicia de Madrid, 19 September 2019, N. 715, which set the classification of TRADE, F. Fita Ortega, 'The 'App-Based' Employment Relationship: The Spanish Case' *in this volume*, sections 2.1 and 2.3; for the 'worker' classification under UK case law, N. Countouris, above n. 1, section 2.

12 See: Turin Court of Appeal, 7 May 2019; Milan Court of Appeal, 10 September 2018, M.T. Carinci, above n. 11, section 2.

13 See in UK case law, N. Countouris, above n. 1, section 3.

14 See Tribunal Superior de Justicia Asturia, 25 July 2019, N. 1818 and Tribunal Superior de Justicia Madrid, 27 November 2019, F. Fita Ortega, above n. 11, section 2.3; State Labour Court of Munich, 4 December 2019, R. Krause, above n. 1, section 3.2; Court de Cassation, 28 November 2018, case 'Take Eat Easy', Court de Cassation, 4 March 2020, 'Uber' case, B. Gomes and T. Sachs, above n. 5, section 2; Criminal Court of Milan, decree 27 May 2020, Tribunal of Palermo, 24 November 2020, N. 3570, M.T. Carinci, above n. 11, section 2; see also A.T.J.M. Jacobs, above n. 3, section 4, who mentions four decisions.

15 N. Countouris, above n. 1, section 4.

(routes to follow, expected delivery times, etc.). Failure to accept most of the assignments and to follow the automated instructions leads to the worker being penalised in subsequent allocation of assignments and even being removed from the platform. The automated system, in fact, monitors every worker's performance, checks the data provided by the app on the worker's smartphone (time taken for each delivery, routes taken, number of deliveries made during the week, etc.) and customers' feedback. Such data, which is processed by the algorithm, allows the platform to prepare a 'ranking' of workers and to select those workers with the highest scores for subsequent assignments and to penalise – by suspending, or even totally excluding – those with the lowest scores.

The clause making it possible for workers to be replaced by others was also carefully examined by the judges. Indeed, they ruled out that a mere standard clause with no significant use or that is difficult to apply could preclude the employment relationship as subordinate.[16]

In any case, even when they are faced with the classification of 'work via platform', the judges generally do not budge from the 'classical' 20th century concept of subordination, which is mainly focused on the employer's managerial power.

In this regard, two French rulings and one Italian ruling are exceptions.

In the 'Uber' case in France, the *Cour d'Appel de Paris*,[17] first, and the *Court de Cassation*, later,[18] made a qualitative leap by straying from the traditional notion of subordination – that is, the existence of the employer's hetero-directive power – and opting for a 'sort of notion of economic dependence'[19] focused instead on the employer's power to organise and set the conditions of the service rendered. Indeed, in these two rulings, the judges gave significant importance to elements such as the possibility for drivers to establish their own clientele or to independently decide the price of the rides or the conditions of the service.[20] According to the rulings, the lack of such elements shows that the alleged self-employed worker does not actually have the power to autonomously organise their activity but that it is the principal – that is, the platform – that organises the service and must therefore be acknowledged as the employer in a real employment contract with the worker.

---

16 F. Fita Ortega, above n. 11, section 2.3; N. Countouris, above n. 1, section 3.

17 Cour d'Appel de Paris, 19 January 2019.

18 Court de Cassation 4 March 2020, B. Gomes and T. Sachs, above n. 5, section 3.

19 Likewise, B. Gomes and T. Sachs, above n. 5, section 3.

20 B. Gomes and T. Sachs, above n. 5, section 2.

Even one Italian ruling on merit (the Tribunal of Palermo)[21] departs from the 'classical' notion of subordination as hetero-direction, highlighting the separate notion of 'dual alienation', as set forth in the past in a famous, but isolated, ruling by the Italian Constitutional Court.[22] According to the Tribunal of Palermo, which echoed, *verbatim*, ruling 30/1996 of the Italian Constitutional Court, subordination does not hinge on the fact that the platform has mere directive power but exists if two other conditions of alienation exist at the same time: alienation in which the end result of the assignment is for the sole use of others; and alienation of the production organisation that renders the service. Thus, this ruling, too, adopts a notion of subordination that is distinct from the employer's directive power but instead focuses on the titleship of the organisation for which the work activity is rendered.

It is too early to say whether a different and broader concept of subordination is emerging in case law that is aimed at ensuring full protection for all those platform workers who – though not technically hetero-directed – can say they are actually as weak as subordinate workers are. Firstly, platform workers do not have their own means of production (except items of very low value: a bicycle, a motor scooter, a smartphone) and are, therefore, committed to providing mainly personal work. Secondly, they are workers without independent market opportunities and are, therefore, forced to render their service to one (or more) organisations assigned by others. Lastly, they are precarious workers because they are hired on short or very short-term contracts and without any guarantee of continuity/frequency of assignments or income.

In any case, the fact that the most recent case law acknowledges that in most of the cases examined (regarding mostly riders and drivers), platform workers having a subordinate employment relationship certainly does not solve all of the problems.

Firstly, the classification of these individuals as subordinate workers can always be called into question if the platforms modify the assignment organisation model adopted (e.g. by eliminating the ranking systems, which are focused on controlling performance and programmed to distribute assignments among the workers) – something that, in any case, has already occurred, as testified by the clause making it possible for workers to be replaced by others.[23] Even if the above were to happen – as is

---

21 Tribunal of Palermo 24 November 2020, N. 7283.

22 Constitutional Court 5 February 1996, N. 30.

23 N. Countouris, above n. 1, section 3; F. Fita Ortega, above n. 11, section 2.2.

indeed happening – no one can have any doubt that 'via platform' workers, due to their inherent weakness, need protection.

Secondly, acknowledgement that there is a subordinate employment relationship does not necessarily mean platform workers are ensured all the protection they need. The extreme precariousness of the constraint and the exasperating fragmentation of the assignments can, in fact, make it difficult to extend to such workers the protection designed for 'classical' 20th-century subordinate work, which, on the contrary, is characterised by stability and continuity. For example, under the Belgium judicial system the classification of 'riders' as subordinate workers could pose significant problems over the exact definition of working time. Is it the time taken to complete a delivery? The time from the moment at which each assignment is accepted? Or the time from which the worker connects to the platform? There are also the consequent issues of remuneration due to the worker.[24] Under the Dutch judicial system, extension of the protection ensured to employees with zero-hours contracts or to subordinate leased employees constitutes insufficient minimum protection.[25]

Based on this analysis, one cannot but conclude that the 'uberisation' of work is nothing but extreme exasperation of that precariousness of work that has long characterised all European legal systems[26] and which clearly needs resolute action by national legislators, as well as a deep rethink of the kind of protection to give these workers.

2.3. NATIONAL LAWS GOVERNING THE EMPLOYMENT RELATIONSHIP OF 'WORKERS VIA PLATFORM': DO THEY ADD OR REMOVE PROTECTION?

Though there is a debate on the need for legislative intervention in favour of 'workers via platforms' in all the legal systems considered, only in three has the legislator intervened: France, Belgium and Italy.

As will immediately become clear, in all three of these countries, legislative intervention was ambivalent, if not downright unfavourable to workers, if it is true it ended up discouraging requests to have their status changed to subordinate and/or to limit the protection afforded them

[24] F. Kéfer, above n. 3, section 4.2. See F. Fita Ortega, above n. 11, section 3 for analogous considerations.

[25] A.T.J.M. Jacobs, above n. 3, section 4.

[26] A.T.J.M. Jacobs, above n. 3, section 11; F. Kéfer, above n. 3, section 7; N. Countouris, above n. 1, section 8.

(so much so as to urge the judges to rule, in two cases, the laws in question unconstitutional). The first country to pass legislation on the matter was France with the *Loi Travail* of 8 August 2016, which contained a provision within the Labour Code that applied to 'workers using an electronic networking platform'.

From careful examination, this law reflects – both in consideration of the language used and the type of protection afforded to workers (among which are the right to strike, the freedom to join a trade union and the taking out of insurance coverage against accidents at work, which gives preference to 'private' insurers over affiliation to general scheme) – not so much a will to protect a weak form of self-employment, but, rather, legitimisation of the organisational model adopted by the platforms by consolidating their decision to only use self-employed workers (for which the law itself ensures few embryonic protections, grouped around the title 'social responsibility of platforms').[27] In actual fact, this law did not fulfil its purpose, since French case law still held that 'workers via platforms', in particular the Uber drivers, were to be classified as subordinate workers.[28]

On 24 December 2019 (after an initial attempt in 2018), the French legislator intervened again with the so-called 'Mobility Act', which was dedicated more specifically to workers of certain platforms: 'for the electronic linking of platforms operating in the sector of driving a chauffeur-driven transport vehicle (VTC) and the delivery of goods by means of a two- or three-wheeled vehicle'. The 'Mobility Act' provided for the platform to draw up the so-called 'social responsibility charter' (known as the 'social charter') in order to define its own rights and obligations as well as those of the workers: 'the platform may draw up a charter determining the conditions and procedures for exercising their social responsibility, defining their right and those of the workers with whom they are in contact'.[29] The content and function of the 'social charter' seem somewhat ambivalent. If acknowledgement of the need for the 'social charter' is itself implicit, then acknowledgement of the power exercised by the platform over the worker – at the same time that the law (art. 44 of the 'Mobility Act') provides that the 'social charter' cannot be taken by the judge as an element of proof in order to classify the contract as subordinate. Therefore, once again, the aim of the law is not so much to extend protection to a weak self-employed worker as it is, instead, to protect the platform that adopts the

27 B. Gomes and T. Sachs, above n. 5, section 2.

28 See, in particular, Court of Cassation, 4 March 2020, B. Gomes and T. Sachs, above n. 5, section 2.

29 For which see B. Gomes and T. Sachs, above n. 5, section 2.

'social charter' against the risk of a reclassification of the relationship and to discourage the worker – who in this way is afforded only a minimum cluster of rights – from demanding application of all the labour law protections, which would naturally lead to the acknowledgement of subordination. In 2019, however, the Constitutional Council (decision N. 2019/794) ruled that art. 44 of the 'Mobility Act' was unconstitutional, while the rules that legitimise the introduction of the 'social charter' are still in force.

Between 2018 and 2020, the Belgium legislator made even more radical provisions. The law had in fact provided that all 'workers via platform' below a certain income threshold (€6,340 in 2020) – regardless of how, concretely, the relationship was conducted – were exempt from all forms of taxation and, above all, exempt from application of a large part of the protective legislation governing subordinate work (Employment Contract Act; Act on Protection of Remuneration; Act on Collective Labour Agreements; Act on Working Hours; Act on Health and Safety at Work), as well as application of all social security laws. By way of order N. 53 dated 23 April 2020, the Constitutional Court ruled that such laws were unconstitutional.[30]

In Italy, a law passed in 2019 governing 'workers via platform' is even more ambiguous (Decree Law 101/2019, converted into Law 128/2019). Italian law has taken two directions: on the one hand, it explicitly confirmed that the 'worker via platform' – no matter the type of activity provided by the platform – can fall into the category of hetero-organised self-employment, for which all the protections provided for subordinate work apply (art. 2, Legislative Decree 81/2015, the so-called 'Jobs Act'). On the other hand, it introduced a mandatory minimum protection (in terms of health and safety, compensation, prohibitions on discrimination, protection of privacy, etc.) in favour of 'workers via platform' who deliver goods on behalf of others using bicycles or motor scooters and who fall into the category of 'pure' self-employment (*titolo* V *bis* Legislative Decree 81/2015).

At first glance, therefore, it seems that the Italian legislator has gone against the trend set by the French and Belgian legislators; this is also in consideration of the fact that the broad notion of hetero-organisation accepted in case law means that in many cases 'workers via platform' (including delivery platform riders) fall into this contractual relationship.[31] However, it should be noted that even Italian legislation is ambiguous. In fact, with reference to hetero-organised work, the law provides that the

30 F. Kéfer, above n. 3, section 4.

31 M.T. Carinci, above n. 11, section 3.

national collective agreements stipulated by the most representative trade unions may depart, in whole or in part, from the discipline of subordinate work, which, in principle, the law says is applicable. That this provision is not destined to remain on paper is proven by a collective agreement signed in 2020 between Assodelivery and UGL explicitly aimed at derogating *in peius* from the protective provision provided by the law on riders (in particular, reintroducing piecework pay, which was banned by law). A contract stipulated, furthermore, by a union whose representational authority for riders is questioned.[32]

It is clear from what has been examined that all national legislators have so far encountered serious difficulties fending off the pressure from those centres of economic power, which are, undoubtedly, the platforms. It is therefore urgent that collective representation of 'via platform' workers be consolidated so that they can not only sit at the negotiating table, which would already be a leap forward, but also influence political power and raise public awareness (i.e. of consumers) to ensure these workers also have the means for a free and dignified life.

3. PLATFORM WORK AS A CHALLENGE FOR INDUSTRIAL RELATIONS

3.1. THE NATURE OF THE *CHALLENGE* FOR TRADITIONAL AND ALTERNATIVE TRADE UNIONS

Historically, systems of collective employment relations have been established in an industrial setting that respects the rules of classical theatre. Workers were acting in conformity with the rule of unity in time and space. They were part of a working community that was physically situated in an establishment. Platform workers, whether they carry out crowdwork or work on demand, often have no idea of each other's existence. A number of notions such as shop rules, shop stewards and workers' assemblies are problematic in the absence of a shop. The workplace has not merely fissured, it has become virtual. In the case of crowdwork, even work has become virtual.

Systems of industrial relations emerged with the rise of trade unions. It presupposes actors organising and representing the workforce. These

32 M.T. Carinci, above n. 11, section 5. Recently the Court of Bologna (Court of Bologna, decree, 30 June 2021) decided in this sense.

actors do not necessarily need to be created nowadays. In all the countries reported here, trade unions exist at the intersectoral level and at the sectoral level. The question arises of whether they have shown an interest in organising and defending platform workers and/or whether the platform workers have tried to organise themselves outside the traditional trade union movement. Subsequently, the further question arises of whether the prerogatives attributed to these (representative) trade unions within an instituted system of industrial relations are suitable tools in order to defend and promote the interests of platform workers.

The country reports show that 'traditional' trade unions in Belgium, Germany, Italy, the Netherlands and the UK have indeed taken an active interest in organising and representing platform workers. In a number of cases, this interest has even amounted to the conclusion of collective agreements. This begs the questions of whether this openness needs to be based upon the presumption that all platform workers are bogus self-employed workers, or whether the trade unions are also open to organising genuine self-employed workers, which, however, do not function as employers themselves and lack the kind of economic autonomy that is essential to qualify them as entrepreneurs. The Dutch trade unions are willing to accept self-employed workers, irrespective of their status. This is an issue that needs to be addressed in the constitution of these trade unions. Insofar as the right to form and join trade unions is regulated by a non-optional legal framework, it is essential that such a framework does not prevent workers, without any discrimination based upon the nature of their work, from being part of a trade union that can defend the interests of these workers, irrespective of the formal qualification of such a structure as a trade union.[33]

The French *Loi Travail* explicitly recognises the right of platform workers to form and join trade unions. Quite remarkably, the law does not refer to a '*syndicat*' but to an '*organisation syndicale*'. Inevitably, the question arises as to whether they could thus deviate from the mandatory '*Loi Waldeck Rousseau*'. The latter does not require members of a '*syndicat*' to be remunerated workers in a state of subordination. It is sufficient that they exercise a professional activity.

This interest of trade unions for platform workers went hand-in-hand with the efforts of the latter to organise themselves outside the traditional trade union movements in a number of countries such as Germany and

33 See *Manole and 'Romanian Farmers Direct' versus Romania*, no. 46551/06, ECtHR, 16 June 2015.

Spain. In Belgium, a collective of riders has set up a Facebook group that comes closer to the virtual exercise of the freedom of assembly than to the exercise of the freedom of association.[34] It has not been set up against the traditional trade unions and is in fact being supported by the socialist trade union. In Germany, the traditional trade union IGMetall and the YouTubers union set up the association 'Fair Tube e.v.'. The German trade union Verdi also established an independent organisational unit for individual counselling of self-employed members.[35]

These experiences show how platform riders in particular have employed the technology that is used to exploit them as a means to organise themselves. Ortega refers in this respect to 'cyberunionism'.[36] The question of whether a platform of workers or a Facebook group can qualify as a trade union fit to be recognised as a representative trade union for the purposes of instituted systems of collective bargaining remains unanswered. Paradoxically, if one takes the discourse of drivers as independent, autonomous and self-employed 'entrepreneurs' (too) seriously, one might wonder if associations of employers – some of which also organise self-employed people – have taken an interest in organising these workers. The national reports provide no evidence of this. The interest of employers' associations in the issue of platform work is obviously key, albeit not essential, in order to arrive at any system of industrial relations. The sole question is: at what level or levels is or should such bargaining be taking place? In practice, one can imagine a bargaining process taking place at the enterprise level or at the sectoral level. For this first level of bargaining, the interest of an employers' organisation is not essential.

The national reports provide evidence of bargaining at both levels. In the UK, the union GMB concluded an agreement with the delivery firm Hermes in February 2019.[37] The Spanish report provides evidence of a collective agreement at the branch level in the hostelry sector, which includes the activity of delivering food and beverages.[38] In view of the overall representativeness of management and labour, this collective agreement binding *erga omnes* can cover the specific subsector of food and beverage delivery. Such a collective agreement cannot be applied to independent or self-employed platform workers. The Italian report provides evidence of

---

34 F. Kéfer, above n. 3, section 5, R. Krause, above n. 1, section 5 and F. Fita Ortega, above n. 11, section 3.

35 R. Krause, above n. 1, section 5.2.

36 F. Fita Ortega, above n. 11, section 5.

37 N. Countouris, above n. 1, section 6.

38 F. Fita Ortega, above n. 11, section 3.2.

an agreement concluded at the branch level between an organisation that represented the formal employers as opposed to platforms in the transport and logistics sectors. It cannot be applied to genuine self-employed or independent drivers. Hence, the creation of an association representing the platforms as economic actors created a steppingstone to conclude a more relevant collective agreement, applicable to self-employed riders. The representative status of the signatory trade union is debated. Hence, the question arises as to the extent to which this agreement allows one to derogate *in peius* from Italian statutory law as far as, for example, the issue of piecework-based remuneration is concerned.

3.2. COLLECTIVE BARGAINING

The examples of collective bargaining described in the national reports highlight both the thresholds and the catalysts affecting the prospect of collective bargaining. It is interesting to observe that the most documented cases of collective agreements (UK and Italy) that appear to be applicable to self-employed workers both concern systems of industrial relations that are not institutionalised on the basis of a heteronomous statutory framework dealing with collective agreements and are both examples of concession bargaining. More institutionalised systems of collective bargaining might prove to be less suitable, insofar as statutory frameworks might describe their scope in function of formal employees. On the other hand, they tend to provide greater leeway for a more universal coverage of collective agreements.

The most important legal threshold for collective bargaining relates to the dark shadow of EU competition law. Hence, an extension of the immunity from competition law should be extended to collective agreements that affect workers who cannot be construed as genuine entrepreneurs. The focus should be less on the issue of whether they are working in subordination. The question of how a directive could ever solve this problem, which is of a constitutional nature, therefore arises. However, the issue of collective bargaining has been integrated into the issues of the first stage of consultation on improving the working conditions of platform work – albeit as Ratti indicates, quoting the directive, it: 'does not address the issue of potential impacts of EU competition law, notably prohibitions under Article 101(1) TFEU, on platform work'.[39]

---

39 L. Ratti, 'Crowdwork and Work On-Demand in the European Legal Framework: Promises and Expectations' *in this volume*, section 5.

3.3. COLLECTIVE ACTION

The willingness of platforms to play a role as bargaining partners should not solely depend upon the advantage offered by *in peius* bargaining. It is inherent in the dialectics of systems of industrial relations that economic actors offering employment are more inclined to bargain under the threat of some collective pressure that is being exerted against them. Inevitably, this begs the question of what kind of pressure platform workers could and are allowed to exercise, if any. The national reports do not highlight examples of massive walkouts (i.e. practices of workers who disconnect). Such massive walkouts presuppose that platform workers get organised and that a vast majority of them would be able to refuse to execute a request to perform a specific task. Several problems come into play. At first sight, many systems of platform work formally allow a worker not to take a specific task on board as an individual. This refusal will be registered by the algorithm, and platform workers might fear retaliation from the platform. Hence, it is crucial that they are protected against such retaliation, insofar as the individual refusal is part of a concerted action.

In this respect, the legislative good practice of the French law needs to be welcomed.[40] Article L 7342-5 recognises that the concerted refusal to offer their services cannot give rise to contractual liability, nor does it constitute a reason for *stante pede* termination of the employment relation, nor a reason for retaliation. This statutory intervention is prefigured by Italian Art. 47 *quinquies*, paragraph 2 of Legislative Decree N. 81/2015. This provision prohibits the exclusion of workers from the platform or the reduction of their work opportunities due to a refusal to accept tasks offered to them. This provision has a narrower scope than the French provision and is solely applicable to self-employed riders. The principle is, however, also applicable in a mandatory way to riders performing subordinated work or work which is organised by third parties.[41] A clause in the Italian 2020 collective agreement states that the refusal of a rider to take on a specific task cannot have an impact on the distribution of job opportunities.

The question of whether these provisions boil down to a recognition of a right to strike is complicated. *Prima facie*, the right to refuse a task comes close to a right to strike. However, some caveats seem warranted. Firstly, domestic laws might consider that the right to strike presupposes

---

40 B. Gomes and T. Sachs, above n. 5, section 1.

41 M.T. Carinci, above n. 11, section 2.

that the status of a worker is in a state of subordination. Such a narrow interpretation is at odds with an ILO approach.[42] Since the right to strike is a corollary right of the freedom of association and since the freedom of association should be granted even to self-employed workers who are acting as employers or entrepreneurs, the notion of a worker who is a holder of a right to strike needs to be construed equally in a wide manner. Secondly, even insofar as such a work relation might be construed as an employment relation, in the case of on-call contracts or zero-hours contracts, the refusal might be interpreted as amounting to a non-conclusion of a subsequent contract. Hence, the relevant notion here might not be the strike, but a boycott, that is, the concerted exercise of a negative freedom to contract. This negative exercise of contractual freedom is reminiscent of older strategies of journeymen associations, known as combinations, or in French, 'coalitions'. In the absence of criminal provisions prohibiting these kinds of boycotts, there is no reason to see why this would be illegal. The difficulty is more of a practical nature due to the unorganised character of the workforce.

At the end of the day, the recognition of a right to take collective action presupposes an effective protection against discrimination based upon participation in such collective action. Given the very loose and precarious nature of the employment relation, there is a continuous risk of disruption of the employment relation with the platform. In this respect, a recent judgment of the Court Bologna of 31 December 2020 could be deemed as ground-breaking.[43] The court concluded that an action of trade unions calling for a negative injunction to end a discriminatory practice conducted by Deliveroo was admissible. The trade unions mobilised to that end the generic provisions combatting discrimination. By not mobilising the more specific and pioneering provisions of the *Statuto dei Lavoratori*, they were able to overcome the question of whether the contractual relation could be seen as a genuine employment relation. They managed to obtain a ruling stopping the practice that allowed Deliveroo to treat riders who did not revoke, in due time (within 24 hours), their availability as being on an unequal footing with those who did, because it was deemed discriminatory, and the union even received compensation. It is questionable whether appropriate use could be made of the *Statuto*

---

42 F. Dorssemont, 'Fundamental Workers' Rights as an Access to Collective Labour Law for Workers in the Gig Economy' *in this volume*, sections 3 and 4.

43 For a comment by Professor Ballestrero, see M.V. Ballestrero, 'Ancora sui rider. La cecità discriminatoria della piattaforma' [2021] *Labor. Il lavoro nel diritto online* https://www.rivistalabor.it/ancora-sui-rider-la-cecita-discriminatoria-della-piattaforma/.

dei Lavoratori to obtain a similar result. A recent attempt by the Italian trade unions before the Court of Florence to mobilise the *Statuto* proved unsuccessful.[44]

The national reports do provide examples of alternative actions. Thus, the German report highlights how the Fair Crowd Work platform has started to rate platforms on a fairness basis.[45] The rating instrument is thus being instrumentalised as a kind of boomerang. This method of labelling platforms is reminiscent of past experiences, as well. In the 19th century, trade unions in France used to promote products and goods produced in a way that was acceptable to trade unions by attributing a trade union label. This served as an incentive for the members of the trade union to buy such goods or services. The non-attribution or withdrawal could thus serve as an implicit boycott.

3.4. WORKER INVOLVEMENT

Last but not least, the Spanish and German national reports highlight the issue of worker representation at the enterprise level. This issue is not directly related to collective bargaining, although work councils can take part in talks that amount to autonomous rules at the enterprise level.[46] The way in which an establishment is defined as a workplace in a number of laws and the way in which certain trade union activities need to be exercised physically in such a workplace do not fit well with the reality of a more or less virtual community. The tragic German example of the constitution of a *Betriebsrat* by Deliveroo in Cologne shows how easy it might be to obstruct the functioning of such a body merely by not renewing work contracts. A better way to frustrate these platforms might be to ask for the establishment of a European work council at the group level. This would force the controlling companies to highlight the structure. It would force them to take into account the workers who are part of the staff and to take into account those workers who are recognised as subordinate workers under the law of the Member State where they are active.

---

44 Court of Florence, 9 February 2021.

45 R. Krause, above n. 1, section 5.2.

46 F. Fita Ortega, above n. 11, section 3.3 and R. Krause, above n. 1, section 5.3.

BIBLIOGRAPHY

AA.VV., *El trabajo en las plataformas digitales de reparto*, [2019] 1 *Estudios*.

ABDELNOUR S. and MEDA D., *Les nouveaux travailleurs des applis*, La vie des idées, Paris, PUF, 2019.

ADAMSKI D., *Lost on the Digital Platform: Europe's Legal Travails with the Digital Single Market*, [2018] 55 *Common Market Law Review* 719–751.

AGIS DASILVA M., *Una revisita a los contornos de lo laboral. Algunas reflexiones*, (to be published in the collective book *Os impactos das novas tecnologias no direito do trabalho*).

AHRNE G. and BRUNSSON N., *Organization outside organizations: the significance of partial organization*, [2011] 18 *Organization* 83–104.

ALAMEDA CASTILLO M. T., *Un nuevo reto para. el derecho de conflictos: el paro profesional reivindicativo*, [2018] 84 *Revista de Derecho Social* 171–192.

ALOISI A. and GRAMANO E., *Workers Without Workplaces and Unions Without Unity: Non-Standard Forms of Employment, Platform Work and Collective Bargaining* in PULIGNANO V. and HENDRICKX F., *Employment Relations in the 21st Century: Challenges for Theory and Research in a Changing World of Work*, Alphen upon Rhine, Kluwer Law International, 2019, 107, 37–57.

ALOISI A., DE STEFANO V. and SILBERMAN S., *A Manifesto to Reform the Gig Economy*, http://www.pagina99.it/2017/05/29/a-manifesto-to-reform-the-gigeconomy/.

ARANGUIZ A. and BEDNAROWITZ B., *Adapt or perish: Recent developments on social protection in the EU under a gig deal of pressure*, [2018] *European Labour Law Journal* 329–45.

BAETHGE C.B., BOBERACH M., HOFFMANN A. and WINTERMANN O., *Plattformarbeit in Deutschland*, Gütersloh, Bertelsmann Stiftung, 2019.

BALES K., BOGG A., NOVITZ T., *"Voice" and "Choice" in Modern Working Practices: Problems With the Taylor Review*, [2018] 47 *Industrial Law Journal* 46–75.

BALLESTRERO M.V., *Ancora sui rider. La cecità discriminatoria della piattaforma*, [2021] *Labor. Il lavoro nel diritto online*.

BALLESTRERO M.V., *Diritto sindicale*, Giappichelli, Torino, 2004.

BAYREUTHER F., *Arbeitnehmereigenschaft und die Leistung fremdbestimmter Arbeit am Beispiel des Crowdworkers*, [2020] 73 *Recht der Arbeit* 241–248.

BEAUDONNET X., *Le droit de négociation collective des travailleurs considérés comme indépendants au regrad des norms de l'organisation international du travail* in DUMONT D., LAMINE A. and MAISON J.B., *Le droit de négociation collective des travailleurs indépendants*, Brussels, Larier, Brussels 2020, 55–83.

BEDNAROWICZ B., *Delivering on the European Pillar of Social Rights: The New Directive on Transparent and Predictable Working Conditions in the European Union*, [2019] 48 *Industrial Law Journal* 604–623.

BEDNAROWICZ B., *Workers' rights in the gig economy: is the new EU Directive on transparent and predictable working conditions in the EU really a boost?* EU law analysis blog, at http://eulawanalysis.blogspot.com/2019/04/workers-rights-in-gig-economy-is-new-eu.html.

BEKKER S., *The European Semester Process: Adaptability and Latitude in Support of the European Social Model* in VANDENBROUCKE F., BARNARD C. and DE BAERE G., *A European Social Union After the Crisis*, Cambridge, Cambridge University Press, 2018, 238–250.

BENNAARS J.H., *Is platformwerk een bedreiging of een kans voor het arbeidsrecht? Het antwoord is ja*, [2018] 28 *ArbeidsRecht* 8–14.

BERG J., *Income security in the on-demand economy: Findings and policy lessons from a survey of crowdworkers*, Geneva, ILO, 2016.

BERSCHTEK I., OHNEMUS J. and VIETE S., *Befragung zum sozioökonomischen Hintergrund und zu den Motiven von Crowdworkern*, Mannheim, Zentrum für Europäische Wirtschaftsforschung, 2015.

BOES A., KÄMPF T., LANGES B., LÜHR T. and STEGLICH S., *Cloudworking und die Arbeit der Zukunft*, Kassel, Beratungsstelle für Technologiefolgen und Qualifizierung, 2014.

BOES A., KÄMPF T., LANGES B., LÜHR T., *Landnahme im Informationsraum. Neukonstituierung gesellschaftlicher Arbeit in der "digitalen Gesellschaft"*, [2015] 68 *WSI Mitteilungen* 77–85.

BOGG A., *Sham Self-Employment in the Supreme Court*, [2012] 41 *Industrial Law Journal* 328–345.

BONIN B. and RINNE U., *Omnibusbefragung zur Verbesserung der Datenlage neuer Beschäftigungsformen*, Kassel, IZA Research Report No. 80, 2017.

BOOTH R., *DPD courier who was fined for day off to see doctor dies from diabetes*, [2018] *The Guardian*.

BORELLI S. and SERRANO GARCÍA J.M., *Il necessario riconoscimento dei diritti sindacali ai lavoratori dell'economia digitale* in ALESSI C., BARBERA M. and GUAGLIANONE L., *Impresa, lavoro e non lavoro nell'economia digitale*, Bari, Cacucci, 2019, 537–556.

BOURAZERI K., *Neue Beschäftigungsformen in der digitalen Wirtschaft am Beispiel soloselbstständiger Crowdworker*, [2019] 36 *Neue Zeitschrift für Arbeitsrecht* 741–746.

BUENDIA R., *The Court of Justice of the European Union's Order on B v Yodel Delivery Network*, [2020] *Comparative Labor Law & Policy Journal* – Dispatch No. 24 – United Kingdom.

CAÑIGUERAL A., *Fundación COTEC para. la innovación*, available at https://cotec.es/media/COTEC_PIA_Ouishare_WorkerTech_EN_ExecutiveSummary.pdf.

CHERRY M., *A Global System of Work, A Global System of Regulation?: Crowdwork and Conflicts of Law*, [2019] 94 *Tulane Law Review* 183–246.

CHERRY M., *Beyond Misclassification: The Digital Transformation of Work*, [2016] 37 *Comparative Labor Law & Policy Journal* 577–602.

CHOUDARY S.P., *The architecture of digital labour platforms: Policy recommendations on platform design for workers wellbeing*, Geneva, International Labour Organisation, 2018.

CLESSE J., *À propos du travail indépendant …* in WESTRADE M. and GILSON S. (dir.), *Le statut social des travailleurs indépendants*, Perspectives de droit social, Limal, Anthemis, 2013, 9–17.

CLESSE J., CORDIER Q. and KÉFER F., *Le statut social des travailleurs de plateforme* in CLESSE J. and KÉFER F., *Enjeux et défis juridiques de l'économie de plateforme*, Cambridge University Press, Limal, Anthemis, 2019, 137–184.

CLESSE J., DELOOZ P., MANETTE R. and NEUPREZ V., *L'assujettissement à la sécurité sociale des travailleurs salariés. Règles générales et questions particulières*, [1993] *Actualités du Droit* 1143.

CLESSE J., *La qualification juridique de la relation de travail* in CLESSE J. AND KÉFER F., *Questions de droit social*, vol. 94, No. 21., CUP, Anthemis, Louvain-la-Neuve 2007, 231-263.

CORDERO GORDILLO V., *La huelga y otras medidas de acción colectiva en el ámbito de las plataformas digitales* in AA. VV., *El futuro del trabajo: cien años de la O.I.T. XXIX Congreso Anual de la Asociación Española de Derecho del Trabajo y de la Seguridad Social. Ministerio de Trabajo, Migraciones y Seguridad Social*, Madrid, Colección Informes y Estudios. Serie General nº. 23, 2019, 1329–1348.

COUNTOURIS N. and RATTI L., *The Sharing Economy and EU Anti-discrimination Law* in DAVIDSON N., FINCK M. and INFRANCA J., *The Cambridge Handbook of The Law of the Sharing Economy*, Cambridge, Cambridge University Press, 2018, 486–498.

COUNTOURIS N., *The Contract of Employment as an Expression of Continuing Obligations* in M. FREEDLAND, *The Contract of Employment*, Oxford University Press, 2016, 326–382.

COUNTOURIS N., DE STEFANO V., EWING K. and FREEDLAND M., *Covid-19 crisis makes clear a new concept of 'worker' is overdue*, [2020] Social Europe Blog https://www.socialeurope.eu/covid-19-crisis-makes-clear-a-new-concept-of-worker-is-overdue.

COUNTOURIS N., *La gouvernance par les algorithmes, et le récit alternatif du travail* in SUPIOT A., *Le travail au XXIe siècle*, Atelier, 2019, 87–101.

COUNTOURIS N., *The Concept of "Worker" in European Labour Law: Fragmentation, Autonomy and Scope*, [2018] 47 Issue 2 *Industrial Law Journal* 192–225.

COURCOL-BOUCHARD C. and PASQUIER T., *Le livreur, la plateforme et la qualification du contrat*, [2018] *Revue de droit du travail* 812–819.

CRUZ VILLAÇA J., *Le principe de l'effet utile du droit de l'Union dans la jurisprudence de la Cour* in *The Court of Justice and the Construction of Europe: Analyses and Perspectives on Sixty Years of Case-law*, Cham, Springer, 2013, 279.

CRUZ VILLALÓN J., *El concepto de trabajador subordinado frente a las nuevas formas de empleo*, [2018] 83 *Revista de Derecho Social* 13–44.

DAGNINO E., *Ancora ostacoli sulla "via giurisprudenziale" alla protezione dei lavoratori della gig economy in Italia* [2019] 1 *Argomenti di diritto del lavoro* 156–167.

DÄUBLER W. and KLEBE T., *Crowdwork: Die neue Form der Arbeit – Arbeitgeber auf der Flucht?*, [2015] 32 *Neue Zeitschrift für Arbeitsrecht* 1032–1041.

DÄUBLER W., *Digitalisierung und Arbeitsrecht*, [2016] 6 *Soziales Recht – Special Issue* 2–44.

DAUGAREILH I., DEGRYSE C. and POCHET P., *The platform economy and social law: Key issues in comparative perspective*, 10, Brussels, ETUI Working Paper, 2019.

DE STEFANO V. and WOUTERS M., *Should digital labour platforms be treated as private employment agencies?* Brussels, ETUI, 2019.

DE STEFANO V., *A tale of oversimplification and deregulation: the mainstream approach to labour market segmentation and recent responses to the crisis in European countries*, [2014] 43 *Industrial Law Journal* 253–285.

DE STEFANO V., *La 'gig economy' y los cambios en el empleo y la protección social*, [2016] 27 *Gaceta Sindical: reflexión y debate* 149–172.

DE STEFANO V., *Non-Standard Workers and Freedom of Association: A Critical Analysis of Restrictions to Collective Rights from a Human Rights Perspective*, [2015] *Working Papers del Centro Studi Diritto del Lavoro Europeo Massimo D'Antona*.

DE STEFANO V., *Non-standard works and Limits on Freedom of Association: a Human Rights-Based Approach*, [2017] 46 *Industrial Law Journal* 185–207.

DE STEFANO V., *The Rise of the "Just-in-Time Workforce": On-Demand Work, Crowdwork, and Labor Protection in the "Gig-Economy"*, [2016] 37 *Comparative Labor Law & Policy Journal* 471–504.

DE VRIES B., *The "Social Market Economy" in a (Heterogeneous) Social Europe: Does it Make a Difference?*, [2019] *Utrecht Law Review* 47–63.

DEACONU-DASCĂLU D., *The scope of the assignment of contract*, [2014] 2 *Public Administration & Regional Studies* 95–103.

DEGNER A. and KOCHER E., *Arbeitskämpfe in der "Gig-Economy"?* [2018] 51 *Kritische Justiz* 247–265.

DEINERT O., *Die heutige Bedeutung des Heimarbeitsgesetzes*, [2018] 71 *Recht der Arbeit* 359–367.

DEINERT O., *Soloselbstständige zwischen Arbeitsrecht und Wirtschaftsrecht*, Baden-Baden, Nomos, 2015.

DEKKER F., *Werken in de kluseconomie*, [2018] 45 *Beleid en Maatschappij* 189–198.

DESBARATS I., *Quel statut social pour les travailleurs des plateformes ? La RSE (CSR) en renfort de la loi*, [2017] *Droit social* 971–983.

DHORAJIWALA H., *Secretary of State for Justice v Windle: The Expanding Frontiers of Mutuality of Obligation?*, [2017] 46 *Industrial Law Journal* 268–278;

DRAHOKOUPIL J. and FABO B., *Outsourcing, offshoring and the deconstruction of employment: new and old challenges*, in SERRANO A. and JEPSEN M., *The deconstruction of employment as a political question*, Basingstoke, Palgrave Macmillan, 2019, 33–61.

ERDSIEK D., OHNEMUS J. and VIETE S., *Crowdworking in Deutschland 2018: Ergebnisse einer ZEW-Unternehmensbefragung*, Mannheim, Zentrum für Europäische Wirtschaftsforschung, 2018.

EVERS G. and POT F., *Platform werk ontwricht ons arbeidsbestel*, Economisch-Statistische berichten 20.12.2018.

EWING K. D., HENDY J. and JONES C., *A Manifesto for Labour Law*, Liverpool, IER, 2016.

EWING K. D., HENDY J. and JONES C., *Rolling Out the Manifesto for Labour Law*, Liverpool, IER, 2018.

FABO B., BEBLAVÝ M., KILHOFFER Z. and LENAERTS K., *An overview of European Platforms: Scope and Business Models*, Luxembourg, Publications Office of the European Union, 2017.

FABRE A., *Les travailleurs des plateformes sont-ils des salariés*, [2018] *Revue de droit du travail*, 547–558.

FAVEREAU O., *Marchés internes, marchés externes*, [1989] 40 *Revue économique* 273–328.

FELSTINER A., *Working the Crowd: Employment and Labor Law in the Crowdsourcing Industry*, [2011], 32 *Berkeley Journal of Employment and Labor Law* 143–203.

FERNÁNDEZ LÓPEZ M. F., *Los derechos fundamentales de los trabajadores autónomos económicamente dependientes*, [2008] 42 *Revista de Derecho Social* 13–44.

FINCK M., *The Sharing Economy and the EU*, in DAVIDSON N., FINCK M. and INFRANCA J., *The Cambridge Handbook of The Law of the Sharing Economy*, Paris, Cambridge University Press, 2018.

FIORELLI E., *Collaborazioni etero-organizzate: l'esistenza di un Accordo collettivo nazionale esclude l'applicazione della disciplina del lavoro subordinato* [2019] 6 *Labor* 699–712.

FLORISSON R. and MANDL I., *Digital age Platform work: Types and implications for work and employment - Literature review*, Eurofound, 2018.

FORD M. and BOGG A., *Between Statute and Contract: Who is a Worker?* [2019] 135 *Law Quarterly Review* 347–353;

FREEDLAND M. and COUNTOURIS N., *Some Reflections on the "Personal Scope" of Collective Labour Law*, [2017] 46 No. 1 *Industrial Law Journal* 52–71.

FREEDLAND M. and COUNTOURIS N., *Employment Equality and Personal Work Relations - A Critique of Jivraj v Hashwani* [2012] 41 *Industrial Law Journal* 56–66.

FREELAND M., *From the contract of employment to the Personal Work Nexus*, [2006] 35 *Industrial Law Journal* 1–29.

FROUIN J.Y., *Réguler les plateformes numériques de travail*, 2020, https://www.gouvernement.fr/partage/11921-rapport-reguler-les-plateformes-numeriques-de-travail.

FUHLROTT M. and OLTMANNS S., *Der Crowdworker - (K)ein Arbeitnehmer?*, [2020] 73 *Neue Juristische Wochenschrift* 958–963.

GALARDI R., *Uber Italy commissariata dal Tribunale di Milano per l'ipotesi di reato di intermediazione illecita e sfruttamento del lavoro* [2020] *Labor. Il lavoro nel diritto online.*

GARBEN S., *Protecting Workers in the Online Platform Economy: An overview of regulatory and policy developments in the EU,* Luxembourg, EU-OSHA, 2017.

GARBEN S., *The Constitutional (Im)balance between "the Market" and "the Social" in the European Union,* [2016] *European Constitutional Law Review* 23–61.

GARBEN S., *The European Pillar of Social Rights: An Assessment of its Meaning and Significance,* [2019] 21 *Cambridge Yearbook of European Legal Studies* 101–127.

GARBEN S., *The European Pillar of Social Rights: Effectively Addressing Displacement?,* [2018] *European Constitutional Law Review* 210–230.

GARCÍA MURCIA J., *Los derechos colectivos del trabajador autónomo,* [2009] 9 *Actualidad Laboral* 1.

GÄRTNER J.A., *Koalitionsfreiheit und Crowdwork,* Berlin, Duncker & Humblot, 2020.

GAUTIER J., FRENKEN K. and STRAATHOF B. in B. TER WEEL, *De match tussen mens en machin,* Amsterdam, Preadviezen van de Koninklijke Vereniging voor de Staathuishoudkunde, 2015, 103.

GERBER C., *Crowdworker*innen zwischen Autonomie und Kontrolle,* [2020] 73 *WSI Mitteilungen* 182–192.

GHEZZI G. and ROMAGNOLI U., *Il diritto sindacale,* Bologna, Zanichelli, 2001.

GIUBBONI S., *Being a Worker in EU Law,* [2018] *European Labour Law Journal* 1–13.

GIUGNI G., *Diritto sindacale,* Bari, Cacucci editore, 2000.

GOERLICH PESET J. M. and GUAMÁN HERNÁNDEZ A., *Los escenarios del conflicto* in AA.VV. *Libertades económicas, mercado de trabajo y derecho de la competencia. Un estudio de las relaciones entre el ordenamiento laboral y la disciplina del mercado,* Madrid, C.E.S., 2011, 52–61.

GOMES B., *Constitutionnalité de la "charte sociale" des plateformes de "mise en relation": censure subtil, effets majeurs,* [2020] 1 *Revue de droit du travail* 42–47.

GOMES B., *Employees or self-employed: what legal protection for platform workers?* [2019] 265 *Open* 1.

GOMES B., *Take Eat Easy: une première requalification en faveur des travailleurs des plateformes,* [2018] 1841 *Semaine sociale Lamy* 6.

GONZÁLEZ ORTEGA S., *Trabajo asalariado y trabajo autónomo en las actividades profesionales a través de plataformas informáticas,* [2017] 138 *Temas Laborales* 85–123.

GORELLI HERNÁNDEZ J., *Indicios de laboralidad en el trabajo a través de plataformas (Crowdsourcing offline),* [2019] 86 *Revista de Derecho Social* 39–62.

GRABEN S., *Protecting workers in the Online Platform Economy: An overview of regulatory and policy developments in the EU,* OSHA, 2017.

GRACEFFA S., *Refaire le monde … du travail: une alternative à l'ubérisation de l'économie,* Valence, Les Éditions Repas, 2016.

GREEF S. and SCHROEDER W., *Plattformökonomie und Crowdworking: Eine Analyse der Strategien und Positionen zentraler Akteure*, Kassel, 2017.

GROSHEIDE E. and TER HAAR B., *Employee-like worker: Competitive entrepreneur or submissive employee? Reflections on ECJ, C-413/13, FNV Kunsten Informatie* in BELLOMO S., GUNDT N., ŁAGA M. and MIRANDA BOTO J.M., *Labour Law and Social Rights in Europe: The Jurisprudence of International Courts. Selected Judgements*, Gdańsk University Press, 2018, 21–39.

HACKER P., *UberPop, UberBlack, and the Regulation of Digital Platforms after the Asociaciòn Profesional Elite Taxi Judgement of the CJEU*, [2018], 14(1) *European Review of Contract Law* 80–96.

HAIPETER T. and HOOSE F., *Interessenvertretung bei Crowd- und Gigwork*, [2019] *IAQ-Report 05*, 11.

HATZOPOULOS V., *The Collaborative Economy and EU Law*, Oxford, Hart, 2018.

HENDRICKX F., *European Labour Law and the millennium shift: from post to Pillar*, in HENDRICKX F. and DE STEFANO V., *Game Changers in Labour Law: Shaping the Future of Work*, Alphen upon Rhine, KLI, 2018, 49.

HENNION S., *Les limites d'application du droit de la concurrence aux conventions collectives conclues au profit de la protection sociale de travailleurs indépendants*, [2015] 12 *La semaine juridique - Édition générale (JCP G)* 549–553.

HENSEL I., *Die horizontale Regulierung des Crowdworking: Wer bestimmt die Regeln?*, in HENSEL I., SCHÖNEFELD D., KOCHER E., SCHWARZ A. and KOCH J., *Selbstständige Unselbstständigkeit. Crowdworking zwischen Autonomie und Kontrolle*, Baden-Baden, Nomos, 2019, 215–254.

HENSEL I., KOCH J., KOCHER E. and SCHWARZ A., *Crowdworking als Phänomen der Koordination digitaler Erwerbsarbeit - Eine interdisziplinäre Perspektive*, [2016] 23 *Industrielle Beziehungen* 162–186.

HEUSCHMID J. and KLEBE T., *Erwerbsarbeit in der Plattformökonomie und Schutz des Arbeits- und Sozialrechts?* in FABER U., FELDHOFF K., NEBE K., SCHMIDT K. and WASSER U. (eds), *Gesellschaftliche Bewegungen - Recht unter Beobachtung und in Aktion. Festschrift für Wolfhard Kohte*, Baden-Baden, Nomos, 2016, 73–84.

HINCK G., *Rider Captain unterwegs in den Aufsichtsrat*, [2018] 3 *Mitbestimmung* 19–21.

HODGES-AEBERHARD J., *The right to organise in Article 2 of the convention No 87. What is meant by workers without distinction "whatsoever"?* [1989] 128 *International Labour Review* 177–194.

HOEKSTRA R.F., *Naar een normalisering van platformwerk*, Wiardi Beckman Stichting, The Hague 2019.

HOUWERZIJL M., *Arbeid en Arbeidsrecht in een digitale platform samenleving. Een verkenning*, [2017] 2 *TRA: Tijdschrift recht en arbeid* 3–8.

HOUWERZIJL M., *European Cross Border Worker Mobility in the Light of Digitalisation of Labour. More Fragmentation underway?* in AHLBERG K. and BRUUN N., *The New Foundations of Labour Law*, Frankfurt, Peter Lang, 2017, 233–254.

HOUWERZIJL M.S., *Juridische vraagstukken rond arbeid in de klusseneconomie*, [2018] 45 *Beleid en Maatschappij* 208–216.

HUWS U., SPENCER N. H., COATES M. and HOLTS K., *The platformisation of work in Europe: results from research in 13 countries*, Brussels, Foundation for European Progressive Studies, 2019.

HUWS U., SPENCER N.H., SYRDAL D.S. and HOLTS K., *Work in the European Gig Economy*, Brussels 2017.

ICHINO P., *Contratto per i riders: è davvero pirata?*, [2020] *Lavoce.info*.

ICHINO P., *Subordinazione, autonomia e protezione del lavoro nella gig-economy* [2018] 2 *Rivista Italiana di Diritto del Lavoro* 294–306.

JACOBS A.T.J.M., *Article 5. The right to organize*, in BRUUN N., LOERCHER K., SCHOEMANN I. and CLAUWAERT S., *The European Social Charter and the employment relation*, Oxford, Hart, 2017, 220–248.

JACOBS A.T.J.M., *Labour and the Law in Europe. A Satellite View on Labour and Social Security Law in Europe*, Nijmegen, Wolf Legal Publishers, 2011.

JACOBS A.T.J.M., *The Netherlands*, in BLANPAIN R., *Encylopedia of Labour Laws*, Hague, Kluwer, 2020, 59.

JAMOULLE M., *Les transformations du droit belge du travail depuis 1975*, [1996] 78–79 *Contradictions* 101–161.

JEAMMAUD A., *L'avenir sauvegardé de la qualification de contrat de travail, à propos de l'arrêt Labbane*, [2001] *Droit social* 227–238.

JEAMMAUD A., *Le régime des travailleurs des plateformes: une œuvre tripartite*, [2020] *Droit Ouvrier* 181–214.

JOHNSTON H. and LAND-KAZLAUSKAS C., *Organizing on-demand: Representation, voice, and collective bargaining in the gig economy*, [2019] 94 *ILO Conditions of Work and Employment Series*.

JULIEN M. and MAZUYER E., *Le droit du travail à l'épreuve des plates-formes numériques*, [2018] *Revue de Droit du Travail* 189–198.

KAGANER E., CARRAN E., HIRSCHHEIM R. and OLSEN T., *Managing the Human Cloud*, [2013] 54 *MIT Sloan Management Review* 23–32.

KAWALAC S. and MENZ W., *Die Verflüssigung von Arbeit. Crowdsourcing als unternehmerische Reorganisationsstrategie – das Beispiel IBM*, [2013] 6 *Arbeits- und Industriesoziologische Studien* 5–23.

KÉFER F. and CORDIER Q., *Le travailleur 2.0. Contribution à l'étude de la dépendance dans l'environnement numérique* in DEAR L. and PLASSCHAERT E., *Le contrat de travail revisité à la lumière du XXIè siècle*, Brussels, Larcier, 2018, 35–87.

KÉFER F., CORDIER Q. and FARCY A., *Quel statut juridique pour les travailleurs des plateformes numériques?* [2019] 31 *Revue de droit social/Tijdschrift voor sociaal recht* 31–62.

KÉFER F., *L'avenir du travail : les défis lancés au droit du travail et de la sécurité sociale …*, available at http://hdl.handle.net/2268/234206.

KELLER B. and SEIFERT H., *Atypische Beschäftigungsverhältnisse in der digitalisierten Arbeitswelt*, [2018] 71 *WSI Mitteilungen* 279–287.

KILHORRER Z., DE GROEN W.P., LENAERTS K., SMITS I., HAUBEN H., GIACUMACATOS E., WAEYAERT W., LHERNOULD J. P. and ROBIN-OLIVIE S., *Study to gather evidence on the working conditions of platform workers*, European Commission, Luxembourg 2020.

KIRCHNER S., *Arbeiten in der Plattformökonomie: Grundlagen und Grenzen von "Cloudwork" und "Gigwork"*, [2019] 71 *Kölner Zeitschrift für Soziologie und Sozialpsychologie* 3–25.

KLEBE T. and NEUGEBAUER J., *Crowdsourcing: Für eine handvoll Dollar oder Workers of the crowd unite?* [2014] 62 *Arbeit und Recht* 4–7.

KLEBE T., *Crowdwork: Faire Arbeit im Netz?* [2016] 64 *Arbeit und Recht* 277–281.

KOCHER E. and HENSEL I., *Herausforderungen des Arbeitsrechts durch digitale Plattformen – ein neuer Koordinationsmodus von Erwerbsarbeit*, [2016] 33 *Neue Zeitschrift für Arbeitsrecht* 984–990.

KRAUSE R., *Die Share Economy als Herausforderung für Arbeitsmarkt und Arbeitsrecht*, in DÖRR J., GOLDSCHMIDT N. and SCHORKOPF F., *Share Economy*, Tübingen, Mohr Siebeck, 2018, 147–170.

KRAUSE R., *Digitalisierung der Arbeitswelt – Herausforderungen und Regelungsbedarf – Gutachten B zum 71. Deutschen Juristentag*, München, C.H.Beck, 2016.

KRAUSE R., *Kollektivverträge für soloselbstständige Plattformbeschäftigte?*, in DEINERT O., KLEBE T., PIEPER R., SCHMIDT M. and WANKEL S., *Festschrift für Michael Kittner zum 80. Geburtstag*, Frankfurt am Main, Bund-Verlag, 2021 (*forthcoming*).

KRAVARITOU Y., *Les nouvelles formes d'embauche et la précarité de l'emploi*, [1990] 42 *Revue Internationale de Droit Comparé* 129–147.

KRUIT P. and OUWEHAND M., *Platformarbeid: de ene platformwerk(nem)er is de andere niet*, [2018] 58 (7/8) *TRA: tijdschrift Recht en Arbeid* 14.

KULLMANN M., *Platform Work, Algorithmic Decision-Making, and EU Gender Equality Law*, [2018] 34 n. 1 *International Journal of Comparative Labour Law and Industrial Relations* 1–21.

LAAGLAND F.G. and KLOOSTRA J., *De Engelse tussencategorie als oplossing voor platformwerk: mythe of werkelijkheid?*, [2019] 7 *Ondernemingsrecht* 41–49.

LAMINE A. and DORSSEMONT F., *Quels droits collectifs pour le travailleur de plateformes?* in LAMINE A. and WATTECAMPS C., *Quel droit social pour les travailleurs de plateformes*, Limal, Anthemis, 2020, 299–350.

LAZZERONI L., *Libertà sindicale e contrattazione collettiva: una norma impegnativa* in GAETA L., *Prima di tutto il lavoro. La costruzione di un diritto all'Assemblea Costituente*, Roma, Ediesse, 2014, 229–254.

LEIMEISTER J.M. and ZOGAJ S., *Neue Arbeitsorganisation durch Crowdsourcing*, Düsseldorf, Hans Böckler Stiftung, 2013.

LEIMEISTER J.M., DURWARD D. and ZOGAJ S., *Crowd Worker in Deutschland*, Düsseldorf, Hans Böckler Stiftung, 2016.

LEIMEISTER J.M., ZOGAJ S., DURWARD D. and BLOHM I., *Systematisierung und Analyse von Crowd-Sourcing-Anbietern und Crowd-Work-Projekten*, Düsseldorf, Hans Böckler Stiftung, 2016.

LEIST D., HIEßL C. and SCHLACHTER M., *Plattformökonomie - Eine Literaturauswertung*, Trier, 2017.

LIANOS I., COUNTOURIS N. and DE STEFANO V., *Re-thinking the competition law/labour law interaction: Promoting a fairer labour market*, [2019] 10(3) *European Labour Law Journal* 291–333.

LINGEMANN S. and OTTE J., *Arbeitsrechtliche Fragen der "economy on demand"*, [2015] 32 *Neue Zeitschrift für Arbeitsrecht* 1042–1047.

LOISEAU G., *Menace sur le modèle économique des plateformes de mise en relation en ligne* [2020] 4 *Communication Commerce Électronique* 29–31.

LYON CAEN G., *The evolution of Labour Law* in AA.VV., *Labour Law in the post-industrial era, Essays in Honour of Hugo Sinzheimer*, Aldershot, Dartmouth Publishing Co Ltd., 1994, 93.

MAIER M.F. and VIETE S., *Plattformbasierte Erwerbsarbeit: Stand der empirischen Forschung*, Mannheim, IZA Research Report No. 81, 2017.

MATSAGANIS M., ÖZDEMIR E., WARD T. and ZAVAKOU A., *Non-standard employment and access to social security benefits*, Brussels, n. 8 Research note, 2015.

MAYR D., *Arbeitsrechtlicher Schutz Soloselbständiger am Beispiel der Plattformarbeit*, Berlin, Duncker & Humblot, 2021.

MAYR S., *Putting a Leash on the Court of Justice? Preconceptions in National Methodology v Effet Utile as a Meta-Rule*, [2012] 5 n. 2 *European Journal of Legal Studies* 8–21.

MEHREZ F., *La délicate sécurisation juridique de la relation des plateformes et de leurs travailleurs*, [2020] *ActuEL RH*.

MEJÍAS GARCÍA A., *Elecciones sindicales. El preaviso electoral*, Valencia, Tirant Lo Blanch, 2016.

MIKKOLA M., *Social Human Rights of Europe*, Porvo, Karelactio Legisactio, 2010.

MOLERO MARAÑÓN M. L., *La representación de los trabajadores en los procesos de subcontratación* in AA.VV., *La representación de los trabajadores en las nuevas organizaciones de empresa*, Madrid, Ministerio de Trabajo e Inmigración, 2010, 71–100.

OGIER-BERNAUD V., *Les droits constitutionnels des travailleurs*, Paris, Economica, 2003.

OJEDA AVILÉS A., *Los trabajos periféricos y el esfuerzo por unificar su regulación*, [2009] 47 *Revista de Derecho Social* 39–57.

PACHA J., *Crowdwork. Arbeitsrechtlicher Schutz einer neuen Beschäftigungsform*, München, ZAAR Verlag, 2018.

PALMER G., *Foodora & Co.: Die Revolte der neuen Dienstbotenklasse*, [2017] 62 *Blätter für deutsche und internationale Politik* (7) 29–32.

PANTAZATOU K., *The Taxation of the Sharing Economy*, in HASLEHNER W., KOFLER G., PANTAZATOU A. and RUST A., *Tax and the Digital Economy: Challenges and Proposals for Reform*, Alphen upon Rhine, WKI, 2019, 215–236.

PASQUIER T., *L'arrêt Uber - une décision a-disruptive*, [2020] *Actualités juridiques contrat* 227–234.

PASQUIER T., *Sens et limites de la qualification de contrat de travail. De l'arrêt Formacad aux travailleurs "ubérisés"*, [2017] *Revue de Droit du Travail* 95–109.

PECINOVSKY P., *Het recht op collectief onderhandelen voor economisch afhankelijke zelfstandigen*, [2019] 4 *Revue de droit social/ Tijdschrift voor sociaal recht* 529–550.

PESOLE A., URZI BRANCATI M.C., FÉRNÁNDES-MACIAS E., BIAGI F. and GONZÁLEZ VÁZQUEZ I., *Platform Workers in Europe (COLLEEM-I)*, Luxembourg, Publications Office of the European Union, 2018.

PESOLE A., URZI BRANCATI M.C., FÉRNÁNDES-MACIAS E., BIAGI F. and GONZÁLEZ VÁZQUEZ I., *Platform Workers in Europe (COLLEEM-I)*, Publications Office of the European Union, Luxembourg 2018.

PIASNA A. and DRAHOKOUPIL J., *Digital labour in central and eastern Europe: evidence from the ETUI Internet and Platform Work Survey*, Brussels, ETUI, Working Paper, 2019.

PONGRATZ H.J. and BORMANN S., *Online-Arbeit auf Internet-Plattformen. Empirische Befunde zum "Crowdworking" in Deutschland*, [2017] 10 *Arbeits- und Industriesoziologische Studien* 158–181.

PRASSL J. and RISAK M., *Uber, Taskrabbit, & Co: Platforms as Employers? Rethinking the Legal Analysis of Crowdwork*, [2016] 37 *Comparative Labor Law & Policy Journal* 619–651.

PRASSL J., *Humans as a service. The promise and perils of work in the gig economy*, Oxford, Oxford University Press, 2018.

PREIS U., *para. 611 a BGB – Potenziale des Arbeitnehmerbegriffes*, [2018] 35 *Neue Zeitschrift für Arbeitsrecht* 817–819.

PREPIN P., *De l'illusion de l'ubérisation à la réalité du salarié*, [2020] 62 *Revue des droits et libertés fondamentaux.*

RATTI L., *Online Platforms and Crowdwork in Europe: A Two-Step Approach to Expanding Agency Work Provisions?*, [2017] 38 *Comparative Labor Law & Policy Journal* 477–511.

REBHAHN R., *Effet Utile – Towards a General Principle of Law?* in TICHY L., POTACS M. and DUMBROVSKY T., *Effet Utile*, Prague, Charles University, 2014, 147.

RECCHIA A., *Contrordine! I riders sono collaboratori eterorganizzati* [2019] 4 *Il lavoro nella giurisprudenza* 403–411.

RECCHIA A., *La Cassazione "consegna" ai riders la collaborazione eterorganizzata* [2020] 3 *Il lavoro nella giurisprudenza* 245–256.

RIESENHUBER K., *Arbeitnehmer(ähnlicher) Schutz von Crowd-Dienstleistern?*, [2021] 52 *Zeitschrift für Arbeitsrecht* 5–43.

RISAK M. and DULLINGER T., *The Concept of "Worker" in EU Law: Status Quo and Potential for Change*, Brussels, ETUI, 2018.

RISAK M., *Crowdwork – Erste rechtliche Annäherung an eine neue Arbeitsform*, [2015] 50 *Zeitschrift für Arbeits- und Sozialrecht* 11–19.

ROBIN C., *La notion d'entreprise, le droit de la concurrence et la convention collective de travail*, [2015] 43 *Revue Lamy de la concurrence* 15–16.

ROCHA SÁNCHEZ F., *La intervención de los sindicatos de clase en la economía de plataformas*, [2018] 5 *Anuario IET de Trabajo y Relaciones Laborales* 77–94.

ROGERS B., *Employment Rights in the Platform Economy: Getting Back to Basics*, [2016] *10 Harvard Law & Policy Review* 480–519.

ROQUETA BUJ R., *Los derechos colectivos de los trabajadores autónomos. Los acuerdos de interés profesional*, [2012] 114 *Temas Laborales* 13–30.

RÖZER J., VAN DER TORRE A. and ROETERS A., *Platformisering en de kwaliteit van werk*, Den Haag, SCP, 2021.

SABATO S. and VANHERCKE B., *Towards a European pillar of Social Rights: From preliminary outline to a Commission Recommendation* in VANHERCKE B., SABATO S. and BOUGET B., *Social policy in the European union: State of Play 2017*, Brussels, Etui/Ose, 2017, 73–96.

SAVIN A., *Electronic Services with a Non-electronic Component and Their Regulation in EU Law*, [2019] 23 *Journal of Internet Law* 14–27.

SAVIN A., *Regulating Internet platforms in the EU – The emergence of the "Level playing field"*, [2018] 34 *Computer Law & Security Review* 1215–1231.

SCHÄFER H., *Crowdwork und Plattformarbeit in Deutschland*, [2019] 79 *IW-Kurzbericht*.

SCHIECK D. and GIDEON A., *Outsmarting the gig-economy through collective bargaining – EU competition law as a barrier?* [2018] 32 *International Review of Law, Computers & Technology* 275–294.

SCHMIDT F. A., *Digital Labour Markets in the Platform Economy: Mapping the Political Challenges of Crowd Work and Gig Work*, [2017] available at https://www.researchgate.net/publication/314719905_Digital_Labour_Markets_in_the_Platform_Economy_Mapping_the_Political_Challenges_of_Crowd_Workand_Gig_Work.

SCHRAMM F.A., *Arbeitsmärkte in der Plattformökonomie – Zur Funktionsweise und den Herausforderungen von Crowdwork und Gigwork*, Bonn, Friedrich-Ebert-Stiftung, 2016.

SCHUBERT C., *Crowdworker – Arbeitnehmer, arbeitnehmerähnliche Personen oder Selbstständiger*, [2020] 73 *Recht der Arbeit* 248.

SCHUBERT C., *Neue Beschäftigungsformen in der digitalen Wirtschaft*, [2018] 71 *Recht der Arbeit* 193–256.

SCHUBERT C., *Tarifverträge zum Schutz von Crowdworkern trotz Kartellverbot?*, in DEINERT O., HEUSCHMID J., KITTNER M. and SCHMIDT M. (eds), *Demokratisierung der Wirtschaft durch Arbeitsrecht. Festschrift für Thomas Klebe zum 70. Geburtstag*, Frankfurt am Main, Bund-Verlag, 2018, 351–356.

SERFLING O., *Crowdworking Monitor Nr. 1*, Kleve 2018, also available in English: https://www.bmas.de/SharedDocs/Downloads/DE/Meldungen/2018/crowdworking-monitor-englisch.pdf;jsessionid=E6FD5DE9F6920F8AE6E3B2ABB31BD556.delivery1-replication?__blob=publicationFile&v=1.

SERFLING O., *Crowdworking Monitor Nr. 2*, Kleve 2019, also available in English: https://www.hochschule-rhein-waal.de/sites/default/files/documents/2019/05/08/discussion_papers_in_behavioural_sciences_and_economics_no5.pdf.

SIMÓN H. J., *Qué determina la afiliación a los sindicatos en España?*, [2003] 41 *Revista del Ministerio de Trabajo y Asuntos Sociales* 69–88.

SMICEK N., *Platform Capitalism*, Cambridge, Polity Press, 2017.

SUPIOT A., *Au-delà de l'emploi*, Lonrai, Flammarion, 2016.

TER WEEL B. A.O., *De opkomst en groei van de kluseconomie in Nederland*, Amsterdam, SEO, 2018.

TEUBNER G., *Law as an autopoietic system*, Oxford, Blackwell, 1993.

TODOLÍ SIGNES A., *El trabajador en la 'Uber economy': ni dependiente ni autónomo, sino todo lo contrario*, [2016] 25 *Trabajo y Derecho* 43–60.

TRAN M. and SOKAS R.K., *The Gig Economy and Contingent Work: An Occupational Health Assessment*, [2017] 59 Issue 4 *Journal of Occupational and Environmental Medicine* 63–66.

URZÌ BRANCATI C., PESOLE C. A., FERNÁNDEZ-MACÍAS A. and E., *Digital Labour Platforms in Europe: Numbers, Profiles, and Employment Status of Platform Workers*, Luxembourg, Publications Office of the European Union, 2019.

URZI BRANCATI M.C., PESOLE A. and FÉRNÁNDES-MACIAS E., *New evidence on platform workers in Europe (COLLEEM-II)*, Luxembourg, Publications Office of the European Union, 2020.

VALENDUC G. and VENDRAMIN P., *Work in the digital economy: sorting the old from the new*, Brussels, Working Paper No. 3, ETUI, 2016.

VAN EECKHOUTTE W., *Handboek Belgisch Arbeidsrecht*, Mechelen, Wolters Kluwer, 2014.

VAN EECKHOUTTE W., *Handboek Belgisch Socialezekerheidsrecht*, Mechelen, Wolters Kluwer, 2017.

VAN EECKHOUTTE W., *Les frères Jacques c. Délubéro* in D'HUART V. and KÉFER F., *Casus de droit social*, CUP, Limal, Anthemis, 2019, 83–104.

VAN EECKHOUTTE W., *Vers une harmonisation du droit du travail pour les travailleurs indépendants?* in GILSON S. and VANHAVERBEKE P., *La rupture du contrat de travail: entre harmonisation et discrimination*, Jeune barreau de Mons, Limal, Anthemis, 2015, 607.

VAN OLMEN C. and DEVLOO K., *De "Uberisatie" van het Belgisch arbeidsrecht* in *L'économie du futur. Le futur de l'économie*, Le droit des affaires en évolution, Bruxelles, Bruylant, 2016, 119.

VAN SLOOTEN J.M., *Ter Visie – Platformarbeid: nog een reden tot rethinking van het arbeidsrecht*, [2017] 6 *Tijdschrift voor Arbeid & Onderneming* 51–52.

VANDAELE K., *Will trade unions survive in the platform economy?*, Brussels, ETUI Working Papers, 2018.

VELGE H., *Elements of Belgian Industrial Law*, Brussels, Librairie Dewit, 1927.

VENEZIANI B., *The Employment Relationship* in HEPPLE B. and VENEZIANI B., *The Transformation of Labour Law in Europe*, Oxford, Hart, 2009, 99–128.

VERHULP E., *Platformwerkers verdienen meer!*, [2018] 1 *Arbeidsrecht* 6.

VERHULP E., *The Notion of 'Employee' in EU-Law and National Laws*, Annual Conference of the European Centre of Expertise (ECE), 2017.

VERICEL M., *Des incidences en droit social de la loi Madelin sur la qualification de salarié*, [1995] *ALD* 54.

VOSS E. and RIEDE H., *Digitalization and Workers Participation: what Trade Unions, Company level workers and online platform workers in Europe think*, ETUC, 2018.

WAAS B. and VAN VOSS G.H., *Restatement of Labour Law in Europe, Volume I, The Concept of Employee*, vol. 1, Oxford, Hart, 2017.

WAAS B., *Crowdwork in Germany* in WAAS B., LIEBMAN W.B., LYUBARSKY A. and KAZUKA K., *Crowdwork – A Comparative Law Perspective*, Bund-Verlag, Frankfurt am Main 2017, 142–186.

WALTERMANN R., *Abhängige Beschäftigung in der digitalisierten Arbeitswelt*, [2021] 38 *Neue Zeitschrift für Arbeitsrecht* 297–301.

WALTERMANN R., *Digitalisierung der Arbeitswelt – arbeits- und sozialrechtliche Fragen*, in KITAIBL C., MOSLER R. and PAČIĆ H. (eds), *Gedenkschrift Robert Rebhahn*, Wien, Manz, 2019, 635–648.

WALZER S., *Der arbeitsrechtliche Schutz der Crowdworker*, Baden-Baden, Nomos, 2019.

WANK R., *Die personelle Reichweite des Arbeitnehmerschutzes aus rechtsdogmatischer und rechtspolitischer Perspektive*, [2016] 9 *Europäische Zeitschrift für Arbeitsrecht* 143–171.

WARTER J., *Crowdwork*, Wien, ÖGB-Verlag, 2016.

WENCKEBACH J., *BAG: Crowdwork ante portas! Von persönlicher Abhängigkeit in der digitalen Arbeitswelt*, [2020] 10 *Soziales Recht* 165–175.

WILLOCX L., *L'arrêt Uber, une conception mixte de la subordination*, [2020] *Revue de droit du travail* 328–331.

WISSKIRCHEN G. and SCHWINDLING J., *Crowdworking im Lichte des Arbeitsrechts*, [2017] 16 *Zeitschrift für europäisches Sozial- und Arbeitsrecht* 318–323.

WOODS L., *Uber: a taxi service or an app? Analysis of an ECJ Advocate-General's view*, in *EU Law Analysis*', http://eulawanalysis.blogspot.com/2017/05/uber-taxi-service-or-app-analysis-of.html.

XHAUFLAIR V., HUYBRECHTS B. and PICHAULT F., *How Can New Players Establish Themselves in Highly Institutionalized Labour Markets? A Belgian Case Study in the Area of Project-Based Work*, [2018] 56 *British Journal of Industrial Relations* 370–394.

ZAHN R., *Revision of the Posted Workers Directive: A Europeanisation Perspective*, [2017] *Cambridge Yearbook of European Legal Studies* 187–210.

ZANDER I., *Naturtalent der Mitbestimmung*, (2018) *Mitbestimmung* (3) 16–18.

ANNEX

The Questionnaire

1. IMPORTANCE OF THE PHENOMENON

Can you give statistical data with regard to the number of workers involved in the platform economy in your Member States? What is the evolution? In which branches, sectors is the phenomenon apparent?

2. THE QUALIFICATION OF THE PHENOMENON

a) Does your legal order have a legal qualification *de iure condito* or à *droit constant* which fits adequately, *id est* which can be applied as such without further modifications to platform workers? Or is the dominating feeling rather that current legal categories are inadequate or too limited and that henceforth a legislative intervention *ad hoc* is required?

b) Does the judiciary rules that platform workers could or indeed must fall within the ambit of subordinated work/autonomous work or indeed other existing categories in your legal system?

c) Does the judiciary in dealing with platform workers in order to assess their qualification, make a distinction according to the nature of the work concerned (driver, babysitter, plumber, web-designer, programmer etc) In other words, is a distinction being made between workers according to the physical or the virtual nature of their working environment?

3. REGULATIONS QUESTIONS:

a) Which parts of labour law protection is being applied, according to the case law,

b) The protection envisaged relates to the employment relation, to the labour market, to social security, or to Health and Safety

b1) The bulk of labour law applicable to subordinated work.

b2) The labour law protection proper to autonomous work.

b3) Or a mixture of both worlds.

b4) Or another configuration.

4. THE ISSUE OF LOOPHOLES IN PROTECTION

a) Does the judiciary creates (throughout interpretation) 'new rights' for these workers.

b) Does the legislator creates 'new rights' for these workers (e.g. the right to be disconnected)?

5. THE ISSUE OF THE APPLICABLE LAW

Have PIL (private international law) problems been identified either in case law or in fact in doctrinal writings related to workers who perform their work remaining in the country of origin?

6. CAN PLATFORM WORK CONSTITUTE A LABORATORY FOR PRODUCTIVE WORK IN THE PRESENT DAY MILLENNIUM?

A characteristic of platform work is the dissociation of the temporal and spatial dimensions of labour, including labour in the era of the Industry 4.0 era

7. PLEASE FEEL FREE TO SUGGEST SOLUTIONS IMPLIED IN COLLECTIVE AGREEMENTS? LEGISLATIVE PROPOSALS UNDER DISCUSSIONS OR PROPOSALS AT EU LEVEL.

INDEX

ABOUT THE EDITORS

FILIP DORSSEMONT is Full Professor of Labour Law at the Catholic University of Louvain (UCLouvain). He is President of the School of Labour Sciences at the UCLouvain. He is also a Visiting Professor at the Free University of Brussels (VUB). He is a previous President and current Co-President of the Belgian Association of Labour Law and Social Security Law. He is part of the Editorial Board of the *Revue de Droit Social* (Belgium), and of the Scientific Committee of European Employment Law Cases.

MARIA TERESA CARINCI is Full Professor of Labour Law and Industrial Relations at the University of Milan. She is also Head of the Department of Private Law and Legal History, Director of the Specialisation Course in Labour Law and Member of the Faculty Teaching Committee at the University of Milan. She is Scientific Coordinator of the double degree between the University of Milan and the University of Cergy Paris. Her recent research focuses on outsourcing, dismissal and the relationship between work and new technologies.